Editorials from
"Lehre und Wehre"

SELECTED WRITINGS OF C. F. W. WALTHER

Editorials from "Lehre und Wehre"

Herbert J. A. Bouman, Translator

Aug. R. Suelflow, Series Editor

Concordia

Publishing House
St. Louis

Copyright © 1981
Concordia Publishing House
3558 South Jefferson
Saint Louis, Missouri 63118

Manufactured in the United States of America

1   2   3   4   5   6   7   8   9   10   WP   90   89   88   87   86   85   84   83   82   81

Library of Congress Cataloging in Publication Data

Walther, C. F. W. (Carl Ferdinand Wilhelm), 1811-1887.
    Editorials from Lehre und Wehre.

    (Selected writings of C. F. W. Walther)
    Bibliography: p.
    1. Lutheran Church—Collected works. 2. Theology—Collected works—19th century. I. Lehre und Wehre. II. Title. III. Series: Walther, C. F. W. (Carl Ferdinand Wilhelm), 1811-1887. Selections. English. 1981.
BX8011.W28213 1981b   230′.41322   81-3095
  ISBN: 0758618190   AACR2

Contents

Introduction 6

Translator's Preface 8

Foreword to the 1856 Volume 11

Consubstantiation and Impanation 15

Is It Heretical to Question the Canonicity of Some New Testament
  Writings? 24

The Distinction of Estates in the Church 27

Foreword to the 1857 Volume 39

Foreword to the 1858 Volume 43

Foreword to the 1859 Volume
[On Doctrinal Development] 49

On Church Language 62

Foreword to the 1860 Volume
[Do We Draw the Lines of Fellowship Too Narrowly?] 74

Foreword to the 1862 Volume
[Do We Lack Creative Activity?] 102

Opening Address at the Convention of the General Synod of
  Missouri, Ohio, and Other States, at Trinity Lutheran Church,
  St. Louis, Mo., Oct. 31, 1866 115

Foreword to the 1875 Volume
[Are We Guilty of Despising Scholarship?] 122

Foreword to the 1877 Volume
[On the 300th Anniversary of the Formula of Concord] 143

Foreword to the 1882 Volume
[The Only Source of Doctrine] 164

Notes 179

Introduction

It is an ambitious project to permit C. F. W. Walther (1811—87) to address English readers. Efforts to do so have occurred in the past from time to time. But this English edition constitutes one of the most significant contributions made to the study of the theology of Lutheranism in America within past years. The stereotype of Walther heretofore imposed upon him by those who were unable to read his German writings will now be significantly altered! It is to be regretted that a rich treasury of many other works from Walther's pen still await a future project.

Dr. Henry E. Jacobs (1844—1932), late president of Lutheran Theological Seminary in Philadelphia, Pa., said of Walther:

> He is as orthodox as John Gerhard, but as fervent as a pietist, as correct in form as a university or court preacher, and yet as popular as Luther himself. If the Lutheran Church will bring its doctrines again to the people, it must be as faithful and as definite in its doctrine and as interesting and thoroughly adapted to the times in form, as is the case in Walther. He is a model preacher in the Lutheran Church ("Dr. Walther as a Preacher, *Lutheran Church Review*, III [October 1889], 319).

In each of the volumes a special effort was made to select the most significant and relevant materials and to have Walther speak contemporary English. We have further endeavored, wherever possible, to quote from the American Edition of *Luther's Works* and to utilize the Revised Standard Version of the Bible for Scriptural references. Quotations from the Lutheran Confessions were keyed to the Tappert edition of the *Book of Concord*. It was helpful to be able to consult some resources which Walther had in his own library.

Walther was an exceedingly involved church leader. A founding father of The Lutheran Church—Missouri Synod, he served as its first president 1847—50 and 1864—78. He was Concordia Seminary's (St. Louis) foremost instructor from 1849 until his death in 1887, and served as its president 1850—87.

His concern for Lutheran unity is demonstrative. He conceived the "Free Conferences" in the aftermath of the confessional crisis in 1855. Later, in 1872, he was elected the first president of a new pan-Lutheran federation, the Evangelical Lutheran Synodical Conference.

The project to translate Walther into English received support from The Lutheran Church—Missouri Synod in 1962, when a special committee was formed. When funds were not available, the project was transferred to Concordia Publishing House. It has now become a pioneer in publishing both Luther's and Walther's select works in English.

Walther's classic *Law and Gospel,* generally considered one of the most important books produced within American Lutheranism, deserves a volume of its own. In it we see him as theological professor, with his students gathered around him.

Another volume acquaints us with Walther the preacher. He made a great impact on his hearers, and much of his sermonic and homiletical material was published in German during his lifetime and in the years following his death. In spite of this, several thousand sermon manuscripts still remain untouched.

In a further volume we see Walther the convention essayist. None of these essays, presented to Western District conventions between 1873 and 1886, with their ever-recurring theme "To God All Glory!" have seen the English light of day until now.

Of particular importance were Walther's writings on the church, and one of our volumes brings a condensation of these. *Church and Ministry* (1852), *The Proper Form* (1863), and *The True Visible Church* (1866) give the theological foundation for the Missouri Synod's strong emphasis on the congregation and on lay involvement.

We include a volume of Walther's correspondence. It lets us see him in his intense and complex relationships with many different people. Concordia Historical Institute, with funds provided by the Aid Association for Lutherans, has in recent years transcribed several hundred original *Fraktur* letters. Only a few have been published in English heretofore, and we too can bring only a selection.

Finally we take a look at Walther the editor—one of his most important functions. Through *Lehre und Wehre* (from which we bring articles never before presented in English) and *Der Lutheraner* Walther exerted a strong influence toward orthodox Lutheranism.

The translators of this edition hope that readers and users will develop a new appreciation for this 19th-century hero of faith, but above all, that Walther, as the preceptor of Luther in America, will direct the readers to the very cross of our Lord Jesus Christ, his and our only hope.

Aug. R. Suelflow, *Series Editor*

Translator's Preface

The June 1887 issue of *Lehre und Wehre* announces the death of C. F. W. Walther on May 7 and refers to him as "a genuine, divinely equipped, truly great theologian." Walther did an astonishing amount of work as pastor, church president, theological professor and seminary president, author, conference lecturer, and participant in an extensive handwritten correspondence. Small wonder that he often complained of being "dreadfully busy" *(entsetzlich beschaeftigt).* Yet in addition, he launched an activity as editor that in itself might be considered a full-time career. After beginning publication of *Der Lutheraner,* a biweekly church paper, in 1844, he promoted the idea of a separate journal of theology, which he referred to as the "preacher's paper" *(Predigerzeitung).* From the first issue, January 1855, until a few months before his death, Walther was actively associated with this periodical as editor, coeditor, and principal contributor. He called it *Lehre und Wehre* [Doctrine and Defense], a title suggested to him by some words of Luther's commentary on 1 Peter 5:2, which graced the masthead throughout the magazine's existence:

> A pastor must not only lead to pasture by teaching the sheep how to be true Christians: but, in addition to this, he must also repel the wolves, lest they attack the sheep and lead them astray with false doctrine and error *(Luther's Works,* American Edition, Vol. 30, p. 135).

Walther kept and read a great variety of Lutheran church papers and theological journals from both America and Germany and commented incisively on what he read. These comments appeared in a department of *Lehre und Wehre* titled "Kirchlich-Zeitgeschichtliches" [The Current Church Scene]. More than half of the 32 volumes published in his lifetime contain Forewords from Walther's pen, although he was sole editor for only the first six years. In addition to his Forewords, often spread over several issues, he contributed various other articles.

The essays in this volume are a selection of Walther's Forewords and a few other pieces. They are presented in chronological order without any attempt to group them around special topics. The reader will discover that certain basic concerns of Walther surfaced no matter what the topic might be. At his ordination to the pastoral ministry of the Evangelical Lutheran Church he had made a solemn pledge of allegiance to the Holy Scriptures and the Lutheran Confessions. He was utterly serious about this pledge and remained passionately committed to it until his dying day. The full implications of that pledge controlled his stance as theologian and churchman. Vigorously he supported and promoted everything that conformed to the Lutheran Reformation and its confessional writings, and just as vigorously he opposed and rejected all that did not.

Walther's uncompromising stand drew him into a number of controversies. Yet he was not contentious. "I am regarded far and wide as a contentious person, but one who gets to know me better will soon realize that I suffer more from faintheartedness than from spoiling for a fight," he once wrote. But he was convinced that, far from causing disunity, his battles on behalf of the truth were the only way to true concord.

Since this volume offers a selection, the editor is necessarily involved in subjective judgments for which he must assume responsibility. To save space many of the extended quotations, especially from post-Reformation Lutheran authors, were greatly condensed, but almost none of Walther's own words were omitted.

Walther frequently emphasized certain words, and we have reproduced this in many cases. Italics for emphasis, even in quotations, are therefore Walther's. He also had quite a few footnotes, here given in the back of the volume. We have indicated these with the letter "W" (for Walther) after the note number. The notes without the "W," given in the back just after Walther's notes for each essay, are our own. Also our own are many of the paragraph breaks, since Walther's paragraphs were often very long. Walther has many references to contemporary and earlier theologians. The interested reader can usually find information on these in the *Lutheran Cyclopedia*, ed. Erwin L. Lueker (St. Louis: Concordia Publishing House; Revised Edition, 1975).

A reading of even a selection of Walther's essays will disclose his far-ranging knowledge of Scripture, the Lutheran Confessions, the writings of Luther and classical Lutheran theologians, and even the ancient church fathers. At the same time, Walther strove to remain completely current with regard to what was going on in the Lutheran church and theology of his day. In the opinion of Francis Pieper, his successor as professor, president, and editor, "with regard to spiritual experience, theological scholarship, logical acuity, and the ability to communicate, Walther was certainly not inferior to most of the old theologians of our church; in my opinion, he was the superior of many of them" *(Lehre und Wehre,* XXXIV, 266). These essays are part of the basis for Pieper's estimate.

Herbert J.A. Bouman

Foreword to the 1856 Volume

Lehre und Wehre, **II, 1, Jan. 1856, pp. 1—5**

Instruction and Defense! This is the motto we expressed when we began to publish this periodical, and we have since been guided by these words. And as long as God gives us strength and opportunity, we shall continue to be guided by this motto.

We are well aware that thereby we set our course against the stream of what is currently popular. People want to be entertained rather than *instructed.* They repeat Pilate's question, "What is truth?" and deride as a fool anyone who dares to assert that he had found the truth and is proclaiming it. The current taste wants to hear nothing but "views," nothing but thoughts "without prejudice," expressed in attractive form. The man of today wants *his* age to be celebrated as the age of maturity and enlightenment, but past centuries to be smiled at as times of childish simplicity, darkness, and superstition. What was proclaimed as truth in a former day must now be relegated to a pigeonhole of history. Let us hear no more about people or about a *church* that always possessed the truth.

But if the current taste wants nothing to do with *teaching,* it is even more averse to *defense.* It thinks that it is all right to wage war for things that have reality, like land, money, honor, and the like, but fight for *the truth?*—folly! Who would and should fight for a phantom, for something that no one has and that no one can conquer? The spirit of the age believes that truth is the riddle of a sphinx that has not yet found an Oedipus. What truth there is on earth is parceled out, if not among the different chief religions, at least among the various parties in Christendom. All the various so-called churches are regarded as different branches of one tree, and the varieties of teaching in these churches are simply different refractions of the one sun, merely different colors of the one rainbow. They are all sisters, and only lovelessness and spiritual pride can stoke the fires of discord among them.

But however prevalent these principles have become in our day and however commonly they are expressed, sometimes in veiled, sometimes in unveiled form, we cannot subscribe to them. By a divine conviction we believe that there is a truth here on earth and that this truth is contained in God's Word, that is, in the divinely inspired writings of the apostles and prophets. We also believe that these sacred writings have the purpose of imparting the light of this one complete truth to man sitting in darkness and in the shadow of death, and that therefore these writings are so *clear* that a human being is able to recognize and draw this one complete truth from them. We are furthermore convinced that there have always been people who possessed this treasure and that in particular our fathers 300 years ago were granted this unspeakable grace by God and deposited this precious treasure in the Confessions of the so-called Evangelical Lutheran Church. Here we recall the beautiful statement of Professor *Philippi* in the Preface to his *Commentar über den Brief Pauli an die Römer* [Commentary on Paul's Letter to the Romans]:

> If it is true that all systems of human wisdom lie like broken keys before the gate of truth, it is equally true that the church's analogy of faith, drawn from the Word that is the truth, is the long-lost but now rediscovered correct key. Even though covered with rust, this key will more easily work the old, well-known lock than all the prettier keys that are new but fashioned after a false model (p. VII).

Thus we cannot voice the truth we have found as our "opinion" that is not determinative, but we must speak of it as of the one old, eternal, unchangeable *truth*. We must advertise and defend it as our most precious possession, on which our own salvation and that of all people depends. We must reject and condemn all contrary opinions of men as dangerous, harmful, and destructive error. If the observation of such principles will close doors to our periodical—so be it! We are not interested in editing a widely read paper. Our sole interest lies in bearing witness to what we have learned to know as the truth; in passing on what we have received; in speaking because we believe. If this magazine cannot serve to keep or gain friends for the old truth, let it in God's name relapse into silence. There are already too many magazines that build Babel.

However, we would be completely misunderstood if the foregoing remarks were construed to mean that at the beginning of a new year we face the future discouraged either with regard to our periodical or the cause of our church in general. We can assure you of the opposite. As for this monthly journal, it does not yet have enough readers to live without the support it has thus far received from its older brother, the *Lutheraner*. Yet the experiences of the first year make us quite hopeful that the time is not too far distant when our *Lehre und Wehre* will no longer need the *Lutheraner*'s charity. As for the cause of the church, especially here in North America, it seems to us that just in the last months the sky has visibly reddened again, giving us promise of brighter days than those recently passed (Matthew 16:2).

When last September the Wittenberg Synod of Ohio published its so-called Definite Platform[1] for a so-called *American* Lutheran Church with its official forsaking of the constitution, the Magna Charta of our church, the Unaltered Augsburg Confession, and urged all who are like-minded to leave too, a severe storm fraught with misfortune appeared to be gathering over the Lutheran Church of our new homeland and seemed about to unleash its fury. But what happened? Only three synods succumbed to the temptation and accepted the proposal, while nearly all other synods that had opportunity to discuss this matter in part turned back the new doctrinal basis as inappropriate and in part rejected and condemned it with a hardly-to-be-expected unanimity as a disgraceful public apostasy from the church of our fathers and from Biblical truth. No paper that purports to be an organ of the Lutheran Church, with the exception of the *Lutheran Observer,* has adopted the cause of an official change of symbol; even the Gettysburg *Lutherische Kirchenbote* and the *Evangelical Lutheran* of Springfield, Ohio, have not done so formally, although the latter gave space in its columns to favorable reactions to the proposal as well as to its refutation. On the contrary, especially the *Lutheran Standard* of Columbus, Ohio, has borne witness against it with Lutheran seriousness and manly determination. Also the *Lutherische Herold* of New York with righteous indignation rejected the disgraceful suggestion to Lutherans to level their own fortifications, and the *Missionary* of Pittsburgh has expressly and unreservedly embraced the condemnatory verdict on the project expressed by the East Pennsylvania Synod, among others.

Surely this constellation fills all who together with us love the Lutheran Zion of this country with equally great joy and hope for the future. It has become evident from this that the number of those who have not bowed, or will no longer bow, their knees to the Baal of the so-called progress and so-called higher enlightenment of the 19th century is undoubtedly greater than our weak faith and faintheartedness had imagined. The more this must strengthen the faith and courage of all loyal Lutherans in this country, the more urgent appears the challenge that we see in this situation, namely that the unity which God by His marvelous grace has already effected in our midst now be nurtured by us with the highest fidelity and the greatest diligence. At least we for our small part feel solemnly obligated to contribute our mite to this cause.

Our brethren in Germany, who do their work scattered among the various territorial churches, have chosen free conferences, church rallies, and the like as the means to nurture their unity of faith and confession. We are convinced that, after a time in which the various particular churches had experienced a serious deterioration of doctrine and discipline (as in the past century), there is nothing more suitable (except public written testimony) for the individual awakening members in the various church bodies to further and strengthen resurging church unity than the means chosen within our German mother church. Do we not have similar circumstances in our country? May we not expect that similar joint conferences could by God's grace be all the more effective here, the more the church is free from the bonds of the state and the more mere theorizing conflicts with all church life in this country? We have no doubt of it.

Herewith, therefore, we dare to make this public proposal: *Would it not be advantageous and helpful for the endeavor ultimately to achieve one Evangelical Lutheran Church of North America to arrange for the meeting of such members of the various synods bearing the Lutheran name as acknowledge and confess without reservation the Unaltered Augsburg Confession of 1530 as the pure and faithful expression of the doctrine of Holy Scripture and of their own faith?* We on our part would be eager to participate in such a conference of orthodox Lutherans, no matter when or where the majority of the participants choose to have it, and we can guarantee that a number of local theologians and laymen are equally willing. For them the well-being of our dear Evangelical Lutheran Church in our new home is no less the deepest yearning of their hearts, and we have already communicated to them the proposal published here.

In fact, also among Lutherans in this land who are sincerely committed to the primary confession of our church there are still some differences of conviction, and a discussion of these differences in our periodicals can easily do more to hinder than to promote the universally desired union of our church. Therefore a personal oral communication and exchange can no doubt only be salutary and, above all, would surely provide the imcomparable blessing that the battle which will, of course, continue to be necessary also within our church would receive and keep the character of a mutual rivalry among brethren for the faithful preservation of the precious treasure of purity and unity of doctrine.

In order not to prejudge the matter for the brethren, we will say no more about our proposal at this time. We commend the cause to the invisible Lord and Head of the church. As for topics, format, time, place, etc., of such joint consultations, we await the opinion, whether through private letters or in our church papers, of those who deem the matter worth considering and discussing. We merely add that the meetings, in spite of their public form, will naturally be only of private character, and all persons present should participate only for their own persons without wanting to represent their respective synods.[2]

Consubstantiation and Impanation

Lehre und Wehre, II, 2, Feb. 1856, pp. 33—43

If the opponents of the Lutheran Church here in America want to be concise in describing the teaching of Luther, the Augsburg Confession, the Formula of Concord, and the entire old Lutheran church on the Lord's Supper, especially as regards the manner in which the body and blood of Jesus Christ are present in this sacrament, they commonly resort to the use of the technical terms in our title, *consubstantiation* and *impanation,* or also *incorporation.*

This labeling is still used in the latest edition of the *Encyclopedia of Religious Knowledge,* 1854, edited by J. Newton Brown. Under the entry "Consubstantiation" we read the following: "A tenet of the lutheran church respecting the presence of Christ in the Lord's supper. Luther denied that the elements were changed after consecration, and therefore taught that the bread and wine indeed remain; but that together with them, there is present the substance of the body of Christ, which is literally (!) received by communicants. As in red-hot iron it may be said, two distinct substances, iron and fire, are united, so is the body of Christ joined with the bread." Under the entry "Lutheranism" we are told that "It has undergone some alterations since the time of its founder. Luther believed the *impanation* or *consubstantiation.*"

It is indeed a pitiable and devastating testimony to the level of theological education in this country when a book claiming to represent that education contains such disfigurements (to say no more) of the teaching of a church that is spread across the entire globe. But it is even more unpardonable and presupposes either the greatest ignorance or evil intent when alleged theologians who call themselves Lutherans are just as incorrect in presenting the teaching of the church whose servants, stewards, and watchmen they want to be. Alas, this is by no means an infrequent occurrence! The whole so-called "American Lutheran" church, led by such men as Dr. B. Kurtz and Dr. S. S. Schmucker, dissociates itself, to be sure, from *consubstantiation* or *impanation* in the Lord's Supper, yet, in spite of all protests on the part of Lutherans in this country who are faithful to the Symbols, keeps on boldly accusing these Lutherans and the whole old Lutheran Church that has remained loyal to Luther's teaching of holding this unbiblical conception of the presence of the body and blood of Jesus Christ in the Sacrament of the Altar. This is so notorious that we may dispense with documentation from the *Lutheran Observer* or the *Evangelical Lutheran.*

To be sure, the warning has often been issued in recent years against reviving the old controversy about the Lord's Supper. However, just those who issue this warning keep on attacking the teaching of the Lutheran Church on this point and not only call it a remnant of the papacy and a product of dark and superstitious days, but they also give that teaching a completely false interpretation and then make their renunciation of it a shibboleth of genuine American Lutherans. Who, then, is responsible for stirring up the old conflict? Those who remain faithful to the teaching of our church as deposited in its Symbols and defend it against attacks and distortions? Or is it not rather those who in the midst of our church oppose and misinterpret this teaching as unbiblical and papistic? Every fair-minded person, even among our opponents, must concede that it is the latter.

For the moment, we will confine ourselves to rejecting the doctrine of a consubstantiation or an impanation that is imputed to Lutherans who are faithful to the Symbols.

First of all, what do these terms mean?—*Consubstantiation,* as the word indicates, means a combination of two substances in such a way that by being mixed together they are fused into one substance or mass, consisting of different ingredients. For example, pouring the substances of water and wine together produces a watered wine *(Weinwasser);* blending honey and water produces mead; mixing meat and flour produces meat pies. Hence, in the Lord's Supper consubstantiation would involve the concept of a spacial combination, mixture, and fusion of the body and blood of Christ with the consecrated elements as a new dual mass, as Eutyches once asserted the fusion of both natures in Christ into one nature. *Impanation* signifies the spacial inclusion, concealment, incapsulation of an item within the bread, as in a capsule containing and enclosing the item. Hence, in the Lord's Supper impanation would express the idea that the body of Christ, compressed into a very small body, lies concealed under the consecrated bread and is enclosed by it as by its container.[1w]

These conceptions of the presence of Christ, that is, of His body and blood, in the Holy Supper are thoroughly *unbiblical,* materialistic, unworthy, and self-contradictory, and they are equally *un-Lutheran* and in contradiction to the Confessions of our church. In his essay, "That These Words of Christ, 'This is My Body,' etc., Still Stand Firm," 1527, Luther writes: "But *how* this takes place or how he is in the bread, we do not know and are not meant to know. God's Word we should believe without setting bounds or measure to it. The bread we see with our eyes, but we hear with our ears that Christ's body *is present "(Luther's Works,* American Edition, Vol. 37, p. 29).

In this confession of ignorance on this point the whole orthodox Lutheran church followed Luther. So that the Word of the eternal Son of God remain true, this church has at all times insisted that the body and blood of Jesus Christ *are there,* but it has never claimed to be able to explain the *how,* the manner of the presence. For that reason the church has called the presence of Christ's body and blood in the Sacrament one that is supernatural, mystical, hidden from reason, incomprehensible, unsearchable, completely unaccustomed *(inusitata,* something for which there is no full analogy, no second species of the same genus). But the church has also explicitly rejected and condemned all those crass, crude, carnal, Capernaitic (John 6:59-64) conceptions of an earthly, physical, spacial presence, that is, a presence that yields or takes up space. All ways of speaking employed by our church have the single purpose of acknowledging and affirming *the reality and verity of the presence* of the heavenly gifts of the Sacrament and at the same time excluding those unworthy conceptions hatched by reason. When the church calls the presence substantial or real, or at times also corporeal, it does not mean to define the mode of presence but to insist on nothing more than that the presence is a true one, that is, that the body of Christ is really there.

The first one to impute the conception of impanation and consubstantiation to Luther was *Carlstadt,* who therefore in a blasphemous way referred to the God of the Lutherans as a "God made of bread" (St. Louis Edition, XX, 577). Zwingli, Oecolampadius, and even Bucer of Strasbourg followed Carlstadt in this matter. *Bucer,* however, revoked his accusation after he had read Luther's "Confession Concerning Christ's Supper" and had talked with Luther. He wrote:

When Luther in the process of this disputation went into greater detail on this entire matter of the Sacrament, I perceived that he did not combine the body and blood of the Lord with bread and wine by a natural bond, nor enclose body and blood spacially in bread and wine, nor attribute to the sacraments the peculiar power through which these achieve the salvation of the communicants, but that he merely affirmed a sacramental union between the bread and the Lord's body, between His blood and the wine. Furthermore, he teaches that the strengthening of faith attributed to the sacraments does not rest on a power which inheres in the external elements as such, but a power which belongs to Christ and is imparted by His Spirit through the words and sacred signs. When I understood this, I was at pains to show and commend this also to others. Therefore here and now I desire to testify to all who read this that Martin Luther and those who truly agree with him and duly follow his teaching *do not assume any impanation* in the Holy Supper, *nor any local inclusion* of Christ's body in the bread and blood in the wine, nor do they ascribe any saving power to the external actions of the Sacrament as such. They assume a *true, substantial presence and distribution* of the Lord's body and blood with the bread and wine in Holy Communion, as both the Lord's own words and the testimony of the apostle clearly express. This presence and distribution is based on the words and institution of the Lord Himself, *without any natural union* of Christ's body and blood with the elements . . .[1] (cf. *Concordia, Instituted at Wittenberg in the Year 1536. A Declaration Concerning the Presence of the Body and Blood of the Lord Is Added.* By M. Bucer.—Urcellis, ch. 3—6).

However, Bucer's retraction did not put an end to the controversy. As late as two years before his death Luther felt compelled to treat this matter again. In his last confession he writes:

Zwingli had a long, absurd talk with me [at Marburg] about local inclusion, that the body of Christ could not be in the bread as it would be in space or in a vessel, just as if we taught that Christ's body was in the bread like straw in a sack, or wine in a barrel. After that some of them excused themselves and said that they had understood that we and the papists taught that Christ's body was in the sacrament locally, like straw in a sack. Oh, that was a useless, insignificant, lame excuse!

For they knew very well that neither the papists nor we had taught that. Even if they had not understood it otherwise (which is entirely unlikely), they had to confess in this way that they, like mad persons, were attacking matters which they themselves had never heard of nor understood. . . .

The papists teach, yes, not the papists but the holy Christian church and we with them (for the pope, as stated, did not institute the sacrament), that Christ's body is not present locally *[localiter]* (like straw in a sack) in the sacrament, but definitively *[definitive]*. That is, He is certainly there, not like straw in a sack, but yet bodily and truly there . . . *(Brief Confession Concerning the Holy Sacrament,* 1544, *Luther's Works,* American Edition, Vol. 38, p. 301).

In fact, Luther could not have expressed more clearly how he wanted the presence of Christ's body and blood in the Lord's Supper taught than by saying, as he does here, that the body and blood of Christ are in the consecrated elements not locally but definitively. Hence he merely wanted to affirm the "where," that is, *the reality of the presence with the exclusion of all spacial forms of existence;* just as, for example, man's spirit, an angel, a glorified body, heaven and hell have their "where," or are definitively somewhere, without possessing space or extension. To them belongs illocality, even though they are indeed somewhere.

Thus, when Luther says that Christ's body is there definitively, he by no means intends to define the manner of the sacramental presence and consider it to be a definitive one *in the sense in which* it applies to angels. Here the point of comparison is solely *illocality,* the taking away of size, weight, extension, in short, of every way of being somewhere as it obtains in this world of the senses.[2] Carpzov is therefore correct in saying in his *Introduction to the Symbolical Books:* "We point out that this presence is *not* a limited or physical, that is, spacial, or angelic, that is, *definitive,* but an unlimited and divine presence, which belongs to Christ's body and blood by virtue of the union of natures. Thereby the power to be present wherever it wills, which belongs to the divine nature, is communicated to the human nature in Christ" (Isagoge, p. 345).

After Luther's death it was *Calvin* who revived the old accusation, as may be gathered from the *Apologia confessionis de coena Domini contra corruptelas Calvini* [Defense of the Confession Concerning the Lord's Supper, Against the Corruptions of Calvin], by Joachim Westphal at Hamburg (Urcellis, 1558, cf. pp. 297 ff.). Therefore our church has spoken clearly about this in the Formula of Concord of 1580. Here it says among other things (in a citation from the Wittenberg Concord, as it had been jointly composed and signed by Luther and Bucer and other Saxon and South German theologians in the year 1536): We "do not believe that the body and blood of Christ are locally enclosed in the bread, or are in some way permanently united with it apart from the use of the sacrament . . ." (Formula of Concord, Solid Declaration, VII, 14; Tappert, p. 571).

In the Formula of Concord our fathers do not even reject the predicate "spiritual" with reference to the presence and reception of Christ's body and blood in the Holy Supper, so long as it is correctly understood. They write:

> But when Dr. Luther or we use the word "spiritual" in this discussion, we have in mind the spiritual, supernatural, heavenly mode according to which Christ is present in the Holy Supper, not only to work comfort and life in believers but also to wreak judgment on unbelievers. Thus we reject the Capernaitic conception of a gross, carnal presence which the Sacramentarians[2W] ascribe to and force upon our churches in spite of our public and oft-repeated testimony to the contrary. In this sense, too, we use the word "spiritual" when we say that the body and blood of Christ in the Holy Supper are received, eaten, and drunk spiritually, for although such eating occurs with the mouth, the mode is spiritual (Solid Declaration, VII, 105; Tappert, p. 588).

Therefore they say in the Epitome:

> Accordingly we herewith condemn without any qualification the Caper-naitic eating of the body of Christ as though one rent Christ's flesh with one's teeth and digested it like other food. The Sacramentarians deliberately insist on crediting us with this doctrine, against the witness of their own consciences over our many protests, in order to make our teaching obnoxious to their hearers. On the contrary, in accord with the simple words of Christ's testament, we hold and believe in a true, though supernatural, eating of Christ's body and drinking of his blood, which we cannot comprehend with our human sense or reason. Here we take our intellect captive in obedience to Christ, as we do in other articles also, and accept this mystery in no other way than by faith and as it is revealed in the Word (Formula of Concord, Epitome, VII, 42; Tappert, p. 486).

Finally, the Formula of Concord, quoting Luther, teaches:

> The one body of Christ has three different modes, or all three modes, of being at any given place.
>
> 1. The comprehensible, corporeal mode of presence, as when he walked bodily on earth and vacated or occupied space according to his size. He can still employ this mode of presence when he wills to do so, as he did after his resurrection and as he will do on the Last Day. . . . He is not in God or with the Father or in heaven according to this mode, as the fanatic spirit dreams, for God is not a corporeal space or place. The passages which the enthusiasts adduce concerning Christ's leaving the world and going to the Father [to refute the possibility of a presence in the Lord's Supper][3] speak of this mode of presence.
>
> 2. There is, secondly, the incomprehensible, spiritual mode of presence according to which he neither occupies nor vacates space but penetrates every creature, wherever he wills. To use some imperfect illustrations, my vision penetrates air, light, or water and does not occupy or vacate any space; a musical sound or tone passes through air or water or a board and a wall and neither occupies nor vacates space; likewise light and heat[3 W] go through air, water, glass, or crystal and exist without occupying or vacating space, and many more like these. He employed this mode of presence when he left the closed grave and came through locked doors,[4 W] in the bread and wine in the Lord's Supper, and, as people believe, when he was born of his mother.
>
> 3. Thirdly, since he is one person with God, the divine, heavenly mode, according to which all creatures are indeed much more penetrable and present to him than they are according to the second mode (Solid Declaration, VII, 98—101; Tappert, pp. 586 f.).

In view of these definite and crystal-clear explanations it would seem to be impossible for the Reformed to continue saddling the Lutherans with impanation and consubstantiation. But behold! When they noticed that their battle against the true Biblical view of the sacramental union presented by Lutherans made even a seeming victory impossible for them, the Reformed clung to their old figment and continued to combat it as Lutheran superstition just as bravely and victoriously as Baron Muenchhausen. Also the later dogmaticians, therefore, saw themselves compelled again and again to repudiate those conceptions as unbiblical and un-Lutheran.

[Editorial Note: Walther offers two lengthy citations from John Gerhard, who presents the same line of argument in opposition to impanation and consubstantiation and in favor of the supernatural mode of the presence of Christ's body and blood by virtue of the sacramental union. Walther continues:]

It should therefore be perfectly clear that we Lutherans want nothing to do with either consubstantiation or impanation and that we are not minded at all to define the mode of the sacramental presence. Nevertheless, it might appear to many people that all our explanations seem to be contradicted by our customary way of speaking: *In, with,* and *under* the bread, the body of Jesus Christ is present in the Holy Supper.

This is not the place to demonstrate whether this grammatical and logical paraphrase of the Lord's words is suitable; we hope to do so another time. Here we simply want to point out that in the light of what was said above it is self-evident that those words are meant to express neither an impanation nor a consubstantiation, but nothing more than faith in the real and true presence of Christ's body and blood in the Holy Supper. We Lutherans are not remotely interested in binding anyone to the explanatory words "in, with, and under," as long as he confesses without subterfuge that he believes that the body and blood are really and truly present. At the same time we are convinced that one who sincerely believes in the real presence as the Lord promises it it in the words, "This is my body," as the bread is given, and "This is my blood," as the cup is given, will not be offended by those words. On the contrary, he will acknowledge them as a human way of speaking that could not be otherwise in view of the faith of his heart.

Therefore Luther says: "When the fathers and we occasionally say, 'Christ's body is in the bread,' we do so quite simply because by our faith we wish to confess that Christ's body is present. Otherwise we may well allow it to be said that it is in the bread, it is the bread, it is where the bread is, or whatever you wish. Over the words we do not wish to argue, just so the meaning is retained that it is not mere bread that we eat in Christ's Supper, but the body of Christ" ("That These Words of Christ, 'This Is My Body,' etc., Still Stand Firm," 1527; *Luther's Works,* American Edition, Vol. 37, p. 65). Gerhard speaks in the same vein: "Only grant us the true, real, and substantial presence of Christ's body and blood in the Holy Supper. Agree that the words of Christ as they read must be taken in their original, natural, and proper sense, and we will easily come to terms with them regarding the use of these particles." *(Loci theologici,* "Locus de sacra coena" [Theological Topics, Topic on the Lord's Supper], par. 98, ed. Cott.).

More weight might apparently be attached to the objection of the Reformed that we do, after all, sing in our church:

> That we never may forsake Him,
> His body gave for us to take Him,
> Hidden in the bread so small,
> And in the wine His blood for all.[4]

This is the second stanza of the incomparable Communion hymn "Jesus Christ, Our Blessed Savior." This hymn is Luther's German version of a hymn by John Hus, perhaps (as Wackernagel[5 W] thinks) originally composed in Bohemian and later put into Latin. In the Latin text the words in question are *Nobis in sui memoriam dedit hanc panis hostiam* [In His memory He gave us this offering of bread]. However suspicious the words "hidden in the bread so small" might appear to those who do not know our church's teaching, the solution of the riddle of this mode of speech, which seems to express impanation, is quite simple. Here the word "hidden" is not an adjective modifying "body," nor does the word "small" refer to the body. Rather, "hidden" is here used as an adverb belonging to the verb "gave," and the word "small" modifies "bread." Therefore the sense is: In a manner "hidden" from our understanding, that is, incomprehensibly, the Lord gave us His body, the highest and greatest gift, to eat in and with so "small" a morsel of bread. So our theologians have always understood these words. To cite just one theologian, *John Andrew Quenstedt:*

> When we sing Luther's translation of Hus' hymn, "hidden in the bread so small" (Latin: *parvo latens in crustulo),* we are not, as the Calvinists accuse us, singing of an inclusion of the body lying hidden in the bread (for we say expressly that no divine presence can be described as lying hidden), but we sing of the depth of the mystery, we praise the ineffable presence, and we lift our spirit to the incomprehensible greatness of the benefit imparted to us in this most sacred meal. The word "hidden" refers to the mode of *giving,* namely that Jesus Christ presents His body for sacramental reception in a manner hidden and beyond all understanding. We are here not concerned about the Latin translator who refers "hidden" to body, as an adjective modifying the noun. But if he takes it

adverbially, he is correct. Therefore "hidden" must not be referred to an inclusion but to an understanding of the matter, since for His most sacred remembrance the Lord Jesus has presented the greatest mystery in a tiny morsel of bread, and has given His body hidden, hidden not in the crumb of bread, but *hidden in the manner of its presence,* as we have learned to know it entirely from revelation and do not acquire by any shrewdness on our part *(Theologia didactico-polemica* [Didactic-Polemical Theology], chapter 6, section 2, question 3, folio 1221).

We hope that this short discussion will settle the question for those who are sincerely concerned about the truth whether our church teaches consubstantiation or impanation. But to try to silence those who substitute desire for reason would be just as foolish and futile as trying to silence an echo by means of louder shouting. By the way, we are firmly convinced that many a person who is still secretly afraid of the Lutheran, that is, Biblical teaching on the Lord's Supper would accept this teaching with joy if he learned to know it as it really is and if it were not presented to him as something monstrous through the unconscionable distortions of our opponents. One who sincerely believes that Holy Scripture is God's Word and that Christ is God and man in one person cannot do otherwise than believe that also the word: "This is My body," is the truth and that the God-man, who gives Himself wholly to us sinners, also desires and is able to impart to us His humanity assumed into His deity.

Is It Heretical to Question
the Canonicity
of Some New Testament Writings?[1]

Lehre und Wehre, II, 7, July 1856, pp. 204—16

We are led to this question by the comments on the Revelation of St. John which Pastor Roebbelen published in *Der Lutheraner,* where he also confessed that together with Luther he did not regard Revelation as canonical. It has come to our ears that this has here and there caused great offense. We, too, cannot agree with our dear brother Roebbelen in this point, since we are convinced that Revelation, that precious book of comfort for Christians and for the church, belongs to the canon. Nevertheless, we believe that it is improper and probably based on ignorance of the situation to regard an otherwise blameless theologian as a dangerous false teacher who makes God's Word itself suspect because, even though he sincerely regards all homologoumena (universally accepted books) as canonical, he questions the canonicity of one or the other antilegomenon (a disputed book). Such an attitude would be thoroughly un-Lutheran, since *our revered fathers in the faith almost without exception until after the writing of the Formula of Concord were of the opinion and so stated that either all or at least some of the antilegomena did not belong into the canon.* They did this not from undue haste or levity over against the Word of God but, on the contrary, out of profound conscientiousness with respect to the same. *Luther's* judgments on the antilegomena are not only no "stain" on our church but rather give testimony to the care which men in our church once took regarding what should be the rule and norm of our faith and life. On the other hand, the summary decrees of papists and Reformed that every Christian on the pain of losing his salvation *must* accept also all antilegomena as canonical is not only no testimony to reverence for the Word of God in these denominations but is in fact a demonstration of how easy it is for those who want to see Scripture interpreted either in a blind collier's faith according to the *church's* (i.e., the pope's) whim or according to the principles of *reason* to receive something into the canon.

It is, therefore, our opinion that this might be the proper place to transmit to our cherished readers some testimonies of what our fathers especially of the 16th and the first half of the 17th century thought about this matter; not because we ourselves share their opinion but only to show that doubts about the canonicity of *disputed* books may be fostered even by those whose reputation of orthodoxy no Lutheran will dare to deny. In this way we hope to clear Luther, among others, of the suspicion that with reprehensible boldness he passed judgment on books of the New Testament canon in a subjective and arbitrary way.

It will not be necessary to print *Luther's* views here, since they are contained in his Prefaces to the New Testament and to the antilegomena.[2]

Of especial importance is the testimony of Martin Chemnitz, chief co-author of the Formula of Concord. He speaks at length on this question in his *Examination of the Council of Trent.* He may lead the procession of witnesses.

At the Council of Trent it was decreed:

> If anyone does not accept as sacred and canonical the aforesaid books in their entirety and with all their parts as they have been accustomed to be read in the Catholic Church and as they are contained in the old Latin Vulgate Edition, and knowingly and deliberately rejects the aforesaid traditions, let him be anathema (H. J. Schroeder, *Canons and Decrees of the Council of Trent,* 4th Session, first decree, p. 18).

On this decree *Martin Chemnitz* writes in his *Examination of the Council of Trent,* among other things, as follows: *[Editiorial Note: In a lengthy quotation covering five closely-printed pages, Chemnitz reviews the matter. He asserts that the church has no authority to wipe out distinctions between New Testament writings universally accepted and those whose place in the canon was disputed in the past, in the early history of the church. Since this is a historical question, the issue must be left undecided. The writings of Eusebius and Jerome clearly indicate that the early church distinguished between* homologoumena *and* antilegomena, *the latter comprising the epistles of James, Jude, 2 Peter, 2 and 3 John, Revelation, and perhaps Hebrews. Chemnitz states that "this whole matter depends on the sure, firm, and harmonious testimonies of the first and ancient church, and where these are lacking, the later church, as it cannot make genuine books out of spurious ones, so also it cannot make certain writings out of doubtful ones without clear and firm proofs." This does not mean, says Chemnitz, that those disputed books should simply be rejected and condemned. The purpose of this dispute is "that the rule of faith or of sound doctrine in the church may be sure." While the antilegomena should not be made the basis of church dogma, they may well be read for the edification of the people.*[3]

Walther then cites statements of varying length from the Magdeburg Centuries *(a 16th-century work on church history by Flacius, Wigand, Judex, and Basilius Faber), Andrew Osiander (died 1617), Aegidius Hunnius (died 1603), Dr. Hafenreffer (died 1619), Conrad Dietrich (died 1639), Friedrich Balduin (died 1627), and Dr. Theodore Thummius (died 1630). Then Walther continues:]*

May God grant that these testimonies may serve the purpose that everyone will strive to become very sure of his faith in these last distressful days and realize that in many points such certainty can be obtained only through conscientious and serious research and great inner struggles of conscience. But may these words also warn everyone against the serious sin of immediately suspecting those of opposing the Word of God who cling to all articles of faith together with the most faithful teachers of our church in its best and most blessed days and acknowledge as the divine rule and norm of faith and life those holy books that have been *universally received* at all times by Christendom, but who nevertheless hesitate to accept as on the same level of authority those books that have been opposed and about whose origin and authority also upright and faithful Christians and teachers of the church have had their doubts at one time or another.

Such people do not attack the divine *teaching* contained in the disputed writings but desire to see them interpreted in the light of the homologoumena, rather than the other way around. If there is no unchristian procedure in the discussion of this question, and if the poor people are not confused by dishonest treatment of this issue through partisan exploitation of a thesis which the people will have great difficulty understanding—which is very easy in this case—then a treatment of this question can only serve to arouse Christians to serious searching and be used as an opportunity to establish them more deeply and more firmly in their faith.

In case any periodical should take note of this matter, we state in advance that we will not deign to answer stupid prattle that may pretend to be a defense of the Word of God. However, we will give appropriate consideration to an objective discussion of this important matter, even though in the process our old teachers, men like Luther, Brenz, Chemnitz, Veit and Conrad Dietrich, and others, should be most severely judged.

The Distinction of Estates in the Church

[First Part:] Lehre und Wehre, II, 10, Oct. 1856, pp. 289—99

Motto: "Temporal authority is concerned with matters altogether different from the Gospel. Temporal power does not protect the soul, but with the sword and physical penalties it protects body and goods from the power of others. Therefore, the two authorities, the spiritual and the temporal, are not to be mingled or confused." (Augsburg Confession, XXVIII, 11-12; Tappert, pp. 82—83). "The writings of our theologians have profitably illumined this whole question of the distinction between Christ's kingdom and a political kingdom. Christ's kingdom is spiritual; it is the knowledge of God in the heart, the fear of God and faith, the beginning of eternal righteousness and eternal life. At the same time it lets us make outward use of the legitimate political ordinances of the nation in which we live, just as it lets us make use of medicine or architecture, food or drink or air. . . . Thus they failed to see that the Gospel brings eternal righteousness to hearts, while it approves the civil government" (Apology, XVI, 2, 8; Tappert, pp. 222—23).[1][W]

In his "Opening Address at the Fifth Convention of the Buffalo Synod" on June 23 of this year Pastor Grabau[1] says, among other things: "I have not yet had the audacity to label the earlier polity of the Lutheran Church a mere ceremony. For what *God Himself* has ordained and prescribed in it is not a mere human arrangement. The reformers did not establish a church government of Christians in general, where the heads of the crowd ruled according to their will and agreement" (very true!); "but with a clear eye they recognized how God Himself fashioned the visible church in its members. They presented it as an obvious truth; that in His true visible church God established three chief members or estates: the *holy ministry,* the *household,* and the *civil government.*[2][W] They took this plain truth as the basis for the polity of the church. They called it the 'estate of teaching, of nurture, and of defense.'

"This teaching of the Lutheran Church has in recent years experienced neglect and contempt, for in practice people preferred letting everything be constructed and built up out of the doctrine of the exclusively invisible universal church. . . . When we speak of the polity of the Lutheran Church and individual congregations we are not thinking of the above-mentioned *human* provisions and constitutions but of the *structuring of the holy*

27

church in its visibleness, as *God Himself* establishes and structures it for communal life and work. Hence those members of the church who are called upon to govern must all be plants planted by God Himself, or else they 'will be rooted up' [Matthew 15:13]. However, in speaking of members of the church we are here not thinking of the individual souls, including the children, as the creed commonly takes it, but we are here speaking of the members whom our Lord God has *specified for government* in the visible church in accordance with their obvious nature and makeup.

"What do we find about this in the Scriptures? We find the holy ministry as the *first member* which God has given to care for and rule over His church (1 Timothy 3; Titus 1; 1 Peter 5, etc.) . . . But *since* the hearers, whether of the household or civil government, are commanded to *obey* the Word of God, and hence their teachers and spiritual leaders who proclaim it (Hebrews 13:17), it follows that obedience to the Word of God" (or, as stated above, teachers and spiritual leaders!) "is the highest and noblest thing in the church. Without it the godly preaching of the teachers could not be done 'with joy' but must be done 'with grief' [Hebrews 13:17 KJV]. The entire church government is directed and oriented toward this obedience to the Word of God.

"The question now is whether God has also placed such members into the visible body of the church as should by virtue of their calling implement this obedience to the Word of God and watch over it. And the Lutheran Reformation answers the question with a resounding YES! For in the Word of God there is the dignity of the *housefather* who is to teach all his household to walk in the fear of God and in obedience to His Word, and there is the strengthening of his power to punish the family members who go astray. In his position the housefather is backed by the divine authority of the Fourth Commandment. Leaning on this pillar, he rules over his domestics and his children, and is also the head of his wife.

"Here, then, we meet the *second member* God has placed into the body of His visible church for the purpose of procuring obedience to the preached Word. Therefore the Lutheran Church rightly sings: 'How blessed is this place where God Himself holds sway, a house which has a head whom God guides in His way.' For it is through this estate that the whole Word of God is to pass into everyday life, because the citizens of Jerusalem with their houses should serve the Lord and not idols. Therefore we must not think that the domestic estate established by God within the church has little or no share in the government of the church. It has the important function of seeing to it that the Word of God holds sway in the circle of its [this estate's] calling, for we read that the women should ask her husband [1 Corinthians 14:35] and the fathers should teach their children (Psalm 78:5). They are to bring up their children 'in the discipline and instruction of the Lord' (Ephesians 6:4). 'Men should pray, lifting up holy hands without anger or quarreling' [1 Timothy 2:8]. They should 'bring back the sinner from the error of his way' (James 5:20). They should 'admonish the idlers,' etc. (1 Thessalonians 5:14). There should be 'glad songs in the tents of the righteous'(Psalm 118:15). In fact, we are told that in this estate even the first and second admonitions are to be given a sinner (Matthew 18), and that in the final admonition in the third step this estate is again involved, as Christ says: 'Tell it to the church.' Hence also the judges in the church" (in what sense?) "must come from the domestic estate. Out of this estate the apostles had the assembly choose seven men as almoners" (not also as preachers?), "'men of good repute, full of the Spirit and wisdom'[Acts 6:3]. The domestic estate elected them, and the apostles appointed them.

"Now, we surely no longer ask whether the Christian household is such a member of the visible church, with a rightful place in church government. For God established it as such before we asked. The gift bestowed by God on this calling should also be used for the common good. Therefore in the structuring of the Christian church it is only a matter of integrating this member as God has prescribed in His Word. Unfortunately, however, the new doctrine of the church sought something else; it sought to give due honor not to the Christian *estate,* but to the number of heads and the will of the crowd, instead of obedience to God's Word" (impudent insinuation!). . . .

"Here we come face to face with the *third member* of the church, which has the same task, namely to plant and to preserve obedience to the holy Word of God. This is the *estate of civil government,* that is, if it"(!) "has entered the believing fellowship of the church by means of a public confession and in faith has kissed the Son (Psalm 2:11). The Treatise on the Power and Primacy of the Pope calls it" (whom?—the estate? God forbid! who then?) "'the chief members of the church'(Par. 54; Tappert, p. 329). Consequently" (in consequence of what?) "it is self-evident that the government and the judges on earth enter the church not only with their own persons but also with their divinely ordained *estate,* just as the housefather does with his estate, and that the persons in the estate of the government must now serve the church with their God-given authority and gift of rule for the common good. As Paul says (Romans 13), they are especially to protect and preserve the pious in their rights and to restrain and punish the wicked according to Christian laws" (!!).

"This does not mean" (??) "mingling spiritual and secular government, for such mingling takes place only if the civil government insists on running the church's affairs alone, without the two other members in the church.[3 w] As long as it governs together with the other two and protects and implements what the church" (here the church is again conceived without the government and probably taken as referring to the pastors) "has said on the basis of God's Word, civil government is thus involved in governing the church in accordance with God's will. Through this active membership of the state in the church of God the church's pronouncements and resolutions receive their authority and emphasis" (God have mercy if the church's pronouncements and resolutions receive their authority and emphasis only through the civil government!). "In this way the reverence and obedience of all church members toward the Word of God and Christian truth and justice will be greatly promoted. In this relationship the civil government does not coerce" (?) "the church but serves it for the protection of the godly and for the common good, which is obedience to God's Word.

"Thus we see that the polity of the Lutheran Church regarded the three estates instituted by God Himself as those members of the church that should constitute the government of the church. In this way our church differed from the Roman church, where only the priests and bishops ruled and told the rest what to do." (As we shall soon see even more clearly, this is precisely what Pastor Grabau is proposing here!). "This is called the Catholic hierarchy. It desired to be completely isolated from joint rule with the domestic estate and the civil government." (This is not true. Rome was always pleased when the government "ruled jointly" in such a way that it "served" the church and "protected and implemented" what the "Catholic" church allegedly said "on the basis of God's Word," and thus gave its "pronouncements and resolutions their authority and emphasis"; or when the domestic estate recognized its task to see to it that the "Word of God proclaimed" by the priests held sway, especially if that estate remained within "the circle of its calling." The whole difference between the papistic priests and Pastor Grabau at this point is that the latter calls this thing "participation in the government of the church," while the former did not use this inadequate expression. But patience! The matter will become still clearer.)

"We have already shown in part what God has given to each estate. Let us summarize it: In the office of the ministry the Word of God and its salutary teaching and whatever belongs to it makes its way publicly." (We know what belongs to it according to Pastor Grabau's teaching; for example, the clergy decision that the building of a school and other "churchly matters" "that are not contrary to God's Word" must be carried out). "The whole church must listen and be subject to it" (to whom?—the clergy or the Word of God?). "In the domestic estate there is the calling to preserve the sway of the Word of God" (naturally as preached by that ministerial office) "and be obedient to it in life, as well as to bear witness against sin. In the estate of civil government lies the protecting authority for God's Word and the just regulations of the church. By its authority the government is to take good care of the church and break the willfulness of the insolent.

"But this raises the question: Is it not risky to have the three estates joined together in one government? . . . We answer: The question is not whether the members who rule the church are still sinners and at times at cross purposes, but whether and in what manner our *God* has integrated these three members into the body of His church. . . . Furthermore, God is a God of order and of peace also in the government of the church. Let the first member, which is to teach the whole church, *be the first to open its mouth;* let the second member, which is to bring the doctrine into everyday life, *follow* with counsel, faith, and wisdom; let the third member, which is to protect doctrine and godly life, use its wisdom and divine authority to provide *support and emphasis* among men for what the church says." (This also demonstrates that in the proposed so-called joint government of the church the preachers are the ones who rule, and the housefathers and civil rulers have been appointed as the preachers' servants and executors at home and on the street!). . . .

"These three members involved in the church's polity, if they are to remain united, must be careful to observe that God wants to use each estate in the government of the church *only to the extent of its calling,* not to the extent of its wishes, desires, and benefit. . . . For that reason the sainted Luther wished that from all estates those most capable be chosen to govern the church, men full of faith and the Holy Spirit and wisdom. . . . Hence, according to the custom of the Lutheran Church, only these three members: pastors, housefathers, and civil officials, should be admitted to the government of the church; under no circumstances the so-called independent members, or those entitled to vote who are only 20 or 21 years old, that is, young people who should be subject to their parents." (Must not also older children be subject to their parents? And were there not 21-year-old consistorial councillors?). "Our old church orders know nothing of this; it is an abuse which the new doctrine of the invisible church has gradually smuggled in, contrary to the church order. Furthermore, also our church boards should, as much as possible, consist of people from these three divinely ordained estates, and one member should honor the other member and each should regard the other as a gift of God for the welfare of the church. For the unity of the church boards and their members we must also bear in mind that the church boards are not representatives of the will of the crowd, for that creates disunity; rather they are representatives of the truth and of justice and the guardians of obedience to God's Word.[4][w] This creates unity."

So far Pastor Grabau.

We cannot help warning earnestly against these principles of church polity, church order, and church government. They are just as false, unbiblical, and un-Lutheran as they are dangerous; all the more dangerous because Pastor Grabau intends on the basis of these principles to propose also in our country a "general ecclesiastical court" that is to seek "a strong support, a final authority from God" in our *secular government* and "draw it into the church's use." In this plan the housefathers are not to be received as *Christians* and as representing Christians, but as official persons authorized because of their specific *estate.*

It is, of course, quite good and fine for Pastor Grabau to concede that a proper church government should be composed, not of persons from one estate but from all of them. Ever since Luther all faithful Lutherans have always testified to that, especially in the matter of the election and call of preachers and in ecclesiastical courts (having to do with excommunication, synodical affairs, etc.). Yet, while conceding this, Pastor Grabau's agreement with our old orthodox theologians is sheer pretense. They wanted men from all estates so that all might be represented in matters that concern all, since according to God's Word the highest court is not in the hands of a privileged few but of all, namely the church or congregation (Matthew 18:15-20; 1 Corinthians 5:4; 2 Corinthians 2:6; Acts 15:22; 21:22).

Pastor Grabau, however, builds up everything on the "estate." Of the various estates, of nurture and defense and as well as of teaching, he says not only that they are in the church (which is quite right), but also that *as such estates* they belong to the church, as such constitute the church, and as such have the privilege of being judges in the church. This contradicts the Word of God, which says: "There is neither Jew nor Greek, there is neither slave nor free, there is neither male nor female; for you are all one in Christ Jesus" (Galatians 3:28; cf. 1 Corinthians 12:13). "My kingship is not of this world; if My kingship were of this world, My servants would fight" (John 18:36; cf. Luke 22:25-26). Of course, even according to this, housefathers and kings, princes and government officials can be in the church, yet they do not *as such* belong to the church, but as believers; otherwise also unbelieving housefathers and government officials would belong to the church. As a result, the corporal chastisements administered to boys by the

32

housefather as a member of the church, and the death penalty imposed by an orthodox government, would by the entrance of housefathers and government officials into the church be transformed into actions of the church, and it would become a kingdom of this world. At least the orthodox domestic estate and governmental estate would as such also have the power of the keys.

As stated, good and fine as it is that Pastor Grabau wants no estate excluded from the government of the church, he nevertheless wants the persons in the domestic and governmental estates moved into the church in such a way that believing Christians are *deprived* precisely of those rights which our fathers sought to *safeguard* for believing Christians through their teaching that all members of the church must necessarily be represented in the government of the church! In addition, Pastor Grabau clearly betrays the intent to construct a church polity that would no longer have the character of a human arrangement but of a divine order. It is impossible to express how dangerous and appalling this is. Furthermore, Pastor Grabau assigns to the domestic estate and the governmental estate such a position in the government of the church that they have only the function of giving power and emphasis to the pronouncements and resolutions of the preachers. Consequently, instead of protecting the laity from possible political ambitions of arrogant pastors by giving laymen a place in the government of the church (as our fathers intended), Pastor Grabau's theory, if put into action, would only confirm and strengthen the rule of imperious pastors and surround the individual Christian with official power and enchain him, so that under this threefold force imposed on him he would not dare to move or utter a sound. Pastor Grabau's theory rests on a serious misunderstanding of the Lutheran doctrine of the three estates.

For further clarification of this matter, which we intend to elucidate in more detail later, in connection with our discussion of Pastor Grabau's project of establishing a general American Lutheran Church Court, we may be permitted to cite a few testimonies from old and new theologians.

When the papistic bishops could not induce the Lutherans to observe their ceremonies, they resorted to the stratagem of asserting that if the people were unwilling to obey them as *bishops,* they should at least obey them as *princes* within the church (a position which many bishops held at the same time). When Melanchthon, who was involved in discussions on this matter, could not gain clarity on this matter, he wrote from Augsburg to Luther at Coburg. On July 21, 1530, Luther replied:[2]

> First, it is certain that these two governments are separate and different, that is, the ecclesiastical one and the secular one; Satan,

through the papacy, has fundamentally confused and mixed them. We have to be sharply alert here, neither to have them brought together so that the two governments may again be mixed, nor to give an inch to any one or consent that he may mix them. For this would mean to make common sense with thieves and robbers, because in this connection we have the divine Word, which says, "But not so with you" [Luke 22:26]. It is the authority, and it commands that the two governments be preserved separate and unmixed.

Second, from this it follows that the same person cannot be a bishop and a sovereign, nor simultaneously a pastor and a housefather. You understand sufficiently well what I want to say here. I want to keep the persons separate, just as the governments, even though the same man can represent both persons, and one Pomer [Bugenhagen] can be a parish pastor and a householder. . . .

Third, as bishop, a bishop has no authority to impose on his congregations any statute or ceremony, except with the expressed or silent agreement of the church. For the church is free and is the lord of all, and the bishops ought not to dominate the faith of the congregations, nor burden or oppress the congregations against their will. The bishops are, after all, only servants and stewards, and not the lords of the church. . . .

Fourth, as sovereign, a bishop may impose even less on the church, since this would mean fundamentally to mix these two jurisdictions. . . .

Fifth, as sovereign, a bishop may impose upon his subjects, as subjects, whatever seems appropriate to him, as long as it is godly and permissible; the subjects are required to obey, since under these circumstances they obey *not as members of the church*, but as citizens. . . .

We are unable, therefore, either on the basis of the ecclesiastical or the secular law, to grant to the bishops the power to impose anything on the church, even if it is permissible and godly, since one ought not to do evil so that good may result . . . (*Luther's Works,* American Edition, Vol. 49, pp. 383—87).

In view of this, who will still dare to say Luther taught that the housefather and the civil government are part of the church's government *as estates?*[25 W] To be sure, Luther himself called on the elector to take charge of the visitation of parishes; not, however, because the elector by virtue of his civil position was part of the church's government or even, because of it, the supreme authority over the church. In the light of what Luther said above this is altogether impossible.

He himself speaks about it in his Preface to the *Instructions for the Visitors of Parish Pastors in Electoral Saxony:*

Now that the gospel through the unspeakable grace and mercy of

God has again come to us or in fact has appeared for the first time, and we have come to see how grievously the Christian church has been confused, scattered, and torn, we would like to have seen the true episcopal office and practice of visitation re-established because of the pressing need. However, since none of us felt a call or definite command to do this, and St. Peter has not countenanced the creation of anything in the church unless we have the conviction that it is willed of God [1 Peter 4:11], no one has dared to undertake it. Preferring to follow what is certain and to be guided *by love's office* (which is a common obligation of Christians), we have respectfully appealed to the illustrious and noble prince and lord, John, Duke of Saxony . . . our most gracious lord and prince, constituted of God as our certain temporal sovereign, that out of Christian love *(since he is not obligated to do so as a temporal sovereign)* and by God's will for the benefit of the gospel and the welfare of the wretched Christians in his terrritory, His Electoral Grace might call and ordain to this office several competent persons[6W] (*Luther's Works,* American Edition, Vol. 40, p. 271).

In an Opinion of 1536 Luther joined others in declaring that the "calling and election of orthodox servants of the church is not properly and originally a business of the civil government but of the church. If the civil ruler is Christian and a member of the church, he calls, *not because he is the ruler, but because he is a member of the church.* For 'My kingship is not of this world'" (Cited in Loescher, *Unschuldige Nachrichten* [Innocent Reports], 1715, p. 383).

Finally, as late as 1543, after many unhappy experiences concerning the corrupting influence on the church exerted by the secular government, to which many things had been entrusted because of emergency conditions, Luther wrote to Pastor Daniel Cresser in Dresden:

My dear Daniel, I can see no good coming from the form of investigation devised at your court. For the courts want to rule the church according to their desires, God will not grant His blessing, and the last state will be worse than the first, for "whatever does not proceed from faith is sin" [Romans 14:23]. But what happens without a call is doubtlessly done without faith and will perish. Let them either become pastors themselves and preach, baptize, visit the sick, distribute the Lord's Supper, and perform all churchly functions, or desist from mingling the callings. They should look after their court and leave the church to those who have been called to this task and who must account to God for it. It is intolerable that others should assume tasks for which we must give account. We want the offices of the church and of the court to be separate, or else we will leave both alone. Satan continues to be the Adversary. *Under the pope he mingled the church into the secular government, and in our time he wants to mingle the secular government into the church.* But with God's help we will resist and do all we can to keep the callings separate (St. Louis Edition, XXIb, 2911 f.).

After many irksome cases Luther finally went so far as to say that it would be better to abolish the consistories in which men from the secular government had a part and tried to exercise control as a governmental estate through their jurists. He writes: "They want to be in the church and rule over consciences; we will not tolerate that. We must dismantle the consistory, for we simply do not want the jurists and the pope to be involved. The jurists do not belong into the church with their legal processes; they rule the world only with opinions and fancies, not with the law" (Walch Edition, XXII, 2160). . . .

Continuation and Conclusion: Vol. II, No. 12, Dec. 1856, pp. 361—70

To repeat what Pastor Grabau said:

> The reformers did not establish a government of Christians in general, where the heads of the crowd ruled according to their will and agreement,[7W] but with a clear eye they recognized how God Himself fashioned the visible church in its members. They presented it as an obvious truth that in His true visible church God established three chief members or estates: the holy ministry, the household, and the civil government. They took this plain truth as the basis for the polity of the church. They called it "the estate of teaching, of nurture, and of defense. . . ."

Pastor Grabau's theory of church polity and church government may appear to many as quite harmless and Lutheran, since he, ostensibly following our orthodox fathers, wants to include persons from each estate in the church's government. On closer inspection, however, it becomes evident that this theory is anything but Lutheran and harmless. In matters dealing with the election and call of preachers, excommunication, ceremonies, judgment on doctrine, synodical resolutions, etc., that is to say, in matters of church government, our fathers wanted all three estates duly represented. *They did this while safeguarding the principle that no one should rule in the church, that the whole church is the highest court, and that therefore the government of the church would be properly structured in an evangelical and fair way only if not just one or the other but all estates in the church were represented.* They accorded Christians in all estates their participation in the government of the church, not to vindicate a certain privilege in the church for the *estates* as such, but in order to preserve to *all Christians* in these estates their Christian liberty; not because the Christians as members of certain estates had the right to participate in church government, but because the members of all estates had that right as *Christians*; not because an estate as such should rule the church, but because no one should be excluded because of his estate, no matter how secular it might appear to be.

Pastor Grabau, on the contrary, includes the doctrine of the estates in his structural system because he wants to get rid of the "rule of Christians in general" and yet create the impression that his system is not hierarchical. What our fathers wanted to *safeguard* and *provide* for the Christians through the application of the relationships of the estates Pastor Grabau wants to *deny* them and *deprive* them of, under the guise of a good appearance. While our fathers employed the classification of Christians according to their estate so that the rights of Christians in general might be exercised in good, God-pleasing, natural, and salutary order, Pastor Grabau employs the same in order to grant Christians as such only the privilege of obeying and in order to be able to subjugate them under a threefold scepter. While our fathers regarded the domestic and governmental estates as something sanctified and used by the church when they have entered the church, Pastor Grabau regards them as a sort of privileged nobility with whom rests the power of government that is present in the church.

Pastor Grabau was not the first to abuse the doctrine of the estates. It is an old error. Already Luther had to denounce it. In a lecture [on Isaiah] in 1544 he said:

> Therefore we shout and fight with the greatest zeal that a definite and clear and unmistakable distinction and a proper limitation of every estate be maintained, so that the domestic estate is assigned to governing children and family, that the parents govern the household, that the secular princes look after the common welfare, and the subjects are obedient. Likewise, that in the church the knowledge of the Son of God is taught. . . . This distinction between the secular government, the household, and the church must be carefully preserved, and each estate kept within its proper sphere. And even though we have done all we could for this distinction, Satan will not stop mixing them up and creating confusion, and there will never be a lack of people who refuse to remain within the sphere of their office.[8] W The proud, fanatical, and rebellious teachers, not content with their office, usurp also the secular government. On the other hand, the civil government and the princes also meddle in someone else's business, lay hands on the helm of the church's government, and here too arrogate the rule. Thus the devil always has his tools that cause us unrest and go beyond the prescribed limits of their calling. . . . We teach that every one of the three chief estates is godly, or instituted by God, and we despise none of them. But our concern is that they not be intermingled. There is no place here for mingling[3] (St. Louis Edition, VI, 170 f.).

37

[Editorial note: Walther concludes his presentation by introducing extended quotations from an article by Dr. A. G. Rudelbach on "The Teaching of the Lutheran Confessions Concerning the Limits of Ecclesiastical and Civil Power, and the Relationship of This Teaching to Theories of Canon Law."[9]W Rudelbach argues that our confessions nowhere say anything about applying the doctrine of the three estates to the organic presentation of the relationship between church and state. On the contrary, they are careful to distinguish between spiritual and secular power and regard this distinction as a precious gift of the Reformation. Rudelbach points out that the abolition of the Roman episcopal government led, as an emergency measure, to transferring some of the bishops' administration to the Protestant princes, a move that was regretted before long, since it led to interference of the secular government in the internal affairs of the church. Rudelbach observes:]

The apostolic church, which should serve as a model for all subsequent structures of the church, had nothing in common with a secular realm, nor was it an association consisting of those who issued orders and those who were subject to them. The church is not a state but a free and equal fellowship established within the state, a fellowship that repudiates all despotism. . . . Let the prince be the guardian of both tables of the divine Law, but only insofar as both tables have to do with civil welfare, since the care for the eternal welfare of the citizens is no more the concern of the prince than that of every Christian for the spiritual welfare of his neighbor. Hence the prince has at his disposal only Christian means of admonition, intercession, etc. But it would be a great mistake to think that the prince as a Christian has rights different from those of all Christians; for the conventional rights of church members can be transferred only by free mutual agreement.

Foreword to the 1857 Volume

Lehre und Wehre, III, 1, Jan. 1857, pp. 1—4

When a year ago we published the first issue of the second volume [1856] of this periodical, we felt compelled to express joyful hopes regarding our dear church in the United States of North America. On the basis of these hopes we proposed without prior conditions a general Lutheran conference of all those Lutherans in this country who acknowledge and confess without reservation the Unaltered Augsburg Confession of 1530 as the pure and faithful expression of the teaching of Scripture and of their own faith. We hoped that the time had finally come to propose without prejudice such a personal approach to each other on the part of all members of the various synods bearing the Lutheran name who are committed to our church, and in connection with that to provide for an oral exchange concerning the foundation that unites Lutherans. Our hopes rested primarily on the fact that on the occasion of a recently made proposal that the church officially alter our fundamental confession (under the title of a so-called Definite Platform) it became evident that the North American church that is called Lutheran has in its most diverse sections a host of witnesses to whom God has granted enough light, faith, and courage to withstand the revolutionary and destructive cravings of the many apostates in their midst.

Our hope was not disappointed. The conference was held not only in spite of all enemy *machinations* against it, but also in spite of the *doubts* which even faithful members and servants of our church harbored particularly with regard to the basis on which the conference was to be organized and assembled. And we do not doubt that all who were formerly agreed with the purpose and method of the conference are now convinced that the stated purpose was achieved not only to some extent, but beyond all we dared ask or think.[1] Our church in America stood among others in a twofold danger, either of being splintered into hostile armies or of falling prey to the lust for conquest that might be entertained by any synodical coalition with its specific slant, swelling in number and influence and swallowing up everything. Now the conference marked the blessed beginning of stemming this twofold danger with a mighty dike and of clearing the way for the eventual formation of an Evangelical Lutheran

Church of North America united in faith, doctrine, and confession, in spite of all differences in constitution and scope of activity on the part of individual segments of our church in this country, according to the measure of their course of development, their local circumstances, and the knowledge and ability of their leading and cooperating personalities. Such a church, because it would be inwardly strong through the true bond of faith and brotherly love, would also stand firm over against the opponents swarming about it on the outside.

We hope furthermore that the conference has dispelled the doubts of some of those who in honest commitment to the treasure of *all* the official confessions of our church were troubled in their conscience about participating in a conference whose basis for the time being was to be only the *Invariata* (Unaltered Augsburg Confession; or, as a faithful member of our church said at the conference, naively but truly, "the *Unalterable* Augsburg Confession!"). It became very obvious at the conference that, in line with the invitations to the conference, all participants honestly accepted with mouth and heart the Augsburg Confession *"without mental reservation"* and looked upon the other confessions as what they are, authentic explanations and commentaries of the Augsburg Confession, and therefore wanted them to be applied as such.

If it is really certain that the other confessions contain the same doctrine as the Augsburg Confession and none other—something no one who has known both and has carefully compared them will deny—why then cannot one who rests on this certainty offer the hand of brotherhood to those who declare that they accept the Augsburg Confession without reservation? Is it perhaps because at one time even Zwinglians and Calvinists placed themselves under the aegis of the Augsburg Confession in order to share in the political religious peace?[2] Or in general because so many appeal to it deceptively? We think that anyone who is so dishonest and unscrupulous as to allow himself to be pledged to the *Augsburg Confession* and to swear to adhere to it, even though he rejects at least in part the Biblical faith expressed there—such a person has a conscience so broad and dulled and branded that, if it is to his advantage, he will subscribe to the *whole Book of Concord,* containing all the Lutheran Symbols, even though he does not believe their teaching and has no intention of conducting his office in accord with them. Just this Definite Platform movement, by the way, showed clearly enough that men who still have some conscientiousness ultimately find it unbearable publicly to make an unqualified commitment even to the Augsburg Confession alone while there is constant inner contradiction.

Or are we deterred by the practice of our fathers from acknowledging

40

those as brothers in whose midst not all parts of the *Book of Concord* enjoy *symbolical* prestige? A person would have to be quite ignorant of the history of our church if he did not know that the Lutheran churches that had adopted the whole *Book of Concord* as their symbol always dealt in a sisterly way with those churches that had introduced only this or that confession, at least the "apple of our church's eye," as authoritative; assuming, of course, that they did not overtly do this out of guile and did not contradict the authentic explanations and commentaries which the other confessions offer on the teaching of the primary confession. Those who were guilty of such procedures, as in the Palatinate-Zweibruecken, among others, soon became manifest as anti-Lutherans and at last openly joined the Reformed.

Finally it could be asked whether it might not be dangerous at least for members of those synods where all the Lutheran Confessions have normative symbolical authority to participate in a conference whose basis is only the Augsburg Confession as symbolical norm. Could this not turn into a device by which Satan might succeed in robbing these synods of the great treasure of so glorious, thorough, and rich a doctrinal confession, which contains the results and victory spoils of such faithful labors and mighty battles of our fathers? It would indeed be foolish to dispute this danger. However, when an action does not injure the faith but is called for by love for the brethren as individuals and for the church as a whole, it would be an act of both unbelief and lovelessness to omit such an action because of the possible danger. Furthermore, if those who by God's grace have come to recognize the glory of all our churchly confessions timidly withdraw from all those who have the same faith but not the same knowledge, an equally dreadful danger would threaten, namely that the one part would become guilty of a pharisaic, carnal, spiritually proud, loveless insistence on its strict confessionalism, while the other part, instead of being filled with confidence and love for the continued building and further fortification of our confessional castle, would more and more be scared off as from a prison tower of the spirit and of faith. In consequence, the work of rejuvenating our church in America on the old tried foundation, a work so obviously begun by God, would be halted even though there was the best intention to further it.

These are not measures of human wisdom to which a company of Lutherans have resorted in arranging such a conference to help the church. Such measures could easily prove to be extremely foolish. God will not tolerate it when men try to preserve and govern the church by their wisdom, for He wants to do that Himself by His Word and His Spirit. These are not new experiments employed through such a meeting because people had lost confidence in the old means for building the church. Such experiments could fail far too easily. In matters of the kingdom of God all actions must be done in faith, or God will not acknowledge them and will not seal them with His blessing. It is not at all a human desire to accomplish something on their own that has brought the participants in the conference together, nor were they looking for something outwardly imposing, something showy and great in the eyes of the world, perhaps an externally grand Lutheran union in spite of inner disunity. Such an endeavor, even though successful, would have no other outcome than that in the land of Shinar [Genesis 11], for God abominates such building projects that have become quite fashionable but are hollow and designed by men to erect a monument to themselves.

No, the purpose of the conference, for the time being, is none other than to bring together from time to time all Lutherans in this country who stand on one ground of faith, but live and work widely scattered, so that above all by means of mutual conversation about the *doctrine* of our church they may strengthen each other in faith and further one another in the knowledge of the truth. The purpose is to clear away what Satan would like to use to separate them and splinter their combined power, and to become ever more fervent in mutual brotherly love as they constantly revitalize the consciousness of belonging together.

These are indeed very simple matters, but matters commanded by God. In this way, of course, one does not build upward to great heights so that also the world can see and admire the building, but one builds downward in depth. That indeed means forsaking one's own "will or exertion" [Romans 9:16] and leaving it up to God whether He wants to erect anything on the deep divine foundation that has been laid.

But what do you think? Would God alone then fail to look after what is now *His* cause and fail to provide for growth and fruit? Never! We may become unfaithful, but not He. Our word will often not accomplish the purpose for which we utter it, but the Word of the Lord must prosper in the thing for which He sent it (Isaiah 55:[11]).

Therefore we look to the future with the most cheerful hopes, for He who has given the willing will also grant the accomplishment [Philippians 2:13]; He who has begun the good work will also complete it [Philippians 1:6]. May it please Him to make further use of our *Lehre und Wehre* as a weak instrument for this purpose!

Foreword to the 1858 Volume

Lehre und Wehre, IV, 1, Jan. 1858, pp. 1—6

When a little more than three years ago we published the prospectus for this our theological periodical, we said:

> The Holy Scriptures and after them the *Book of Concord* of our Evangelical Lutheran Church will be the norm for all essays to be printed—Scriptures as the *norma normans* [the norm which establishes the norm], and the symbol as the *norma normata* [the norm which conforms to the norm]; both in their simple understanding as provided by the incontestibly orthodox fathers of our church, first of all Luther, and then Chemnitz, John Gerhard, and other holy witnesses to the truth.

We offered this explanation in full agreement with our synod, whose distinctive character consists in this very thing that by a most vivid conviction it recognizes our Evangelical Lutheran Church as the visible, pure, orthodox church of God on earth and therefore sees it as its holy obligation to *take seriously,* in doctrine and defense, in theory and practice, the commitment to the faith deposited in the symbols of our church and developed and defended so thoroughly by its most enlightened teachers in their immortal writings.

As little as we then, when we began publishing this periodical, concealed from ourselves the fact that on the basis of such principles we could count on little agreement in our time, so little, and even less, do we sustain ourselves with the hope of receiving much approval now that we are three years richer in experience.

It is true, both here and in Germany, especially in the last decade, the name "Lutheran" has again been used and respected more and more. More and more, therefore, we heard the rallying cry: "Lutheran Church! Lutheran Confession!" But if we look only briefly at the company of those who utter this slogan and are regarded as people who fight for the treasure entrusted to our church, we usually will soon be more or less disappointed. Here we are not thinking of those who now in large numbers do not want to give up the name "Lutheran" at any price but still want to retain the liberty of departing from the confession of our church even in the so-called distinctive teachings and to hold and disseminate Reformed error and Methodistic enthusiasm *(Schwaermerei),* yes, even overtly rationalistic tenets (as is the case particularly in synods belonging to the so-called General Synod). No, we are thinking here especially of those who with their mouth are expressly committed to the whole number of our symbols and fight for them to a certain extent, also for that reason are stigmatized by the partisan label of "Old Lutherans." Even among these so-called confessors and fighters only a very small minority represent the pure old Lutheran faith as that is deposited in our church's confession.

First of all, even a large proportion of these reveal all too clearly that they have never taken the trouble to study the doctrine of our church thoroughly and for that reason do not know it, no matter how much they may praise it. Consequently they are like the Athenians with their "unknown god" whom they "worship as unknown" [Acts 17:23]. What such a cultus is worth may be observed in the Athenians. When Paul actually proclaimed that "unknown God" to them, some of them cried indignantly, "What would this babbler say? He seems to be a preacher of foreign divinities!" Others, so as not to be disturbed in their lounging about, simply yawned and said, "We will hear you again about this" [Acts 17:18, 32].

It is indeed in the nature of the case that those who buy Lutheranism sight unseen, and claim allegiance to it as to a certain party in politics, fanatically advocate the product of their fancy which they call Lutheranism, and that the more cheaply they themselves bought their orthodoxy, the more demanding they are toward others. They do not realize that pure Lutheran doctrine is not something you find on the street like a stone that you put into your pocket and then carry around with you, but that Scripture says: "Men of violence take it by force" (Matthew 11:12). They think that if today they have resolved to be strictly and purely Lutheran, they will be so tomorrow and can then occupy the inquisitor's chair. They imagine that if they know that according to Lutheran teaching the body and blood of Jesus Christ are truly present in the Lord's Supper and that Baptism really effects regeneration they are dyed-in-the-wool Lutherans, even great pillars of the Lutheran Church, although (in spite of having the correct confession) they do not have the faintest idea, let alone a clear understanding, of what Lutheran teaching really is. This class of Lutherans has come up in great numbers in Germany in opposition to the Union,[1] and in our country in opposition to the many enthusiastic sects.

There are, however, also those who have a better understanding of what Lutheran doctrine really is but, while they are firmly committed to the Lutheran Church in a formal way, still believe that in many respects this our church has some not inconsiderable shortcomings even in doctrine and does not possess symbols that are entirely pure. Most of them,

44

however, do not say this openly. They fear that if they did, they would lose their reputation as convinced Lutherans, yes, the true props of Lutheranism in our time they really consider themselves to be, and this would do great harm to the kingdom of God. Curiously, they are particularly the ones who maintain the teaching that the visible orthodox church is the church in the proper sense of the word to which all the glorious promises given to the church of Christ, such as uninterrupted permanence, possession of the keys, the presence of Christ and of salvation, etc., apply exclusively. We say curiously, for if they were only somewhat consistent, they would necessarily have to hold firmly with us that the symbols of our church contain a *thoroughly pure and flawless* presentation of the doctrines laid down in them. But, as stated, it is quite obvious that, for example, they regard the doctrine of the church given in the Apology of the Augsburg Confession and the development of the doctrine of the office and the power of the keys contained in the Smalcald Articles[2] as highly defective. They do violence, apparently on purpose, to the pertinent message that in the most unequivocal words directly contradicts their view of the points in question, in order to interpret these passages to suit their own understanding.

This inconsistency has undoubtedly reached its highest degree in a man who is otherwise perhaps the most consistent among all theologians of this class, Prof. Dr. *von Hofmann* at the University of Erlangen. He deviates precisely in the core teachings of the Lutheran Church, the doctrine of the Holy Trinity, the atonement, Christ's vicarious sacrifice, and justification by faith, but nevertheless he places himself at the head of those who want to support the preservation of our church's confession and claims that he is only observing a new way to teach the old truth![1] [w]

Others who also want to be regarded as faithful sons and servants of our church in spite of their deviations are more open and admit that they cannot subscribe to the symbols of our church without qualification. Among these is Dr. *Rudelbach,* who in his quarterly in the first issue for the year 1854 clearly states that "the concept of ordination does not receive its due" in the Smalcald Articles [Treatise on the Power and Primacy of the Pope, 70], where ordination is described as *nothing more* than the confirmation of a call. Rudelbach continues: "Alongside Luther's conception *another* type developed in the church, a type which in a number of ways adopted *what we can regard as the only proper teaching.*" In what follows Rudelbach adopts the Episcopalian doctrine of ordination, saying among other things: "In our opinion the Anglican Church has comprehended the essence of ordination most clearly of all." In the course of years Rudelbach's critique of Lutheran doctrine has become ever bolder, but already in his *Einleitung in die Augsburgische Confession* [Introduction to the Augsburg Confession], 1841, he plainly indicates that he regards this confession's teaching on Sunday as incorrect (p. 186).

Besides Rudelbach there is also Pastor *Loehe* in Bavaria. In his essay *Unsere kirchliche lage* [The State of our Church], 1850, he says among other things:

I also believe that without detriment to my insistence on confessional unity I may be permitted to wish that *here and there* a statement in the symbols might have received a more comprehensive *purer* formulation. So, for example, the doctrine of the ministry was not given nearly enough consideration in the days of the Reformation. The decisions of the symbols, to the extent that there are any, suffer from some inadequacy (p. 19). In the *Book of Concord* I distinguish between what is said confessionally and what is not so said—*and I distinguish still more.*[2W] I have no intention of sticking to the letter. I have often indicated my simple opinion with regard to the Smalcald Articles.—The Smalcald Articles were written by Luther entirely with that originality which controlled him, beyond which he was lifted only rarely. With the *lack of restraint* on the part of this hero the objective style so much desired for a confession is entirely missing *and at times a quatenus* ["as far as"] *subscription has much to recommend it;* for who can be obligated to put the seal of approval on every original utterance, even of a Luther? What would be the sense of making originality and individuality symbolically binding?[3W] . . . One may justifiably have his doubts about saying, "The pope is the Antichrist" (Smalcald Articles). . . . Similarly with regard to other passages of the Smalcald Articles, in which the claim is made that Christ did not give the keys to one person but to the *church,* so that in an emergency (?) a church could ordain its own bishops or pastors. If these passages are taken one-sidedly, we get into a dilemma, for Christ really did give the keys also to individuals,[4W] and Paul not only ordains elders himself but also commands his pupils to do so. But with regard to those passages we must assume only the most *extreme* emergency, where the church would be thought of as having *no pastors at all.* As long as pastors belong to the church and are available, the other passages apply where episcopal power as well as the power of the keys and ordination are ascribed to pastors (Treatise, 60 ff.). Only by combining the respective passages will the truth be obtained. For neither will anyone on the basis of Scripture deny the church with no pastors the cited right in an extreme case that can hardly happen, *nor will anyone grant the church this right apart from the presbyterium* (rule by elders) that belongs to the church, if and as long as such a *presbyterium* is present.[5W] . . . *No single (passage) by itself,* but all of them together, can be subscribed with a cheerful heart (pp. 60f.).

Hence Loehe thinks there are many such passages in the symbols, but that these have their *corrective* in other statements.

Besides Rudelbach and Loehe there is also Superintendent *Muenchmeyer*. He strongly emphasizes his commitment to the Lutheran Church and for that reason was assigned a special place in Germany among the convinced confessors of the Lutheran name; and yet he has declared that he discovered error in the symbolically fixed doctrine of our church.

Now, we are far from wanting to put these men on the same level with those who with the mouth are unreservedly committed to the symbols but in their hearts take a position opposed to several important points expounded in the symbols and reinterpret them so as not to have their orthodoxy called into question. At the same time, also the former are of the company of those because of whom we should like to infer from the ever more audible slogan, "Lutheran Church! The Church's Confession!" that a regeneration of our Lutheran Church has begun in our time.

The saddest thing about it is that in this situation some people cherish the illusion, on the one hand, that all is well or at least extremely promising, while, on the other hand, where people recognize what is wrong, they resort to the use of all kinds of human means to help the church.

As indicated, this condition of the church at the beginning of a new year for our theological periodical inhibits our hope of making much of an impact with it. Nevertheless, in the name of Him who has so earnestly commanded us to confess the truth and has promised it the victory we dare to continue cheerfully with our testimony in the confident hope that the Lord will either inaugurate the day of eternal glorification for His church or once again grant it a time of gracious visitation. But just as three hundred years ago the gracious visitation which the church experienced through the Reformation was nothing else than a renewal of the apostolic church, so we now hope for no other visitation than that the church of the Reformation may experience a new springtime. We do not look for a church of the future that would arise in consequence of new disclosures regarding a higher unity of the confessions and thus encompass hitherto separated parties. Far from being tempted by our hope to forsake our established basis to pave the way for the church of the future, our hope rather exhorts and encourages us to make our own the words of the confessors of the Formula of Concord:

> We are not minded to manufacture anything new by this work of agreement or to depart in any way at all, either in content or in formulation, from the divine truth that our pious forebears and we have acknowledged and confessed in the past, for our agreement is based on the prophetic and apostolic Scriptures and is comprehended in the three

Creeds as well as in the Augsburg Confession, submitted in the year 1530 to Emperor Charles V, of kindest memory, in the Apology that followed it, and in the Smalcald Articles and the Large and Small Catechisms of that highly enlightened man, Dr. Luther [and, may we add, in the Formula of Concord].[3] On the contrary, we are minded by the grace of the Holy Spirit to abide and remain unanimously [with all the members of our Synod] in this confession of faith and to regulate all religious controversies and their explanations according to it *(Book of Concord, Tappert Edition, General Preface, pp. 13 f.).*

Foreword to the 1859 Volume

[On Doctrinal Development]

[First Part:] *Lehre und Wehre,* V, 1, Jan. 1859, pp. 1—12

The Roman Church has always claimed and still claims that also with regard to articles of faith and divine precepts the church constantly receives more light in the course of time. Just a few years ago we ourselves experienced that the present pope declared *ex cathedra* that the doctrine of the Immaculate Conception of the Blessed Virgin is an article of faith. At the same time he stated that this was by no means a new article, but one only revealed at this time.

This last allegation was no new figment. Already the Spanish Jesuit *Maldonatus,* famous exegete of the Roman Church (died 1583), although in part under a cloud among his peers just because he denied that faith in the immaculate conception was necessary, writes the following in his commentary on the Gospel of St. John in connection with the words "I have yet many things to say to you, but you cannot bear them now" (John 16:12).

> This passage makes clear that Christ did not say everything He considered necessary for our salvation, and we must believe that the Holy Spirit did the same, *namely that He did not reveal everything to the church at once, because it could not bear everything at once, but that it would grow in understanding as it increased in age.*

It is known that also the Enthusiasts, particularly the Anabaptists, dreamed of a constantly new light that would arise for the church through them and guide it to "the stature of the fulness of Christ" [Ephesians 4:13]. Already *Carlstadt* insisted, as *Luther* observes in his commentary on 1 John (5:1), that "the Holy Spirit was revealed in part but *not yet in His fullness" (Luther's Works,* American Edition, 30, 307).

As has become all too evident, similar ideas have now laid hold of most of the respected theologians also within our Lutheran Church.[1 w] They do not regard it as their calling to bring the teaching of the church of the past back to light and to defend it against the new alleged wisdom of our day, but obviously it is rather this: To present that teaching in a better way, to supplement it, purify it, and develop it further. This view has become so current, particularly in Germany, that, to cite only one example, Pastor *Loehe* suggested to the Iowa Synod to include the following passage even in its *congregational* constitutions: "Since within the genuinely Lutheran Church there are nevertheless *different tendencies, we do not fail herewith to pledge ourselves publicly to that* tendency which, *by way of* (!) the symbols at the hand of the divine Word, is striving toward *a greater consummation of the Evangelical Lutheran Church."* [2 W]

The greater the inroads of this stated principle, which is becoming more general all the time, and the more decisive it is for the future of our church, the more necessary we deem it to express ourselves on it as we begin another year of our theological periodical.

To say it at once without beating about the bush, we regard this principle as thoroughly false. We do so because we believe not only that there *can* be a visible church which has and confesses altogether pure doctrine but also that our Evangelical Lutheran Church *is* such a one, on the basis of the Lord's word: "If you continue in My Word, you are truly My disciples, and you will know the truth, and the truth will make you free" (John 8:31-32).

On the basis of this promise we believe, in the first place, that the saving truth is not a problem waiting for men to solve, but that it is already contained clearly and plainly in Christ's Word; it is not a kind of philosophy that requires or is even capable of an everlasting evolution, higher development, and improvement, but something already lying before us complete in Scripture; it is not a tower of Babel on whose erection theologians must work until Judgment Day, but it is a heavenly building long completed, on which the prophets and apostles did the final work. Every addition, every ostensible supplement from any philosophical discipline is for us nothing but drops of poison in the pure well of heavenly truth, as we remember the apostolic warning: "See to it that no one makes a prey of you by philosophy and empty deceit, according to human tradition, according to the elemental spirits of the universe, and not according to Christ" (Colossians 2:8).

We do not, indeed, deny that there is a salutary use of philosophy on the part of theologians. We do not agree with the Helmstedt theologian Daniel Hofmann, who wrote: "The more human reason is trained by the study of philosophy, the better armed an enemy it is, the more vehemently it attacks theology, and the more plausible it makes errors."[3 W] We do not reject the *service* but the *rule* of philosophy in the domain of revelation; we do not condemn the *formal* but the *material* use of philosophy. And even the material use we reject only with regard to such concepts as are drawn only from revelation.

But our venerable teachers have written about this better than we are able to do. Therefore we will let them speak.

John Gerhard, for example, writes thus: *[Editorial note: Here Walther introduces a very long quotation from John Gerhard on the nature of philosophy, its various branches and functions, its proper role in theological work, and areas of revelation where it has no place.[1] Philosophy may never be employed as a source of theology, which must be drawn exclusively from the Scriptures. To human reason, blinded by the fall into sin, the mysteries of the Christian faith appear unreasonable. Therefore philosophy has no competence in spiritual matters. The final paragraph of the material from Gerhard reads:]*

So much for the use and misuse of philosophy in theology. The conclusion of the whole matter is that in theology philosophy must be assigned a servant role, not a magisterial one, as Philo explains in his book on the cherubim by means of this parable: "Theology should óccupy the place of Sarah in the house, while philosophy is to be admitted as a servant girl and do Hagar's work in Abraham's house." Luther used to compare philosophy to the donkey and theology to Christ who sits on the donkey. The donkey, he says, must not be placed on Christ, but Christ on the donkey.

Continuation and Conclusion: Vol. V, No. 2, Feb. 1859, pp. 33—45

After this lengthy discussion, which we hope has not wearied our dear readers and made them impatient, but which they certainly have received as a costly pearl from the treasury of our fathers, we now return to the subject.

In theory, at least, all so-called believing theologians of our day will perhaps agree with us that the saving truth is already completely given in *Scripture* and therefore we do not need the new revelations of a Montanist Paraclete or the so-called inner light of the Enthusiasts (Anabaptists, Quakers, Inspirationists, Schwenkfelders, Weigelians, Swedenborgians, and others), nor papistic traditions as the alleged unwritten Word of God, nor finally supplements from the stores of the light of nature and of reason, of philosophy. But now the question arises: "Is it possible, too, that there exists a *visible church* which possesses the full saving truth contained in Scripture?"

Many in our day deny this possibility, although they concede that the full truth is contained in Scripture. Therefore they either regard Scripture as an eternal means of exercise in the search for truth instead of a revelation of the truth, the Sisyphus stone which the church must keep on rolling uphill until the end; or they think that this is precisely the task given to the church in this world, gradually to bring to light the heavenly ore of the full truth out of the dark mine of the Bible. If the church would finally accomplish this, it would have reached its goal—it would then have attained to that "mature manhood, to the measure of the stature of the fulness of Christ" (Ephesians 4:13), and would then celebrate its millennial feast of victory.

But as little as we want anything to do with the overt, naked *skepticism* of the former, with that despair of finding the truth which may be appropriate for a pagan Pilate who asks, "What is truth?" but not for a Christian—so little can we ever become reconciled to the *evolutionary theory* of the latter. It is, indeed, a horrible error for the Roman Church to claim that the church *cannot* err. Gerhard calls this papal axiom "a kind of general retreat to which the Papists flee for refuge in all controversies and a sort of Pandora's box with which the papacy covers all its corruptions and errors and all its superstition" *(Loc. de ecclesia,* 104). However, there is a difference as wide as heaven between saying that the church in general or any church in particular *has* not erred with respect to the full saving truth and saying that the church *could* not err. To insist on the latter is as much against Scripture as it is against experience.[4 W] But wanting to *deny* the former is to make a lie of Christ's promise: "If you continue in My Word, you are truly My disciples, and you will know the truth, and the truth will make you free" (John 8:31-32). Therefore Gerhard is right when he comments on John 16:13 in his Gospel harmony: "As long as the church hears the voice of Christ, its Bridegroom, Shepherd, and Head, and insofar as it follows the leading of the Word, permits itself to be guided by the Holy Spirit through the Word, submits to His teaching authority, to that extent it will be led into all truth and *does not err.* "If this were not so, all certainty of faith would be lost.

However, as certain as it accordingly is that there *can* be a visible church that possesses the full truth (of course only according to a perfection of *parts* but not according to a perfection of *degree),* this is a far cry from the claim that such a visible church always really exists. It is, alas, all too obvious that the church often experienced long centuries of eclipse with regard to its public teaching.

For the elucidation of this important point[5 W] we cannot refrain from here letting *Gerhard* speak again. In his *Loci* he writes about this as follows: *[Editorial note: Here Walther inserts another extended quotation from Gerhard. Gerhard argues that we must distinguish between the church triumphant in heaven, which is altogether perfect and not exposed*

52

to even the slightest error, and the church militant on earth, which is constantly involved in combating error. Here, too, we must distinguish between fundamental errors, which overturn the foundation of faith, and nonfundamental errors, which do not touch the foundation. Of the church catholic, which embraces all believers, Gerhard asserts that it does not err. Even though there are times when corruptions dominate the public exercise of religion, the whole church catholic of all times does not err, because from time to time God always raises up prophets and other faithful ministers who rebuke those corruptions in doctrine, reform the divine worship, and restore the church to its pristine splendor. And even though at times no part of the visible church is pure and uncorrupted, the whole church never errs to the extent that there will not be some who remain faithful to the Word and are kept by the power of God through faith unto salvation, even though their number is small and they are completely hidden from view. Historically, in Gerhard's view, the church was 1. sparklingly pure in the days of the apostles and martyrs; 2. somewhat spotted at the time of the heretics and church fathers; 3. wholly disfigured under papal rule; and 4. restored to the original splendor of the apostolic faith by the Reformation. (Loc. de ecclesia 104.) Then Walther continues:]

Although Gerhard here admits that the church was not always free from errors but was in fact often thoroughly corrupted, he nevertheless insists that the church of the Reformation possessed an apostolic purity. And we believe it with him. Or what? Does the saving doctrine in all visible churches still flow from a murky fountain even after the Reformation? Is each one only one color of the rainbow so that only by putting them all together does the heavenly rainbow of pure and complete truth become visible on earth? Does none have the completely pure teaching? Is there only a comparatively orthodox church, better than others, or the best of all, but none that deserves the predicate of a true visible church in the proper sense of the word? Does even this "best" church possess doctrinal purity only approximating the picture of a true church? Are there still doctrines which belong into the context of saving revelation like links in a chain, *articles of faith* (we are here speaking only of such truths), which are not presented by a single church, or at least not presented purely and correctly by any? Is there no truly reformed church which therefore needs no reformation as far as doctrine is concerned?

As we have seen above from Gerhard, our fathers of 300 and 200 years ago sincerely believed that, after the revelation of Antichrist, God truly gave grace for the presentation of such a visible church—and they praised God for it with cheerful voices. They were, of course, far from believing that the Lutheran Church was in no need of reformation with regard to *life*.

53

They well knew that every single *Christian* must pray until he dies, "Forgive us our trespasses," and is therefore in need of daily putting off the old man and daily putting on the new law, that is, of *sanctification*. They also knew that the *church* as a whole is in need of a constant *reformation of life* until it has left the battlefield of this world and is celebrating its triumph in heaven. They well knew that just this continuous reformation of life is one of the indispensable life symptoms of a true church. They also knew that, as far as life is concerned, the greater the grace especially the Lutheran Church experienced with regard to doctrine, the more it stood in need of adorning that doctrine by its life in a better way than in the past. Nevertheless our fathers have conceded that our church was for that reason also impure in its *teaching*. *Luther* writes:

> . . . there is a great difference between teaching and life, just as there is a great difference between heaven and earth. *Life* may well be impure, sinful, and frail, but the *teaching* must be pure, holy, clear, and steadfast. *Life* may well be in error and not keep everything which the teaching commands, but the *teaching* (says Christ [Matt. 5:18]) must not lack one tittle or letter, whereas life may perhaps lack a whole word or line of the teaching. The reason is this: the teaching is *God's* Word and God's truth itself, while life includes *our* actions also. Therefore the *teaching* must remain altogether pure. If someone falls short and is frail in *life,* then God can indeed have patience and forgive, but in the teaching itself, by which one is supposed to live, God can and will tolerate no changing or cancellation, and he ought not tolerate anything of the sort, either, for there his divine majesty itself is affected. There it is no longer a question of forgiving or having patience, and consequently it is best to leave the teachings in peace and not tamper with them ("Commentary on the Alleged Imperial Edict," *Luther's Works,* American Edition, Vol. 34, 77f.).

However, our fathers not only made doctrinal purity, as opposed to purity of life, a *requirement* but they also unqualifiedly *vindicated* it for our Lutheran Church. This was done even by those fathers who otherwise were particularly earnest in lamenting the deterioration of our church and with great zeal pressed for a new reformation. So, for example, *Andrew Kesler* (died 1643), author of the hymn *Keinen hat Gott verlassen* (God has forsaken no one), wrote in the preface of his (written in German) *Prudentia Christiana:*

> In the past many zealous theologians have clamored for a reformation of *life,* and not without cause. *As far as the doctrine of the Gospel is concerned, by the grace of God we have it pure and unadulterated (praise and thank Him for it eternally!), and here no reformation is needed.* But when it comes to the ministerial office and the life of

Christians that should accompany the pure religion, a reformation according to the divine Word is highly necessary in all estates.

The old Strasbourg theologian *Conrad Danhauer* [spelled Dannhauer in the *Lutheran Cyclopedia*] speaks in a similar vein. In his *Casuistics* he raises the question: "Are there some things in our churches that need reformation?" He answers:

> More indeed than can be stated and enumerated. It is true that the *substance of the doctrinal articles is so pure that nothing more can be desired,* but the *method* of teaching demands, for the sake of greater glory, that much be improved, so that the glory of the second temple may be greater than that of the first. With regard to morals and conduct, everything is saturated with papistic and pagan leaven. As for church customs and manner of worship, who would not wish for uniformity and unity everywhere? Would that all other churches, including our Strasbourg church, be conformed to the Saxon churches, from whence the again-purified Gospel went forth! *(Liber conscientiae,* I, 941).

Luther speaks still more plainly. For example, in the Preface to the Smalcald Articles of 1537 he writes:

> But let us return to the subject. I should be very happy to see a true council assemble in order that many things and many people might derive benefit from it. *Not that we ourselves need such a council, for by God's grace our churches have now been so enlightened and supplied with the pure Word and the right use of the sacraments, with an understanding of various callings of life, and with true works, that we do not ask for a council for our own sake, and we have no reason to hope or expect that a council would improve our conditions.* But in the dioceses of the papists we see so many vacant and desolate parishes everywhere that our hearts would break with grief *(Book of Concord,* Tappert, p. 290).

Furthermore, *Luther* writes in his book against Duke Henry of Brunswick (1541):

> And what have you yourselves (the papists) done that you now desire a council, now promising it, then again postponing it, and at other times refusing it? If your church is holy, why does it fear a council? Why does it fear a reformation or a council? If it needs a council, how can it be holy? Do you want to reform your holiness too? *We, for our part, have never desired a council to reform our church. God and the Holy Spirit already sanctified our church through his holy word and, indeed, purged away all papal whoredom and idolatry, so that we have* **everything** *(God be praised) pure and holy–the word, baptism, the sacrament, keys, and everything which belongs to the true church–without the addition and filth of human doctrine. Life* (as was said above) is not lived completely

according to our insights and wishes, a fact bewailed by the prophets and apostles themselves; for this belongs to the time when we shall be like angels [Matt. 22:30].

But we desire a council so that our church may be examined and our doctrine come freely to light—and your whoredom in the papacy be recognized and condemned. Thus everyone who is misled by it may, together with us, be converted to the true holy church and sustained in it. *(Luther's Works,* American Edition, Vol. 41, p. 223).

This conviction that our Lutheran Church is the *truly reformed* church[6 W] as far as *doctrine* is concerned has almost entirely disappeared especially in those theologians who are now regarded as pillars. There is hardly a teaching which is not believed to be in need of a better presentation than that offered by our fathers. Even the doctrine of God, of Christ, of the church, of the ministry, of the sacraments, of heaven and hell and the last things generally—it is alleged that our church in the past either left these teachings undeveloped or presented them very inadequately. We offer several examples in support of our charge.

In his dogmatics *(Christi Person und Werk) Thomasius* first of all sets out to reform the teaching of the entire old Lutheran Church about God's properties. At the close of his presentation of what the Lutheran dogmaticians taught concerning God's properties he writes: "We see that the older dogmatics leaves undecided whether the properties express definite realities or modes of revelation or merely subjective conceptions of the divine essence" (I, 42).[7 W] To pave the way for his doctrine of Christ's person he denies what our old dogmaticians demonstrated so superbly, namely God's simplicity and the resulting identity of the divine properties with the divine essence. We have already documented (in last year's October issue) how Thomasius along with Delitzsch and Hofmann have in essence deviated from the model of our church's teaching especially in the doctrine of the person of Christ.

Far from standing alone in their allegedly necessary further development of the doctrine of Christ's person, the Erlangen theologians are here following an ever more general trend on the part of the newer so-called believing theology. In his book *Die Lehrfortbildung* [Doctrinal Development] (Hamburg and Gotha: Perthes, 1847) the Hessian theologian *George Reich,* formerly Reformed, now member of the Union, writes:

> While the doctrine of the *Reformed* church did not advance beyond upholding the twoness of the natures next to one another without inner communication and posits only a *normal* communication (by alloeosis) of the peculiarities of both to the person, the *Lutheran* doctrine moved ahead to construct a *real* communication by transferring the properties

of one nature to the other (communication of properties [or attributes]), and has thus made considerable progress in solving the problem of describing the person of Christ according to its inner essence in a conceptual way. But this, too, is still inadequate, since it does not go all the way with this communication but only one-sidedly. For while it ascribed the properties of the divine nature to the human, *it did not, in a restrictive way, ascribe the properties of the latter to the former,* so that here, too, the divine side still maintains an undue preponderance(!). It is at this point that the dogma will be taken up by the doctrinal development we are about to describe (p. 40).

From this we see that the Reformed Nestorian doctrine of Christ's person is to pass through the Lutheran doctrine in such a way that it will emerge on the other side in worse condition. *Ebrard* ("Jesus Christus der Gottmensch," in Herzog, *Real-Encyklopaedie)* writes:[8][w]

That the Logos in his own person *became* a man, that He condescended to the form of existence of an embryonic infant's soul, that He in whom all the fulness of the Godhead dwelled in the form of the eternal *present* reduced (!) Himself to a being in which that fulness lay in the form of a *seed* capable of development—that He became an infant's soul, a germinating human center of life and as such *entered* the human womb, the germ cell, and out of earthly-physical matter fashioned for Himself a body—first of all an animated fiber which developed into a body—and gave life to it and had it grow into a body—this is the truth that was misunderstood *equally* by those *two* erroneous views. As soon as that truth is grasped and maintained, it is impossible to arrive at the absurd statement that the Logos united Himself with a man, the Son of God with a son of Mary.

Furthermore, on the basis *of this theory,* Ebrard does not hesitate to acknowledge a communication of attributes that is "not a verbal one." Consequently we can only be deeply saddened by the praise which Ebrard accords the Erlangen theologians at the close of his article and regard it as a disgrace burdening the Lutheran Church of our day. Here are Ebrard's concluding remarks:

The newer Lutheran theology, especially that of the Erlangen school, has made a serious and praiseworthy effort to overcome that view which was taken over from medieval scholasticism. Dr. *Thomasius* first dared to express the opinion in 1845 *(Zeitschrift fuer Protestantismus und Kirche* [Journal for Protestantism and Church], Vol. 2) that in the state of humiliation the Logos *limited Himself* and thus, as it were, assumed the properties of the human nature. Yet the Logos thus limited is said to have *united* Himself with *a* "human nature" in the concrete sense. In the state of exaltation the divine nature reassumed its divine properties and communicated them also to the human nature. The view of the two natures as two component parts was here still retained, *yet a first step had been taken to recognize the untenableness of the Lutheran scholasticism of 1577* (of the Formula of Concord). In a much more energetic way Dr. Hofmann in his *Schriftbeweis* recently carried out the teaching that the Logos *became* a man. Hofmann's form of presentation (the Son of God *"ceased being God* in order to become man") is askew and goes beyond limits (for He did not cease *being God,* but He only gave up the "form of God" [Philippians 2:6].—It might well be the most substantive task of theology in our time to rectify the doctrine of the God-man.

Here we see again that Luther is right in saying that at all times the article concerning Christ is the most offensive to human reason and that all heretics begin here. Satan is aware that in the old form he cannot renew his fight against Christ, God and man united in one person, if he wants to beguile the few believers still remaining in these last times. For that reason he comes strolling along under the cloak of necessary "development" of the old doctrine and so hopes to use plausible words to talk the unsuspecting Christians into a "believing" Arianism and to talk them out of their Christ.

A further sad example to show how the consciousness that the Lutheran Church really has the marks of *pure* preaching has been extinguished in theologians who now pose as leaders of the Lutheran chorus is Dr. *Rudelbach.* Not to repeat what we said elsewhere, we only call attention to an essay of the famous theologian in the fourth quarterly issue of his *Zeitschrift [Journal],* 1842. Among other things he says:

> In the Reformation the concern was in fact so completely with the innermost hearth of the Christian conscience, the center and root of the Gospel, that *many other questions* had to be ignored, all the more since otherwise the battle for altar and hearth could not have been rightly waged. The Reformers could and had to deal at length *only* with what in all of dogmatics again put the doctrine of justification into practice, or what necessarily tied in with it, or wherever Pelagianism had been brought in to sell its gold leaf as the genuine article. Thus they fought against purgatory, and rightly so, because it obscured Christ's merit and endangered the basic concept of the Reconciler in His death. But in removing this conception they pushed aside in a more or less indifferent way the concept in the faith that deals with the *intermediate state* in general and with the *place where souls are kept* until the universal resurrection, which undeniably has the testimony of Scripture. As a result the article in the Apostles' Creed, "He descended into hell," to some extent *did not receive the same complete treatment* as others also in the Lutheran Church, *and least of all the appropriate doctrinal development. . . .* [9][W] The author (of *Die Lehre von Christi Hoellenfahrt*

[The doctrine of Christ's descent into hell], J. L. Koenig) undoubtedly is not doing justice to the presentation in the Formula of Concord when he draws on Luther's oft-mentioned sermon for supplementary material, *but we certainly do not mean to say that the doctrinal development in question is always the appropriate one;* a deeper and clearer one is called for. . . . Without a doubt every great age in the kingdom of God must in a preeminent sense develop one or several aspects of the total scope of Christian doctrine. This has often been noted and just as often been fully confirmed in history. The heretical elements themselves which the church must combat, as well as the church's own innermost consciousness, all converge on this central point. Such a central point is given to the *current great era in the kingdom of God* in the doctrine of the *church* as well as the doctrine of the *last things.* . . . It cannot be denied that perhaps no teaching is farther removed from the faith consciousness of our time than the doctrine of *Hades* and the Lord's *descent into hell.* Therefore nothing could perhaps lead to the goal more quickly than showing how this entire doctrine *is enmeshed in the whole economy of evangelical history just as necessarily as an indispensable member in the whole of the Christian faith,* so that it supports the other members no less than it is supported by them.[10 W] We need only point to Christ's consoling promise to the penitent thief (Luke 23:43) to realize at once *that the usually proposed conception of an immediate arrival of the departed at all-inclusive salvation, the beatific vision of God, is the most untenable of all.* For if that were the case, then the Prince of life, having commended His soul into the Father's hands at the moment of death, would undoubtedly not have gone to that place in "the lower parts of the earth" (Ephesians 4:9), but directly to heaven. . . . Just as little is there any doubt that the *paradise* to which the godly malefactor came is the place to which the Lord went,[11 W] that in the opposite case the Lord's word contradicts His deed, or His deed contradicts His word, but in either case it would nullify His prophecy concerning His stay of three days and nights "in the heart of the earth" (Matthew 12:40), on the analogy of what happened to the prophet Jonah. . . . Hence we are surely not mistaken when we infer, on the one hand, that here also, as in death, the Lord was made like His brethren, yet in such a way that He would become the captain of their salvation also in this respect and, on the other hand, that here too the members will follow the Head; for the disciple is not above his master. . . . However, just as clearly, dogmatically and historically, the true doctrine of Christ's descent into hell is linked with the question concerning the fate of the *heathen* who have not heard or received God's Word. . . .[12 W] If, as always in revelation, and especially in the doctrine of Christ's descent into hell, the light of divine mercy is wedded to the light of truth, this must by no means be extended to the fate of those who have despised the gracious invitation of the Gospel and who will without doubt go "to their place" just as much as the rich man who had spurned God's call to him through Lazarus; still less are we justified thereby to accept an intermediate state in the sense of purgatory. Yet we cannot utterly reject as unfounded the prophetic hope that an extraordinary arrangement of grace, similar to the evangelizing of the dead at Christ's descent to Hades,[13 W] will be made for those who have heard nothing of the Word of Life and thus at least have not entered into an explicit relationship to the Light that has appeared to all men (pp. 145—156).

Sad, furthermore, is the effect which the new discoveries in the field of the natural sciences have produced even in those who otherwise desire to be faithful to our church. Most of them believed that nothing needed to be done more quickly than attempting to show how the Bible is to be harmonized with the allegedly incontestible results of the research in the cited field. This has led to the most monstrous assertions. To cite just one example, Kurtz, at the time in Mitau, so well thought of by Lutherans otherwise, wrote in his essay *Bibel und Astronomie. Ein Beitrag zur biblischen Kosmologie* [Bible and Astronomy. A Contribution to Biblical Cosmology], Berlin, 1849:

> We have an earth already in prehuman times, and no less a history that has unfolded upon it and with reference to it. The prophet of primeval history saw this earth as *without form and void. . . . The desolation resulted from the fall of the angels,* which leads us to conclude *that the primitive earth was the dwelling place and training ground of those angels who rebelled against God* and thus lost their position and were forced to vacate their dwelling.[14 W] The restitution,[15 W] however, was the result of a divine decree according to which God will not allow His plan for the world to be upset . . . from which we conclude further that *man, put in place of Satan and his angels,* has been called also to carry out the unfulfilled task to restore the broken harmony of the universe and to defeat and judge Satan himself, the destroyer and rebel. . . . Now we can understand what an immediate interest Satan had in doing all in his power to seduce man to apostasy. . . . It was a natural enmity against the newly created upstart who took over the dwelling from which he himself had been evicted (p. 96).

In this manner Kurtz accommodates himself to the geologists with their millennia which they think were required for the formation of the earth.

These citations should suffice to show what the theological spokesmen within our church mean by the further development and further construction of Lutheran doctrine. In the narrow limits set for us we are not in a position at this place to name and document all the departures from the doctrine of our church which are now permitted under the heading of further construction of the Lutheran doctrinal system. Just as little will our readers here expect inductive proof for the assertion that no teaching included by our church in its confessions is there presented wrongly and is therefore in need of improvement, and that there is no article of faith that has not already become a possession of our church. For our present purpose it will suffice that we herewith publicly repudiate a further development of doctrine that aims at something else than setting forth the immeasurably rich treasure of divine thoughts contained in the saving truth already entrusted to our church, an approach that has in mind rectifying our good confession and thus *actually* is not a further development but a dissolution of our doctrinal jewel. Moved by a living conviction that our Evangelical Lutheran Church bears the marks of the church listed in Article VII of the Augsburg Confession, we recognize in every *alteration* of its doctrine a *falsification* of the same. And, convinced in our conscience that the Lutheran Reformation was a genuine and authentic reformation granted by God to His church in these last days, we regard every *new* so-called truth as an *old* or also new—error. Therefore nothing will ever induce us to abandon the ark of our beloved church and plunge into the bounding waves of changing current opinions.

Let people not object that according to our own lament the Lutheran Church itself is full of false teachers, for when we declare our church to be pure we do not mean to say that it is not disturbed by false teachers just like the apostolic church, but only that *error, no matter in what form it may arise, never has even a formal right to exist in it.*

May, therefore, the faithful God take pity on His poor Lutheran Zion, bring the erring in its midst back to the light of the full truth, strengthen the weak, and again make it a city upon a high hill.

On Church Language

[First Part:] *Lehre und Wehre,* V, 3, March 1859, pp. 65—71

An old axiom states: "Let us be tolerant about words, as long as we agree about the substance." This axiom agrees fully with God's Word, for the apostle expressly writes: "Charge them before the Lord to avoid disputing about words, which does no good, but only ruins the hearers" (2 Timothy 2:14). Augustine comments: "To dispute about words means not being concerned about how error may be overcome by the truth, but how your way of saying it should be preferred to that of another" *(On Christian Doctrine,* Book 4, ch. 28). In his *Biblia illustrata* Calov adds: "Logomachies are not only utterly useless but they also harm the hearers, who are thrown into confusion by such disputations and begin to have doubts about what they believed. In this way their faith is shaken and turned into skepticism." A Christian, and above all a theologian, must never forget what Jerome writes: "Heresy lies in the sense, not in the words." If this were not so, no one could be orthodox except one who is not only himself master of the language but who is also fully conversant with the language of model theologians. In that case orthodoxy would depend not on faith but on speech.

Furthermore, church history shows that it was always the heretics, seeking to conceal their errors under ambiguous turns of speech, who first compelled orthodox teachers of the church to express the proper meaning of the faith in terms behind which the heterodox teachers could not hide their heresy. For that reason, as long as certain heresies had not yet arisen, the purest teachers of the church spoke concerning the respective teachings *securius,* as our theologians like to express it, that is, more securely, less carefully and precisely, than the teachers who were compelled by later heretics to employ words that prevented them from concealing and spreading their poison. Also pure teachers, for example, who lived and taught before the onset of Arian, Nestorian, Eutychian, Pelagian, Zwinglian, Calvinist, Crypto-Calvinist, Pietistic, and other controversies, often made use of terms that only became suspect in these controversies and were then no longer used by orthodox teachers. As little as false teachers can appeal to the old faithful witnesses and their language in support of their own teaching, it is equally improper to accuse older orthodox teachers of being guilty of the same error as new heretics because their *expressions* are alike, since the correct teaching of the former is expressed in other passages. *Luther* is quite right in saying in his *Theological Disputation that in Christ the Divine and Human Natures Are United in Such a Way that Christ Is Only a Single Person, as Well as Regarding the Fact that He Has the Properties Peculiar to Both Natures:*

In such high truths transcending all reason we must therefore see to it that the language of the fathers must be expounded in a fitting manner where that becomes necessary. *There is something ungodly and spiteful if one tries to make someone guilty of error because of unsuitable words, even though one knows that he teaches correctly in other matters.* For in this way we shall nowhere find a church father or other teacher in the church who has not made use of unsuitable language, if we are out thus to twist their words. The very Christian poet, Sedulius, sings, "The blessed Creator of this world has *donned* the body of a servant," and the whole Christian church sings it after him. Yet, if we wanted to haggle about words, nothing could be said more heretical than that the human nature of Christ is the *dress* of His deity; for dress and the body inside the dress do not together constitute one *person* the way God and man are one person in Christ. Nevertheless, the rest of the poems of this Sedulius prove that he was a pure and orthodox teacher. . . . Hence heresy never consists in the *words* but in the meaning they have, as St. Jerome quite properly told his detractors. . . . *On the contrary, one who has fallen prey to a perverted understanding should not be tolerated even when he uses correct words and zealously appeals to Scripture.* For Christ did not permit the demons to speak when they acknowledged Him as the Son of God, because they know how to disguise themselves as angels of light. The *Holy Spirit* is so good and so artless that those who are His, even though they do not speak too well as far as grammar is concerned, still speak the truth with regard to understanding and meaning. The guile and malice of the *devil,* on the other hand, are so great that his followers speak no truth in the theological sense even when they observe the correct rules of grammar. Here we might say, "If you are a liar, you will be regarded as a liar even when you speak the truth" (Chrysippus).[1] But if you are devoted to speaking the truth, even the untruth that may slip in will be true nevertheless (St. Louis Edition, X, 1143 f.).

Here the old adage applies: "If two *say* the same thing, it *is* not (therefore always) the same." Heterodoxy can easily be concealed under orthodox language, and an orthodox sense under a heterodox expression. Finally, where is the person who always finds the proper *word* when he speaks of the high mysteries of divine revelation, even though he holds the right *faith* in his heart? "For we all make many mistakes, and if anyone makes no mistakes in what he says he is a perfect man" (James 3:2). Every day, therefore, the whole church prays, "Forgive us our trespasses." Even Augustine, the great dialectician, who also had a mastery of the language as did few mortals, writes of himself: "Perhaps I do not worthily *will* how one *should* speak; yet I *cannot* even speak as I *will;* how much less as one *should* speak!" (Commentary on John 1, IX, 43). For all that, if a contentious person wants to engage in logomachies, then, as the Apology observes, "nothing can be said so carefully that it can avoid misrepresentation" (Apology, VII, 2).

As vigorously as all this speaks in opposition to that inquisitorial, heresy-smelling haggling about words that has at times played a big role in the church and has caused untold mischief, it would nevertheless be wrong to conclude that the way of *speaking* about items of faith is a matter of complete indifference as long as one combines the correct *sense* with the words used.

The history of the church shows so clearly and plainly that also the way of *speaking* is highly important that no one who has even a little knowledge of history can deny it. All too often the root of emerging errors was obviously nothing but wrong terms used by Christian teachers with regard to important Christian concepts. The well-known line, "He who coins new words also brings forth new doctrines," applies not only to heretics. The saying contains a warning also for orthodox teachers, although they do not always heed it and so do great harm to the divine truth and hence to the church. History shows us that many expressions, originally taken in the best sense but inappropriate, have become the fertile seeds of the most dangerous and most deeply rooted errors. Such terms are, for example: *Priest* and *cleric* for minister or pastor, *sacrifice* for the Lord's Supper, *transformation* for the change that takes place with regard to the consecrated elements in the sacrament of Christ's body and blood, the *chair of Peter* for the Roman ministerial office and "principal church" *(ecclesia principalis)* for the church in the capital of the empire, *territorial bishop (Landesbischof)* for the civil head of the members of the territorial church, *church and spiritual estate (Geistlichkeit)* for preachers, etc. For that reason *Luther* writes, for example, about the word *priest:*

> On this account I think it follows that we neither can nor ought to give the name *priest* to those who are in charge of Word and sacrament among the people. The reason they have been *called* priests is either because of the custom of heathen people or as a vestige of the Jewish nation. The result is *greatly injurious to the church.* According to the New Testament Scriptures better names would be ministers, deacons, bishops, stewards, presbyters (a name often used and indicating the older members) *(Luther's Works,* American Edition, Vol. 40, p. 35).

Therefore old *William Leyser* is quite correct in writing: "It is a mark of modesty not only to *believe,* as the church believes, but also to speak as the church speaks" *(Syst. theol. exeget.,* p. 494). There is not only a special *Bible language*[W] but also based on it, a special *church language.* As for the Bible, it contains a large number of words and forms of expression that are used in a sense which they did not have before and which they received only from the Spirit of God who inspired them, a sense that can be gathered and learned from no secular author but only from the context in the divine Scriptures. Here belong such words as faith, believing in Christ, works, doing works, righteous, righteousness, justification, election, the elect, the called, edification, Baptism, old and new man, flesh and spirit, cross, church, Word (Logos), God the Father, Son of God, Holy Spirit, begetting and proceeding from (used about God), dead in sins, dead works, sin unto death, perfection, etc. Also the *church* speaks in these Biblical terms. Indeed these are and remain the church's inexhaustible mine of divine revelations. Nevertheless, since it is called not only to preach and expound the Word of God to the world but also to defend and preserve it against false teachers, the church must use other words besides the Biblical ones, by means of which it expresses the correct understanding it has of the Biblical words and repels their perversion by heretics. Thus, in addition to the special Bible language, a special *church language* also gradually developed, that is to say, a way of expressing certain concepts contained in Scripture and discussing them, a way not contained in Scripture as far as the sound of the words is concerned and yet based on Scripture according to the sense. This method of expression is characteristic of the orthodox church and constantly employed by it.

Of the church's right to express the divine truths in words different from those used in Scripture there can be no doubt, for the prophesying, that is, expounding of Scripture, that is necessary in the church for its edification is nothing else than presenting the content of Scripture not only in a language different from the original (a translation), but also in different words of the same language, or by way of circumscription. In addition, heretics have always sowed their errors in spite of the use of Biblical terms, in fact, under their cover. Therefore the church was compelled to find and employ terms under which no heretic could conceal his perversions and misinterpretations of Scripture. Therefore, having shown how the cunning of Arius had compelled the orthodox to use ever more precise terms and finally put the word *homoousios* (of the same substance) in opposition to him, *Luther* continues:

It is certainly true that one should teach nothing *outside of Scripture* pertaining to divine matters, as St. Hilary writes in *On the Trinity,* Book

65

I, which means only that one should teach *nothing that is at variance* with Scripture. But that one should not use *more or other words* than those contained in Scripture—this cannot be adhered to, especially in a controversy and when heretics want to falsify things with trickery and distort the words of Scripture. It thus became necessary to condense the meaning of Scripture, comprised of so many passages, into a short and comprehensive word, and to ask whether they regarded Christ as *homoousios,* which was the meaning of all the words of Scripture that they had distorted with false interpretations among their own people, but had freely confessed before the emperor and the council. It is just as if the Pelagians were to try to embarrass us with the term "original sin" or "Adam's plague" because these words do not occur in Scripture, though Scripture clearly teaches the meaning of these words, that we are "conceived in sin," Psalm 51[:5], that we are "by nature children of wrath," Ephesians 2[:3], and that we must all be accounted sinners "because of the sin of one man," Romans [5:12]. *(On the Councils and the Church, Luther's Works,* American Edition, Vol. 41, pp. 82 f.)

Even *Calvin* here agrees with Luther. In his *Institutes* he writes:

What wickedness, then, it is to disapprove of words that explain nothing else than what is attested and sealed by Scripture!

It would be enough, they say, to confine within the limits of Scripture not only our thoughts but also our words, rather than scatter foreign terms about, which would become seedbeds of dissension and strife. . . .

If they call a foreign word one that cannot be shown to stand written syllable by syllable in Scripture, they are indeed imposing upon us an unjust law which condemns all interpretation not patched together out of the fabric of Scripture. . . .But what prevents us from explaining in clearer words those matters in Scripture which perplex and hinder our understanding, yet which conscientiously and faithfully serve the truth of Scripture itself, and are made use of sparingly and modestly and on due occasion? There are quite enough examples of this sort of thing. What is to be said, moreover, when it has been proved that the church is utterly compelled to make use of the words *"Trinity"* and *"Persons"?* If anyone, then, finds fault with the novelty of the words, does he not deserve to be judged as bearing the light of truth unworthily, since he is finding fault only with what renders the truth plain and clear?

However, the novelty of words of this sort (if such it must be called) becomes especially useful when the truth is to be asserted against false accusers, who evade it by their shifts. Of this today we have abundant experience in our great efforts to rout the enemies of pure and wholesome doctrine. With such crooked and sinuous twisting these slippery snakes glide away unless they are boldly pursued, caught, and crushed. Thus men of old, stirred up by various struggles over depraved

66

dogmas, were compelled to set forth with consummate clarity what they felt, lest they leave any devious shift to the impious, who cloaked their errors in layers of verbiage. Because he could not oppose manifest oracles, Arius confessed that Christ was God and the Son of God, and, as if he had done what was right, pretended some agreement with the other men. Yet in the meantime he did not cease to prate that Christ was created and had a beginning, as other creatures. The ancients, to drag the man's versatile craftiness out of its hiding places, went farther, declaring Christ the eternal Son of the Father, consubstantial with the Father. Here impiety boiled over when the Arians began most wickedly to hate and curse the word *homoousios*. But if at first they had sincerely and wholeheartedly confessed Christ to be God, they would not have denied Him to be consubstantial with the Father. Who would dare inveigh against those upright men as wranglers and contentious persons because they became aroused to such heated discussion *through one little word,* and disturbed the peace of the church? Yet that mere word marked the distinction between Christians of pure faith and sacrilegious Arians *(Institutes of the Christian Religion,* Library of Christian Classics, XX; Book I, Chapter XIII, 3 and 4, pp. 123 ff.).

Calvin then goes on to show how the ancients were compelled to use and introduce the words "Person" and "Trinity" also. But after the truth drove Calvin to bring this testimony, he added: "Indeed I could wish they [ecclesiastical terms] were buried, if only among all men this faith were agreed on: that Father and Son and Spirit are one God, yet the Son is not the Father, nor the Spirit the Son, but that they are differentiated by a peculiar quality" (ibid., p. 126). On these words of Calvin our own John Gerhard remarks quite correctly: "This cannot be approved out of hand and without the addition of an appropriate interpretation. This must be taken with regard to the cause and origin of these terms, namely the perversity of the heretics, but not with regard to the use of these terms themselves" *(Exeges., Loc.* 3, par. 43).

Conclusion: Vol. V, No. 4, April 1859, pp. 97—104

In what follows *John Gerhard* himself demonstrates the church's justification for speaking its special language:

> While the church does not have an autocratic (arbitrary) power to create new articles of faith, since it is bound to the voice of the Bridegroom, which is heard only in Scripture (Deut. 4:2; 12:32; Is. 8:20; Matth. 17:5; John 10:27), the church may nevertheless explain Scriptural articles of faith also by means of words different from those in Scripture. We prove this 1. *from necessity.* For although the *heretics* teach what is different from and even in opposition to the *sense* of the church's dogmas, they yet imitate the Scripture's *modes of speaking,* "speaking

67

the same, but thinking something else," as Irenaeus says of them in the preface to his first book. They resemble the hyena that approaches the sheepfold at night and imitate the voice of the shepherd, and then slaughters and devours the sheep that come out.

Therefore *necessity* compelled the church to use such words in explaining the mystery of the Trinity in order to draw the heretical guile out of its hiding places and to make a clear distinction between the church's orthodoxy and the errors of the heretics.

We prove this 2. *from usefulness*. These words are useful in a threefold way, for they have been employed in part for the sake of a fuller *explanation*, in part for the sake of better *distinction*, and in part for the sake of more thorough and comprehensive *refutation*. When the three *persons* of the Deity are asserted, and their *homoousia* (same substance) is defended, nothing is added to Scripture as far as the matter is concerned, since this is precisely the teaching of Scripture, if not in the same number of words, yet in other words that mean the same thing. Meanwhile the church derives from the use of these words the benefit that they tersely and concisely summarize the sound doctrine concerning this mystery in words which the adversaries of the heavenly truth cannot apply to an alien and heretical sense" *(Exeg. art., Loc.* III, par. 39 and 40).

Since what has been said shows that church language is fully justified, the individual Christian and especially the minister of the church without doubt has a certain obligation to conform in general to the church's language. What is and remains *absolutely* necessary is, of course, the same *faith*. Hence no one can force an obstinate man, who outwardly appeals to his Christian liberty in opposition to accepting church language, not only to believe with the church but also to *speak* its language. In such a case we must leave it to the Discerner of hearts to judge whether a knave is concealed behind this provocation. After citing Socinian utterances in opposition to the church's common technical terms, John Gerhard continues: "Let them concede to us that Father, Son, and Holy Spirit are God and yet there is only one God, and we will not press them to use those ecclesiastical terms." (ibid., par. 42).

It is, however, a cause for concern when an individual refuses to speak the church's language. It would be difficult to cite an example of an individual who rejected the church's words and yet sincerely accepted the church's concepts. Almost always the opposite has manifested itself, namely that those who refused to adopt the church's way of speaking did so because they had already come into conflict with the church's faith. In the case of the Socinians this is obvious. It is the same with the Sacramentarians. Hardly had *Carlstadt* forsaken the church's *faith* with regard to the sacraments when he also felt a strong aversion to the ecclesiastical *term* "sacrament." In his *Dialogue* of 1524 he writes, among other things: "One or the other must necessarily follow: Either Christ was not *wise* enough or not *kind* enough when He instituted His Supper and did not specify that His bread and cup should be called a *sacrament*"(St. Louis Edition, XX, 2317 f.). *Zwingli expressed similar opinions after he had given up the church's teaching* on the sacraments. In his book *On the True Religion* he says: "I wish very much that the word 'sacrament' had never been adopted by the Germans, unless it would have been understood correctly. *For when the people hear this word 'sacrament' they understand by it something great and holy that would by its power free the conscience from sin.*"

There are mainly two reasons why an orthodox Christian should not only *believe* together with the orthodox church but also choose to *speak* the same language. The first reason is that also in this way he might demonstrate his sincere oneness with his spiritual mother and also manifest his loyalty to her thereby, and conversely renounce all heretics, schismatics, and conceited eccentrics and withdraw from them. In truth, if there were no other reasons, this alone should be enough to move every orthodox Christian to conform to the church also in this respect. The apostle St. Paul writes to his beloved Timothy: "Do not be ashamed then of testifying to our Lord, *nor of me His prisoner*"(2 Timothy 1:8). If, then, Timothy should not be ashamed of the single person of Paul, how much less should we be ashamed of the whole rightly believing and rightly confessing *church*. "It behooves obedient children not to be ashamed also of their mother's *voice*," as Gerhard remarked with reference to the church. Refusing to acknowledge the church is nothing else than refusing to acknowledge the truth. Incidentally, one who knows what it means to stand alone in a fierce battle and who has experienced some of the encouragement in the battle resulting from the knowledge that in it one has the whole orthodox church behind and alongside, and that one is fighting as only one of many thousands of members—for such a person the actual commitment to the orthodox church will be a priceless privilege rather than an obligation resting upon him.

The second reason why an orthodox Christian should not only *believe* together with the orthodox church but also *speak* the same language, is that he has the duty not to impede but to help advance, for his part, the important goals which the church is trying to achieve with its way of speaking about the revealed truths. But, as stated, the chief purpose of church language is that none of its members be deceived by the "fair and flattering words"(Rom. 16:18) of the heretics and that the whole church be preserved without schisms in the true unity of the right faith. For that

69

reason the apostle, addressing all Christians, writes: "I appeal to you, brethren, by the name of our Lord Jesus Christ, that all of you agree [speak the same thing, KJV] and that there be no dissensions among you, but that you be united in the same mind and the same judgment" (1 Corinthians 1:10). *Balduin* explains:

He (the apostle) commands that all adopt the same *language* and *mind.* For these are the fountains of dissensions, when people want to be unique in speech and mind. Therefore he admonishes 1. that they speak the same thing, that is, that in matters of faith they use the same ways of speaking and the same terms (peculiar to the orthodox), so that by the novelty of their expressions they do not offend others with whom they may perhaps agree in the matter itself (Balduin, *Commentar zu den Briefen Pauli [Commentary on the Epistles of Paul],* p. 282).

This is Balduin's aphorism on the cited words:

True concord is planted by two things: By speaking the same thing and by meaning the same thing. These two will easily preserve unity in life and in faith. In everyday life nothing is more hated than a double-tongued person, who intends and speaks different things; but in faith nothing is more destructive than an eccentric who has his own special opinions and ways of speaking, merely to create the impression that he has discovered something new. In this way a window is easily opened wide to schisms and sectarian groups. Let us therefore preserve harmony in modes of speech and opinions, in endeavors and customs, and thus we will easily remain free from the guilt of schism. Those who bear one name from the name of Christ should also be one, teach one thing, and confess one thing[2w] (ibid., p. 288).

Similar remarks on 1 Corinthians 1:10 are made by *Calov* in his *Biblia illustrata.* He writes:

In order to exclude every dissension, the apostle admonishes that they speak the same thing, for as a rule one who coins new words at the same time also brings forth new articles of faith. Hence new expressions and formulas should be avoided, both that no strife, disunity, and dissensions arise and that no new articles of faith are thereby introduced. On the contrary, according to 2 Timothy 1:13 we must solemnly and steadfastly cling to the pattern of sound words, both as regards the modes of speech *contained in Holy Scripture* as well as those modes of speech that *explain them,* expressions that have been adopted in the church and that serve to exclude erroneous opinions and that expound and preserve the genuine sense of Scripture. Such expressions are: consubstantiality, incarnation, personal union, communication of attributes, and similar ways of speaking customary in the church and confirmed by symbols of public confession.

For an orthodox and informed Lutheran all this is beyond question. A principal reason why our church pledges its teachers to its common confessions of faith is that thus the teachers guarantee that they not only *believe* what is there confessed but that they will also *teach* it and will not depart from it with regard to the sense or *with regard to the language.* The first signers of the Formula of Concord therefore testify explicitly:

We repeat once again that we are not minded to manufacture anything new by this work of agreement or to depart *in any way at all, either* in content *or* in formulation, from the divine truth that our pious forebears and we have acknowledged and confessed in the past, for our agreement is based on the prophetic and apostolic Scriptures and is comprehended in the three Creeds as well as in the Augsburg Confession, submitted in the year 1530 to Emperor Charles V, of kindest memory, in the Apology that followed it, and in the Smalcald Articles and the Large and Small Catechisms of that highly enlightened man, Dr. Luther. On the contrary, we are minded by the grace of the Holy Spirit to abide and remain unanimously in this confession of faith and to regulate all religious controversies and their explanations according to it (Preface, *Book of Concord*, Tappert, pp. 13 f.).

Those first signers state at the same time that one of the purposes of the church's confession and especially of the Formula of Concord was

that pure doctrine can be recognized and distinguished from adulterated doctrine and so that *the way may not be left free and open to restless, contentious individuals, who do not want to be bound to any certain formula of pure doctrine,* to start scandalous controversies at will and to introduce and defend monstrous errors (ibid.)

Furthermore,

to insure that the truth may be established the most distinctly and clearly and may be distinguished from all error, and likewise to insure that *familiar terminology may not hide and conceal something,*[3W] we have collectively and severally come to a clear and express mutual agreement concerning the chief and most significant articles which were in controversy at this time. This agreement we have set forth as a certain and public testimony, not only to our contemporaries but also to our posterity, of that which our churches believe and accept with one accord as the correct *and abiding* answer in the controverted issues (Formula of Concord, Solid Declaration, Rule and Norm, 16; Tappert, p. 507).

Therefore the symbols often note that certain turns of phrase indeed admit of an orthodox interpretation, but for the sake of avoiding misunderstanding an orthodox person must decline to use them. *Urban Regius* (a theologian highly esteemed by Luther)[2] devoted an entire booklet to ecclesiastical language, a writing that also achieved [some]

71

symbolical status. It has the title *De formulis caute loquendi,* that is, *How One Must Speak of the Chief Articles of Christian Doctrine Cautiously and Without Offense.* Chemnitz incorporated this piece in the so-called *Corpus Julium,* first published in 1576, the collection of those symbols that were acknowledged in the Lutheran Church of Brunswick-Lueneburg. After at least 17 editions of Regius' work, Feustking prepared a new one (Wittenberg, 1710). The best edition is that of Martin Sylvester Grabe, who published the book with ample notes and a biography of Regius (Wolfenbuettel, 1714).

In conclusion we offer a little catalog of expressions which ought to be avoided by one who desires to speak in concert with the orthodox church.

Among unchurchly expressions that are in part openly heterodox, in part very ambiguous and therefore to be avoided are the following:

Apart from its *use* and if the Holy Spirit does not *accompany* it, Scripture has *no power* and is a *dead letter.*[4W] One who is *not* himself *converted* can convert others even less.

God is single in essence and *threefold* in Persons.—The Father is the Son.—Three are *One.*—The Father is something *other* than the Son and the Holy Spirit.—The Father begot the Son by His *will.*—The Son is begotten of the Father in a *figurative* sense.—Christ's flesh belongs to the *essence* of the Holy Trinity.[5W]—The Son is the *instrument* through which God created the world, etc.—In God there is a threefold *will.*

All that happens *must* happen in just that way.

God is or becomes *accidentally* and *indirectly* the cause of sin.

Satan left man seduced by him lying *half dead.*[6W]—Man's will is *not idle* in conversion but does *something* too.—Conversion has three *active causes:* God's Word, the Holy Spirit, and *man's will.*—The free will of the unregenerate person cannot *by itself* accomplish anything in conversion; the Holy Spirit must *support* it.—God must draw us if we are to come to Christ, but He draws only those who are *willing.*—You need only have the *desire,* and God will oblige you with His grace.

The elect are chosen not only in consideration of faith in Christ but also *because* they believe; their faith, foreseen by God, was the eternal moving *cause* of their election.

When a person does as much as he *can,* God will give him His grace.—Man is justified not only *through* faith but also *because of* faith and for the *sake* of faith.—Man becomes righteous through faith because Christ, the *essential righteousness, dwells* in him and is united with him.—Faith does not justify apart from *works.*—Faith justifies *insofar* as it bears love within it.—The believers are righteous before God, on the one hand, by imputation of the righteousness of Christ, on the other hand through their inchoate *righteousness of life.*—The promise of grace is appropriated to us through the faith of the heart and the *confession* of the mouth.

We become righteous by faith alone, but it is impossible to be *saved* without works.—Good works are necessary to *preserve* faith, righteousness, and salvation.[7W]—Good works are *not necessary* for the believer.—Good works are *necessary* to salvation.—Good works are *harmful* to salvation.—The doctrine of the *law* is no longer for the believer, is not necessary for him, and should therefore not be preached to him.

Christ has *begun* to be.—Christ is a *creature.*—To say that God is man and man is God is a *figurative* expression.—Christ as man was *adopted* by God as His Son.—In Christ the divine and human natures were *intermingled.*—Christ has only *one* will and one nature. The *incarnation* of the Son of God is the first stage of His humiliation.—Christ *humbled* Himself according to His *divine* nature and was *exalted* to the Father's right hand according to His *deity.*—For the sake of the work of redemption the *deity limited* itself in Christ.—In the state of humiliation Christ did not yet *possess* omniscience.—With the state of exaltation Christ's humanity *received* the divine properties.—By His holy life and innocent suffering and death Christ *earned* exaltation for Himself.—Insofar as He was human, Christ was *obligated* to keep the Law. Christ was also *able* to sin or fall into sin, but He did not want to.—Christ is omnipotent *according to* His human nature. Christ's humanity is *God.*—Already in the state of *humiliation* Christ was present to all creatures and, sitting at God's right hand, ruled over heaven and earth the same way as in the state of exaltation, except with this difference, that He kept this majesty secret or *concealed* it.—With the incarnation of the *Son of God* the Divine properties became *equal* with the divine.

Prayer, the ministerial office, the church, repentance, watchfulness, etc., are *means of grace.*

Baptism is *not necessary* for salvation.—One who has broken the baptismal covenant and thus has lost baptismal grace, must save himself on the plank of repentance *instead of baptism.*

Bread and wine in the Lord's Supper are *pledges* and *assurances* that the communicants become partakers of Christ's body and blood.

Also hypocrites and ungodly persons are *members* of the church.

With most of these expressions a teacher might conceivably combine a tolerable sense.[8W] But they are all unchurchly expressions and not in accord with the pattern of sound words. To these expressions applies what Augustine wrote concerning the man who wanted to use the word "fate" in an acceptable sense: "Let him keep the right sense but improve the way of saying it" *(City of God,* Book 5, ch. 1).

Foreword to the 1860 Volume

[Do We Draw the Lines of Fellowship Too Narrowly?]

[First Part:] *Lehre und Wehre*, VI, 1, Jan. 1860, pp. 1—13

When *Der Lutheraner* appeared some years ago, and later this theological journal, the accusation was at once raised against these periodicals that in them, as in the synod of Missouri generally, the bounds of orthodoxy and hence also of church fellowship are being drawn too narrowly. Far from allowing this to disconcert us we had rather hoped that at least all those who acknowledged the Word of God as "the only rule and norm according to which all doctrines and teachers alike must be appraised and judged" [Formula of Concord, Epitome, Rule and Norm, 1; Tappert, p. 464] would soon change their minds and finally be convinced by our presentations that members and servants of the orthodox church cannot do otherwise. But this hope has not been realized. Accusations are increasing. From all sides voices are raised in opposition to the "tendency" *(Richtung)* followed in the periodicals of our synod and by the synod itself, and they condemn this "tendency" as *producing heresy.*[1W] Even some of those who earlier had expressed themselves approvingly and encouragingly are now beginning to occupy a stance in opposition to us.

In support of these our observations we offer only a few recent pieces as documentation.

Thus the *Lutheran Observer* of Nov. 18, 1859, writes:[1]

> If we are permitted to judge from what appears in the Alt-Lutheraner, and the Lehre und Wehre, we would be constrained to believe that they can find or see Christ nowhere but in the sacraments. They presumptuously denounce all others who do not hold to their views, and would exclude from the Lord's table any Lutheran who may be connected with the General Synod. There is scarcely a week that they do not anathematize the General Synod and the Observer, because it is planted upon the basis of this body. To hope for union or fraternization with such selfish, such exclusive views, would be worse than folly. They are a class of spiritual Ishmaelites; their appropriate place is in the Church of Rome, where men believe what they are told the church believes, and not what the Bible and the Holy Ghost teach them. An inanimate congregation of wax or clay might be formed by passing them

through the same *iron mould,* but a community of immortal minds, whose divinely-delegated prerogative it is "to search the Scriptures," "to prove all things, and to hold fast to that which is good," never, no never! Revolutions do not go backwards; the Reformation of the 16th century was emphatically a revolution in the sentiments and dogmas of Christendom, and you will never turn the church back into that night of barbarism and spiritual bondage out of which she emerged at the Reformation, while the Holy Spirit makes men free with the liberty of Christ.

If, therefore our good brother of New York (Dr. Stohlmann[2]) indulges the hope of giving these extremists a heart of brotherly kindness, or expects to inspire them with tolerant christian sentiments by exhibiting a gentle bearing towards them, we regret that we must dispel his agreeable illusion. We have great confidence in the power of christian love, for it has often subdued the most stubborn natures, but upon men who have imbibed with their mother's milk their prejudices, who have been cradled in their superstition, and their souls have grown into the exact shape of their doctrinal mould, and been expanded to the utmost limit, even the sun of Righteousness may not woo from such indurated soil the graces of brotherly kindness and charity.—For years we have abstained from making such strictures on their intolerant spirit in their issues, as the character of their articles might well provoke, and that too with the hope that they might be improved by exhibiting that forbearance which we are taught to manifest towards erring brethren, but it was like casting pearls before the wrong persons, for they never appear to be in their true element so much as when they abuse the *General Synod,* or some of its leading members and friends.

So much from a recent article in the *Lutheran Observer* about our synod and its periodicals.

Not so openly hostile to all that is Lutheran, but just as much in opposition to the principles and modes of procedure in our synod and its periodicals, and if possible even more unfavorable to our good name in Germany, is the representation of another tendency. This is *Pastor Loehe,* who airs his views in his *Kirchliche Nachrichten aus und ueber Nord-Amerika,* [Church News from and About North America], No. 8, 1859. First of all, he erroneously maintains that his "emergency assistants by his direction provided the stimulus for the founding of the synod of Missouri and did in fact found it," indeed, that our synod's activity and he, Loehe, are in the relationship "of the harvest to the sower, the movement to its first impulse, the effect to the cause." Then he writes:

The sad experiences which the former Stephanites had with their hierarch, Stephan, have made their hearts very receptive to the *doctrine* of the ministry *held by Luther and subsequent theologians, a teaching also reflected in the Lutheran Symbols,* especially since this doctrine not only *commends itself highly to the Christian mind* but also seems made to order for American circumstances. Conversely, some of *us* were led by experiences of an opposite and different nature to have an eye for a *different* conception of ministry and church, a conception which was present already at the time of the Reformation in the church of the Reformers and had been recommended particularly in some parts of southern Germany.[2W] Where it differs from the specific-Lutheran and Lutheran-theological course *(Richtung),* it *seems* to commend itself by virtue of a more artless attachment to *Holy Scripture* and *antiquity* and by greater truth in *practice.* Formerly and in its best sides *(Seiten)* [Walther corrects this, with a question mark, to "times" *(Zeiten)*] the Lutheran Church knew how to bear *its (?) tendency (Richtung)* and understood to what extent unity could be demanded in order to have unity. But in the 19th century and especially in the tendency with which the leader of the Missouri Synod (it has none) is identified, there is a striving for such a measure of consensus as cannot exist without ongoing disintegration and dissolution of the church. Lutheran theology of the 16th and part of the 17th century provides a standard for exegesis (?) and dogmatics and everything—and where this standard cannot be applied, there peace is at an end, or at least the love that delights in bringing people together.

Loehe then points to the synod's procedure with regard to one of its members who proclaimed chiliasm. He says:

> Oh, how we are overwhelmed by holy horrors of an inquisition on reading whither the traditionally Lutheran view has driven Missouri and its pastors![3W] And what emotions stirred within us when we realized that particularly our more outstanding workers sent abroad *(Sendlinge)* had to serve and must still serve as tools of the consequences of a system of church government which must have a paralyzing and strangling effect, must rear hypocrites in the bosom of the synod,[4W] must produce an inner dissolution, since it is left to itself and is allowed to hold sway without the influence of a salutary antithesis.[5W]

So far Loehe.

Friendliest of all is the attitude of Kirchenrat *Ehlers* of Liegnitz in his *Kirchenblatt fuer die Ev.-Luth. Gemeinden in Preussen* [Church Paper for the Ev.-Luth. Congregations in Prussia]. Yet even his friendly remarks reveal all too clearly that he, too, is unable to approve the principles observed by our synod especially in recent years and set forth and supported in its periodicals. In the issue of Sept. 1, 1859, of the above-named paper, there is an essay with the title "Chiliasten und Nicht-Chiliasten in ihrem kirchlichen Verhaeltnis zu einander" [Chiliasts and

Nonchiliasts in Their Church Relations to Each Other]. Among other things, this article says:

[Editorial note: In a lengthy quotation Ehlers faults Missouri for refusing to have fellowship with chiliasts. In his view chiliasm is not enough to warrant separation and the opponents of chiliasm are unable to offer a satisfactory exegesis of the proof-texts cited by chiliasts. Ehlers also chides Missouri for saying that Pastor Schieferdecker denied the article of faith regarding the "general resurrection of the dead on the last day," since neither Scripture nor the Creeds nor our Confessions speak clearly on this matter. Only if chiliasts come into conflict with a "genuine" article of faith should they be put out of the fellowship if they persist, or if they insist on imposing their opinions on others as necessary to salvation.

In support of his claim that Loehe's chiliasm is not divisive, Ehlers quotes mission inspector Bauer of Neuendettelsau (where Loehe labored) to the effect that they do not regard chiliasm as an article of faith and that they grant every Lutheran complete freedom to adopt whatever view his conscience dictates. Bauer prays that Lutherans may be preserved "from the deification of Lutheran theology and from the fanaticism of dogmatism and scholasticism and every mania for systems." Ehlers pleads that opponents of chiliasm might find it within themselves to acknowledge as full brothers in the faith such Christians as the people of Neuendettelsau. To mistrust them would be doing them an injustice.

Ehlers' article provoked two letters which were critical of his position. One of these made the point that the real question at issue is whether chiliasm can be preached in an orthodox Lutheran church.]

Through these responses Ehlers saw himself compelled to become the advocate of the chiliasts and to demonstrate the harmless nature of these dreamers. May God protect this revered man so that in his attempt to prevent the loveless treatment of chiliasts and an eruption of the fire of dissension and schism that is already smoldering beneath the surface of the Prussian Lutheran Church he may not himself run the danger of falling prey to error. Satan is cunning; if he cannot reach a pure teacher on the left, he will try it on the right.

To go back to the above-mentioned representatives of a threefold opposition that we experience within our church (for the battle with those who are without is a legacy of the fathers into which every one must enter as soon as he wants to bear the Lutheran name in truth), we will perhaps need no special defense and justification as far as the party of the *Lutheran Observer,* that is, the General Synod, is concerned. Whoever grants us the right to be Lutherans must at the same time assert that we are not only justified but also solemnly obligated to keep our distance from the General

Synod. If a Lutheran has drifted into the circle of this church from ignorance or by God's ordaining, there may be a question as to what he should do. But if a Lutheran or a Lutheran Synod in this country has been preserved by the grace of God from being swallowed up by that group, it is completely out of the question to have even the least fellowship with them. The General Synod is an enemy of our church with more power and more to be feared than all other sects infesting this land, just as the enemy within is always more dangerous than the enemy outside the walls of a well-fortified castle.

Therefore let the *Lutheran Observer* and its cohorts judge ever so venomously about our adhering to orthodox church fellowship and about our eschewing fellowship with manifest false teachers who even want to remove grace from the means of grace—this will make no other impression upon us and all true Lutherans, whose faith is not only on their lips and in their head but is a genuine faith of the heart, than the impression made on Luther when a month before his death he heard of the ranting and raving of the Swiss against him. On Jan. 17, 1546, he wrote to Jacob Probst, preacher at Bremen:

> The fact that you report how indignantly and insolently the Swiss write against me and condemn me as an unfortunate man and most unfortunate rationalist makes me very happy. For that is what I wanted; that was my intention with the very writing with which I made them so angry, so that they would affirm by their own public testimony that they are my enemies. This I have now achieved, and, as I have said, I am glad of it. I, the most unfortunate of all men, am content with this beatitude of the psalm, *"Blessed is the man who walks not in the counsel of the sacramentarians, nor stands in the way of the Zwinglians, nor sits in the seat of the men of Zurich."* There you have my opinion (St. Louis Edition, XVII, 2177 f.).

The spokesman of a second opposition directed at our synod is Pastor *Loehe*. It is true, with an honesty that is, alas! becoming ever rarer, he concedes that our teaching is that of *Luther* and the theologians succeeding him, and that it "shines again also in the *symbols,"* but that he inclines toward a "different" conception, for example of the ministry and the church and certain eschatological questions, which "is differentiated from the specifically Lutheran and Lutheran-theological orientation." At the same time he voices a double reproach against us, namely that we demand a measure of agreement which, in the first place, goes beyond what our church in its best days demanded and which, secondly, "cannot be demanded without an ongoing disintegration and dissolution of the church."

In the first place, it is indeed undeniable that "already at the time of the Reformation in the church of the Reformers" there were views on doctrine different from those contained in Luther's writings and those deposited in the Lutheran Symbols. More than that, even the coarsest heresies were voiced there. But when Pastor Loehe writes: "Formerly, and especially in its best days, the Lutheran Church knew how to bear its tendencies"—we do not understand what he means. If by those tendencies Pastor Loehe meant only that individual peculiarity according to which some are oriented primarily toward theory in their activity and others more toward the practical; according to which in practice some follow the principle of freedom to a greater degree while others are more inclined to strict order; some proceed more conservatively in matters of church ordinances, arrangements, customs, and ceremonies while others proceed more radically and puristically; some are legalistically stricter while others are evangelically milder in the church's ethical discipline, etc.—in that case we would have no objections. But then the cited reproach would not strike us either, for we too know how to bear such divergent tendencies as our church in its best days indeed knew how to bear, and we know how to distinguish them clearly from separations and offenses contrary to the doctrine we have learned.

But in connection with different *tendencies* Pastor Loehe obviously thinks of different *doctrines* which concern important articles of the Christian faith, such as the church, the holy ministry, and the last things. This involves a difference in which one party makes the church's confession its own without reservation, while the other party does so with substantive restrictions. But *such* different tendencies our church did *not* bear, particularly in its best days. Rather, as often as such differences arose, they evoked a contrary witness and resistance in our church, and the latter did not rest in those days until the false tendencies appearing in it were overcome. Only after Pietism had swamped our church like an irresistible deluge did our church finally get into its present state where the practice of doctrinal discipline seems incompatible with the continued existence of our church as an organized fellowship.

It is true that Luther put up with *Melanchthon* with admirable patience. But here the following must not be forgotten. First of all, Melanchthon accommodated himself often with great reluctance and revulsion, to the still-living Luther. In his notorious letter of 1548 to Carlowitz, counselor of Elector Maurice, in connection with the introduction of the Interim, Melanchthon admits, surely to his own discredit: "Even though I will not approve what the prince may decree, I will nevertheless do nothing seditiously, but either *keep silent* or *tolerate*

79

whatever may happen. *Even in the past I bore an almost shameful servitude,* when N. (Luther) often served his own nature, in which there was no little contentiousness, more than [he served] either his person or the common good" [cf. *Concordia Triglotta,* Historical Introductions, p. 106; we have omitted a footnote in which Walther gives Melanchthon's words in Latin]. This admission can cast no shadow on Luther, for the same Melanchthon himself gave Luther this testimonial in his funeral address:

> Everyone who has come to know him (Luther) and has been much in his company must attest that he was a very kindly man and socially gracious, friendly, and amiable in speech, and *not at all insolent, tempestuous, headstrong or contentious.* Yet at the same time there was in his words and demeanor a seriousness and courage as befitted such a man. . . . *It is therefore manifest that the hardness he displayed in his writings against the enemies of pure doctrine did not spring from a cantankerous and malicious spirit but from a great earnestness and zeal for the truth.* All of us and many strangers besides, who saw and knew him, must give him that testimonial. . . . I myself often came upon him when with burning tears he prayed for the whole church. For every day he set aside a special period of time to recite a number of psalms, into which he mingled his prayers to God with sighing and weeping (St. Louis Edition, XXIb, 3429 f.).

If Melanchthon nevertheless writes, as cited above, that under Luther he sighed in an almost unendurable servitude, he only reveals thereby that he did not dare to oppose Luther openly but only outwardly gave in to him with inner aversion. Consequently Luther did not know many things that Melanchthon was doing behind his back already during Luther's lifetime. Hence it may *seem* that against Melanchthon's doctrinal aberrations Luther displayed a patience that now puts us to shame. How Melanchthon and his colleagues, who with him later openly deviated, acted toward Luther as late as 1544 may be inferred from a letter which Luther wrote on April 21 of that year to people in Hungary who had heard a rumor that the Wittenbergers had deviated in the doctrine of the Lord's Supper. In this letter Luther writes: *"I do not harbor the slightest suspicion against Master Philip,* nor against anyone among us. For, as I have said, Satan does not dare even to utter a sound *in public"* (St. Louis Edition, XXIb, 2971). Yet Melanchthon had long sided with the opponents of pure doctrine and cast suspicion on Luther.[6w] Honest and unsuspecting Luther had no idea of this. However, his eyes were soon to be opened. When he saw that the sacramentarians were again coming forward ever more boldly and his colleagues observed a suspicious silence, he said that he must once again bear witness to the truth.

Melanchthon heard this with trembling. He saw that the execution of his plan to introduce in the Lutheran Church a so-called "moderate" form of teaching that would make a union with the Swiss possible would be gravely imperiled. Therefore he wrote to Veit Dietrich as early as Aug. 11, 1544: "It is also reported that he (Luther) is going to publish I know not what. If the strife over the Lord's Supper is rekindled, there will be larger and more tragic separations. I was surprised that you wanted to show Luther the writings of Bullinger and Bucer. He has plenty of others to provoke him" *(Corpus Reformatorum,* V, 461). The next day he wrote to Musculus at Augsburg: "At the moment our Pericles (as Melanchthon often titled Luther during this time) is stirring up internal wars. He thunders against those who speak of the symbols of the body and blood of Christ differently than he, and *he even attacks me occasionally.* Therefore I do not know what will become of me. Perhaps at this age I will shortly have to go into exile" (ibid., p. 464). He wrote the same to Bucer on Aug. 28 and to Bullinger on the 30th. Thus the matter finally became public knowledge.

Luther therefore decided to write not only against the Swiss but also against Melanchthon. We read:

His Electoral Grace fears that when especially Dr. Martin or he, the elector, lay down their head, the split will be mightily undertaken and promoted. . . . His Electoral Grace is also worried that the students will notice and understand and then have the audacity to defend this as correct in opposition to the doctrine that is acknowledged and confessed. For the sake of his conscience it would be burdensome if during his and Dr. Martin's lifetime he were knowingly to tolerate such a thing in his university and allow it to take root, and permit further schisms and offenses to come up in the future. And even though His Electoral Grace had graciously endowed the university and was well disposed toward it, and it was experiencing growing prestige not least because of Master Philip Melanchthon, he does not want to conceal from both, Dr. Luther and Bugenhagen, that before he would tolerate and suffer this split he was minded to let matters take their course, *even though only an insignificant university or finally none at all should be and remain,* something he surely would not want. . . . For if Duke George for the maintenance of *untruth* permitted his university at Leipzig to fall largely into ruin, His Electoral Grace would also have to consider whether the same thing should happen with regard to this university for the preservation of the *truth* (St. Louis Edition, XVII, 2170 f.).

Subsequently Brueck reported to the elector on the results of his negotiations with Luther:

Dr. Martin states and avows that he never realized Philip was still so deeply stuck in fantasies. He also indicated that he had various concerns and could not know how Philip stood with regard to the sacrament. He had also brought arguments since he had been in Cassel that showed him [Luther] that Melanchthon was almost Zwinglian in his views,[7W] but he did not yet know how it was in his heart. However, the secret writings and counsels that under tyrants one might receive the sacrament under one kind gave him strange thoughts. But he intended to share his heart with Philip. He would be happy if Philip, an eminent man, did not leave them and the school, for he was doing outstanding work. *However, if he persisted in his opinion* expressed in the letter to Dr. Jacob, *God's truth would have to have priority.* He would pray for him. . . . It was, he said, no longer a matter of weakness. . . . I told him how Your electoral Grace regards Philip's opinion and believes that he, Melanchthon, was waiting for the opportune time, and especially that he would postpone action until the doctor's death. Dr. Martin said, *"If he does it, he will become a wretched man and his conscience will give him no peace."* In my opinion it will do no harm for Dr. Martin to keep the pressure on Philip and have a serious, heart-to-heart talk with him. There is here a chain which links these matters together (St. Louis Edition, XVII, 2171 f.).

Luther followed through on this, and Melanchthon took cover.

Now, if this conduct on Luther's part toward Melanchthon is an example of "knowing how to bear different tendencies within our church in its best days," then we heartily agree with Pastor Loehe. In that case, however, his rebuke does not strike us, because it is that very conduct of Luther's that has always served us as a model for our own conduct.[8W]

Or are we to regard as the best days of our church, when it knew how to bear the different tendencies of its members, the time after Luther's death until the writing and acceptance of the Formula of Concord? Probably not, for that period is the time when the "fury of the theologians," about which Melanchthon complained shortly before his death, was at its most vehement. Or does this accusation of "fury" apply only to the Anti-Philippists? No one who knows history will dare to say that. Or did the Formula of Concord finally signal the beginning of those best days of our church? Men like Loehe will hardly want to assert that. It was particularly the Formula of Concord that owed its origin to maintaining Luther's principle:

> *With the utmost rigor we demand that all the articles of Christian doctrine, both large and small—although we do not regard any of them as small—be kept pure and certain.* This is supremely necessary. For this doctrine is our only light, which illumines and directs us and shows us the way to heaven; if it is *overthrown in one point,* it must be overthrown completely. And when that happens, our love will not be of any use to us.

. . . Therefore, as I often warn you, doctrine must be carefully distinguished from life. *Doctrine* is heaven; *life* is earth. In *life* there is sin, error, uncleanness, and misery, mixed, as the saying goes, "with vinegar." Here love should condone, tolerate, be deceived, trust, hope, and endure all things (1 Cor. 13:7); here the forgiveness of sins should have complete sway, provided that sin and error are not defended. But just as there is no error in *doctrine,* so there is no need for any forgiveness of sins. Therefore there is no comparison at all between doctrine and life. "One dot" of doctrine is worth more than "heaven and earth" (Matt. 5:18); therefore we do not permit the slightest offense against it. But we can be lenient toward errors of *life.* For we, too, err daily in our life and conduct; so do all the saints, as they earnestly confess in the Lord's Prayer and the Creed. But by the grace of God our *doctrine* is pure; we have all the articles of faith solidly established in Sacred Scripture. The devil would dearly love to corrupt and overthrow these; that is why he attacks us so cleverly with this specious argument about not offending against love and the harmony among the churches *(1535 Commentary on Galatians, 5:10. Luther's Works,* American Edition, 27, 41 f.).

Continuation and Conclusion: Vol. VI, No. 2, Feb. 1860, pp. 33—47

Or is Pastor *Loehe* perhaps speaking of the time *after* the adoption of the Formula of Concord when he writes: "Formerly, especially in its best days, the Lutheran Church knew how to bear its tendencies and was aware of the degree of unity that must be demanded in order to have unity"? This we can hardly accept. For it was just at this time and thereafter that the *oath* demanded of all servants of the church in commitment to the symbolical books of our church was made even more distinct and the *doctrinal discipline* based on it ever more strict.[9W] In regard to that *oath,* we refer the reader to an essay on this subject which the Western District of our synod adopted in the year 1858 and published in its *Proceedings,* also in the *Lutheraner,* and by means of a special pamphlet.[3] With regard to the *doctrinal discipline* practiced in our church since the adoption of the Formula of Concord, we will cite a few examples of many.

In 1592 the learned and gifted Swiss theologian *Samuel Huber,* who had come to the Lutheran Church from the Reformed Church (mainly because of the Calvinistic doctrine of predestination), became professor of theology in Wittenberg. Increasingly he promoted his teaching that he had already begun to set forth in Tuebingen, the teaching of a universal election of all people, of a universal regeneration of all the baptized, and of a universal justification of all the redeemed. He did this with the pretense that all these teachings could well be harmonized with the symbols of our church, including the Formula of Concord. His colleagues

Polycarp Leyser, Aegidius Hunnius, and Sal. Gesner admonished him but were able only to persuade him to refrain from affirming the last two teachings. The concession was made to him that if by a universal *election* he meant only God's universal *love,* his *opinion* need not be rejected, but that in any case his *language* was offensive and should therefore be avoided. So, for example, the Tuebingen and Stuttgart theologians Jacob Heerbrand, Stephen Gerlach, Matthew Hafenreffer, Luke Osiander, Felix Bidembach, and others, whom the Wittenbergers had called upon for help, wrote to Huber:

[*Editorial note: Here follows an opinion of several pages in which the theologians point out his errors to Huber, plead with him to cease teaching them, and, if he really wants to teach correctly, to conform his language to that of the orthodox church. Refusal to take their advice would lead only to confusion and schism and would assuredly destroy his teaching career. Walther continues:*]

When also this admonition and the negotiations of several commissions appointed by the elector could make no headway with Huber, he was dismissed the following year and given 200 talers travel money. But when he continued in Wittenberg as a private tutor and sought to keep the unrest alive, he was finally ordered by the court to leave Wittenberg within eight days. Revealing himself to be an erring spirit, Huber now reaffirmed even what he had already admitted as an error and had recanted, and tried to gain a following. Prominent among his followers was one Caspar Hirsch of Wuerttemberg, who was then deposed and exiled. But when Huber died in 1624, the storm ended forever.[4]

Another remarkable example of doctrinal discipline in our church after the adoption of the Formula of Concord can be seen in the proceedings against *John Melchior Stenger,* deacon and inspector of the college *(Gymnasium)* at Erfurt (born there in 1638).[10w] He was a man extremely zealous for seriousness in Christianity. Misled by the observation that so many people seemed only to toy with repentance and thought the fall from grace was no big thing, since one could always repent again and regain grace, Stenger wrote a book with the title *Einschaerfung zweier nuetzlicher zum wahren Christentum gehoeriger Lehrpuncte* [Inculcation of Two Useful Points of Doctrine Belonging to True Christianity], 1670. He wrote:

The *great repentance* is not repeated by the true children of God as often as some imagine. Either the true children of God destined for eternal life are never in need of the great repentance or certainly not for a second time, not to speak of a third, or tenth, or hundredth time (p. 1). One who relapses into wilful sins for the third time will surely not be renewed to a proper repentance. If it should happen and it was clearly evident from the wholly different sanctified life which the penitent person is now manifesting, we would have to call that an extraordinary event.

When he was criticized for this and when he received the unfavorable opinions of the theological faculties of Wittenberg and Jena and the ministerium of Frankfurt,[11w] he apparently backed down. But when he was once more attacked publicly, he returned to his opinion and said: "I hold with those who believe that ordinarily the elect are capable of no more than one relapse" *(Antwort auf das Laesterbuch Hartnacc's* [Answer to the Slanderous Book by Hartnacc]).

Stenger worded another error in this way: "One who at his death does not have the good witness of a life in this world that was holy and in accordance with Christ's commands will die unsaved and will not come (to speak of what happens as a rule and ordinarily) into the kingdom of God" *(Einschaerfung).* In another writing he remarked that while it does not follow from this statement that one merits eternal salvation through one's piety, yet "those who *repent late in life* will not be saved in the ordinary manner" *(Buch fuer die, welche ihr Christentum wollen lernen besser verstehen* [Book for Those Who Would Like to Have a Better Understanding of Their Christianity], p. 239).

A third point was Stenger's assertion that there is a difference between the law of Moses and the law of Christ. 1. Moses forbids also original sin and human mistakes, while Christ forbids only willful sins; 2. the law of Moses applies to the unregenerate, while the law of Christ concerns the regenerate; 3. whoever transgresses the law of Moses will not be condemned on that account, since there is no human being who does not transgress it, while the person who does not observe the law of Christ will be condemned.

Finally, in the fourth place, he taught about willful sins that "one who notices such sins in himself as cannot be found in other pious Christians may conclude that his sins must not be ordinary ones but gross and *willful* sins" (ibid., p. 17). He classified all sins of the unregenerate not only (correctly) as *mortal sins,* but all of them also as *willful* sins. David's sin, however, he did not regard as willful, but only as a human slip, and later conceded only that while the sin was indeed premeditated, it was not a mortal sin. He further made the incidental assertion that true Christians were permitted to boast of their righteous conduct. Faith included five parts: knowledge, assent, confidence, a strong desire for grace, and pleasant rest in Christ, and other similar ideas.

It is true that in these matters Stenger appealed, undoubtedly not against his better knowledge, to the fact that he acknowledged all the symbolical books of our church and rejected the errors of the papists, Reformed, Socinians, Anabaptists, and other sects. However, he did not want to recant decisively, and although there was a desire to deal gently with him because of his zeal and because he obviously did not see the consequences of his assertions, he was first suspended for some time and finally removed from office on Nov. 18, 1670. On pain of severe penalties he was forbidden to preach and to teach in the city and in the entire territory related to the city.

How unreliable Stenger was in his repeated yielding up to a certain degree became evident soon after his dismissal, as in the case of Huber. When in the following year the official record of his case was published under the title *Causa Stengeriana oder wahrer Abdruck der Bedenken,* etc., he responded with a *lampoon* under the title *Palinodia Stengeriana, d. i., demuetigster Widerruf aller der schrecklichen ketzer haften Lehren, in denen J. M. Stenger sich seither leider sehr vertieft gehabt,* etc. [A Most Humble Recantation of All the Dreadful Heretical Teachings into Which J. M. Stenger Had Unfortunately Plunged Very Deeply], 1671. In later years he became involved with the well-known Dr. John Frederich Mayer in so violent a quarrel that they sent their polemical writings to each other's home by hangman's assistants (cf. Walch, *Einleitung in die Religionsstreitigkeiten der ev. luth. Kirche* [Introduction to the Religious Controversies of the Ev. Luth. Church] IV, 919 ff.).

As a third example of Evangelical Lutheran doctrinal discipline in the period following the adoption of the Formula of Concord we cite the case of Pastor Johan Mercker at Essen (born 1658, died 1728). He equated the spiritual priesthood and the public ministry and would admit a difference only when the preachers ruled as bishops (by human right) at the same time. Otherwise, if a Christian had the necessary gifts of the Holy Spirit he had the same right to preach as a called preacher. He denied a special divine institution of the public teaching office and the preacher's authority to forgive sins in God's stead. Logically he therefore also rejected the church's institutions for the training of preachers, because only those thus educated were called to the ministry. He conceded only that the license to teach which he demanded could not be introduced at once because of the confusion that would arise; but the church must work toward that goal. When also in his case all admonitions and theological opinions concerning his teaching proved fruitless, he too was finally deposed in 1703 (Walch, V, 121 ff.).

The same thing happened to Pastor *Johan Crasselius* at Sara in the territory of Altenburg, when he refused to give up his assertion that dancing *per se* (and not only accompanying circumstances) was sinful and when he practiced church discipline accordingly (Walch, V, 151 ff.). Furthermore, in 1703 Magister *Siegmund Beerensprung,* pastor at Tautenhayn, was removed from office by the electoral Saxon consistory, because he stubbornly taught that believers who are in the state of grace have no need to come to confession and again obtain forgiveness; what one already has one need not acquire; hence believers received nothing through the absolution (Walch, III, 127 ff.; cf. Valentine Loescher, *Unschuldige Nachrichten* [Innocent Reports], 1707 p. 496). In 1723 Magister *J. G. Cuntius,* head pastor at Toenningen in the territory of Holstein, was deposed because he had written in favor of union and against the so-called coercion of the symbols and refused to recant. For that reason those who shared his views celebrated him highly as a "martyr for the cause of union" (Loescher, 1723, pp. 494 f.; 1725, p. 760). The same fate befell Magister *G. Klein-Nicolai,* pastor at Friessdorf and Rammelburg in the county of Mannsfeld. He was removed from office in 1706 because in the first place he stubbornly insisted that private absolution could have a salutary application only 1. at Baptism; 2. at one's reinstatement after an excommunication; 3. in connection with a specific concern; and 4. in an act of brotherly reconciliation. In the second place, he taught that unworthy communicants received the Lord's body only as in the form of an offer *(anbietungsweise)* (Loescher, 1706, pp. 229 f.).

How overt *chiliasts* were dealt with in our church was demonstrated at length in the *Lutheraner* (XIV, nos. 8 and 9) with the example of the preacher *George Laurentius Seidenbecher.* He was deposed from office on Dec. 12, 1661, on the basis of several requested opinions offered in the name of the entire theological faculty of Jena by the great and godly theologians Ernst Gerhard and Johan Musaeus,[5] and with the knowledge of the Gotha consistory and the approval of Duke Ernest the Pious.[6]

Finally, a remarkable example of conscientious doctrinal discipline as practiced by our church in its best days is the conduct observed over against *Stephen Praetorius* (from whose writings Statius later excerpted and published the well-known and beloved *Schatzkammer* [Treasury]). This dear man lacked deeper theological insight and as a result allowed his writings, which were otherwise filled with a genuinely evangelical spirit, to be infiltrated with a number of quite dubious, notably antinomian statements. A commission was appointed to show Praetorius his errors. In consequence the honest man signed the following revocation:

I, Magister Stephen Praetorius, of Salzwedel New Town, declare in my own handwriting that I have issued several small tracts which run counter to and are against the norm and model of sound words and especially the ancient Augsburg Confession delivered to emperor

Charles V in 1530, as well as our Christian Formula of Concord which I have subscribed with heart and mouth. 1. I have employed antinomian phrases with regard to the third use of the Law; 2. concerning actions of the saints against conscience, that thereby they do not lose the Holy Spirit and the grace of God; 3. I did not maintain or observe the distinction between mortal and venial sins; 4. I have unfairly reviled and condemned the Christian Questions attached to Dr. M. Luther's Catechism. The official visitors convinced me by means of God's infallible Word and set me right. Therefore, by virtue of this and on pain of losing my position, I reverse myself. During this visitation I will surrender all copies of my questionable booklets mentioned above to the official visitors, and henceforth I will publish nothing further in theology without the inspection and approval of the venerable consistory of Coeln on the Spree or of the theological faculty of Frankfurt on the Oder. Herewith I pledge that I have accepted this judgment and will abide by it. Given in Salzwedel Old Town, June 4, 1600 (cf. *Unschuldige Nachrichten* [Innocent Reports], 1727, pp. 916 f.).

Even Spener writes about this matter in his *Theologische Bedenken* [Theological Thoughts]:

Also Praetorius in his time revoked some things, and this did not lead to his disgrace or to rejection of his writings. On the contrary, as in the case of Augustine, it should serve as a testimonial to his honesty. *At the same time it serves notice on his readers to look at everything cautiously and first put it to the test* (I, 164).

These examples, which could be multiplied by a great number of similar cases, may suffice to show how the Lutheran Church, "especially in its best days, knew how to bear its tendencies and understood to what extent unity must be demanded in order to have unity." We think we have clearly shown that our synod by the grace of God is in fact walking in the footsteps of our church in its best days with regard to doctrinal discipline. As already indicated, we do not deny that later on through the irresistible inroads of Pietism and, still later, of moralism and rationalism, and the unionism in our church resulting from both, all doctrinal discipline gradually either ceased or was turned directly *against* pure Lutheran doctrine. But surely no one will call this period the best days of our church, when it was and to a large extent still is the time of its deepest decline.

Or do people want to call attention to some peculiar opinions which a few of our older theologians expressed here and there on certain points without being challenged on that account? If so, we remind people that such peculiar expressions found here and there did not indicate a special *"tendency"* which they followed but only an inadvertent *weakness* which can easily be forgiven. Yes, we even readily admit that the foremost

Lutheran theologians of the 17th century did not remain completely in line with the model of the *Book of Concord* in some points, *evidently without being aware of it themselves*. We mention only the teaching about Sunday. But we do not doubt for one moment that, like Augustine, they would have retracted if their unwitting departures had been clearly shown to them. However, in the 17th century there were no such watchmen who could or would in all humility call some misstep to the attention of even their fathers. That those theologians could stray in a few points without being called to account for it was not, therefore, because people at that time understood to what extent unity could be demanded in order to have unity. On the contrary, it was because the straying ones were the *leaders* of their time, and gone was the era of the Luthers and Chemnitzes,[12W] whose eye was so keen that they themselves could be leaders of the leaders.

Nevertheless Pastor Loehe reproaches our synod with demanding a degree of consensus which not only goes beyond what our church demanded in its best days but which also "cannot exist without ongoing disintegration and dissolution of the church."

Now, we admit that there is indeed a degree of consensus which, if insisted upon, will necessarily lead to the church's disintegration and dissolution. In the first place, the proper degree is obviously exceeded when agreement not only in the *doctrine* of the Gospel and the administration of the sacraments, but also in *ceremonies,* usages, constitutions, and the like is demanded as necessary. But as strong a preference as we have for the ceremonies, usages, and constitutions transmitted to us by our fathers, we are nevertheless far from making uniformity in these things a condition of church unity. Rather, with a loud voice we confess with our fathers in Article VII of the Augsburg Confession:

> For *it is sufficient* for the true unity of the Christian church that *the Gospel be preached in conformity with a pure understanding of it and that the sacraments be administered in accordance with the divine Word. It is not necessary* for the true unity of the Christian church that *ceremonies,* instituted by men, should be observed uniformly in all places. It is as Paul says in Eph. 4:4, 5, "There is one body and one Spirit, just as you were called to the one hope that belongs to your call, one Lord, one faith, one baptism" [Tappert, p. 32].

Although Loehe calls the *"IT IS SUFFICIENT"* of Article VII *"the great word,* if not for our time *the greatest word, of the Augsburg Confession"* (cf. the Preface to the first edition of his Agenda), a comparison of the practice in our synod with the one whose "existence has no other purpose than to represent Loehe's [theological] position in America" (cf. note[5W]) will quickly show that our synod takes the cited statement of the Augsburg

Confession no less seriously, in fact takes it more seriously, than Loehe's group.

In the second place, we cheerfully concede, furthermore, that the proper measure of necessary agreement is also exceeded when consensus even *in nonfundamental articles* is made the condition of church fellowship. We have in mind all such teachings as may indeed impinge on a treatment of fundamental articles but are neither clearly and plainly revealed in the Word of God nor constitute necessary deductions from those clearly and plainly revealed. We include such dubious teachings as: On which day of creation the angels were created; what specific sin led to the apostasy of certain angels; in what manner human souls since Adam came into being, whether by creation or by transmission through procreation (traducianism); whether the visible world will perish on the last day according to its essence or only according to its accidental condition, that is, whether it will be annihilated or only transformed and transfigured; whether Paul, or Barnabas, or some other apostolic man wrote the Letter to the Hebrews, etc. We concede to no man the right and still less claim it for ourselves to deny church fellowship to a Christian because of the way these questions are answered. We will rather let these questions remain what they are—theological *problems* about which one may argue in either direction without danger to salvation.

But, of course, it is a different matter when it comes to *those fundamental articles of faith* that are clearly and plainly revealed in God's Word. In regard to these we do indeed demand *full agreement* for entering into church fellowship. But we demand it because, according to the Word of God, 1. there is only one church (John 10:16); 2. because this one church is not built upon human ideas but solely on the *foundation of the apostles and prophets,* that is, upon Christ and His Word (Ephesians 2:20); 3. because there is only *one faith,* which the church has and through which it is one body and one Spirit (Ephesians 4:4-5); 4. because also the seemingly *smallest error,* like a little leaven, can *pervert the whole doctrine that is otherwise pure* (Galatians 5:9); and finally 5. because every error with regard to an article of faith is a departure from God's Word and command and hence a serious *sin* which can never, never be granted any sort of right to exist in the church. On the contrary, Christ says: "Truly, I say to you, till heaven and earth pass away, not an iota, not a dot, will pass from the Law until all is accomplished. *Whoever then relaxes one of the least of these commandments and teaches men so, shall be called least in the kingdom of heaven;* but he who does them and teaches them shall be called great in the kingdom of heaven" (Matthew 5:18-19; cf. James 2:10).

All of this shows so incontrovertibly that agreement in all articles of faith is the necessary condition for church fellowship that Pastor Loehe himself wrote 10 years ago: "Within one and the same church body *(Confession)*, agreement is rightly demanded not only in the fundamental articles but also in all those articles about which the Confessions have spoken definitively.[13w] Here belongs what is said in the Formula of Concord (Epitome, X, 7): 'There must be mutual agreement in doctrine and in *all* (underscored by Loehe) its articles[14w] as well as in the right use of the holy sacraments' "[Tappert, p. 493] *(Unsere kirchliche Lage* [The State of Our Church], Noerdlingen, 1850, p. 18). If, however, by adding the qualifier "about which the Confessions have spoken definitively" Loehe, as is clear from the context, is offering a restriction, then the qualifier is obviously false. The orthodox church is definitive not only about those articles that are set forth in its symbols but implicitly about all articles contained in the Word of God.

Therefore it is idle to raise the complaint against us that the principles we maintain with regard to requirements for church fellowship must necessarily lead to the church's disintegration and dissolution. With equal justice our opponents could accuse the Lord Himself that He did not come to send peace but a sword. The cause of the disintegration lies not in the correct principle but in the sin of those who would rather sever the bond that united them with the orthodox church than surrender their pet opinions and be willing to subject themselves and their church to the clear Word of God. They accuse the church of harshness because it will not permit them to depart from the Word of God, and they refuse to see that their own rigidity with which they cling to their fantasy is the only cause of the church's disintegration and dissolution. Must truth yield to error, or should not rather error yield to truth?

It remains for us to comment on the judgment which Kirchenrat *Ehlers* pronounced on our synod's position.

With regard to his wish that our synod would state clearly and definitely whether it denies church fellowship to all "professed chiliasts," that wish has already been granted. In 1857 our synodical convention unanimously confirmed the resolution of the Western District adopted the previous year:

We reject and condemn every form of chiliasm which teaches that before the last day a period is to be expected in which *the devil will no longer hold sway and influence on earth, Christ will return visibly, all nations will be christianized, and all deceased believers, or a number of them, will rise physically* and together with Christ will *rule over all the heathen* in a new and unprecedented manner; we regard as erroneous and a perversion of Scripture every interpretation of the following and related

91

C. F. W. Walther and his wife Emilie *nee* Buenger (courtesy Concordia Historical Institute).

Walther's parents, Gottlob Heinrich Wilhelm and Johanna Wilhelmina Walther (courtesy Concordia Historical Institute).

The parsonage in Langenchursdorf in Saxony, where Walther was born (courtesy Concordia Publishing House Library).

Walther pictured at the organ, illustrative of his musical interest and talent (cf. *The Lutheran Hymnal,* No. 198).

Lehre und Wehre.

Jahrgang I.   Januar 1855.   No. 1.

Zur Lehre vom heiligen Predigtamt.

Von Pastor O. Fürbringer.

Die Frage von Kirche und Amt ist unbestritten eine Zeitfrage. Sie bewegt nicht bloß die lutherische Kirche, sondern auch außerhalb derselben stehende Gemeinschaften. Das Resultat dieses Streits wird aber doch kein anderes sein, als daß die evangelische Lehre von Neuem als gerechtfertigt aus Gottes Wort erkannt werden wird von Allen, welche die Wahrheit ernstlich suchen. Die rechte Kirche hat längst entschieden über diese Streitfrage. Was wäre das auch für eine Kirche, die achtzehn Jahrhunderte lang nicht im Klaren mit sich gewesen, was sie selber sei und ihr Amt! (Matth. 28, 20. 1 Tim. 3, 15. Joh. 16, 13.) Es kommt nur darauf an, daß man das Wort der reinen Lehre auch wiederum recht scheide und auf solche Weise je mehr und mehr im Bewußtsein sich vertiefen lasse. Wegen des innigen und unzertrennlichen Zusammenhangs der Artikel von Kirche und Amt mit dem vornehmsten von der Rechtfertigung aus Gnaden in Christo Jesu durch den Glauben konnte es nicht anders kommen, als daß der ganze Kampf der Reformation nächst diesem hauptsächlich jenen galt. Was unsere Väter uns als Erbteil hinterlassen haben, das lasset uns immer klarer in den Verstand und immer lebendiger in das Herz aufnehmen, nicht in blindem Köhlerglauben, sondern aus eigener Gewißheit durch den Heiligen Geist, auf die Zeugnisse Seines Bibelworts gegründet.

Auch der würdige deutsche Pfarrer, Johann Friedrich Wucherer, hat über Predigtamt ein Büchlein veröffentlicht. Er verspricht durch dasselbe „einen ausführlichen Nachweis aus Schrift und Symbolen, daß das evangelisch lutherische Pfarramt das apostolische Hirten- und Lehramt und darum göttliche Stiftung sei." Dasselbe ist auch uns von vornherein gewiß. Das öffentliche Predigtamt in der Kirche Gottes bis an den jüngsten Tag ist göttliche Stiftung und nicht wesentlich verschieden vom heiligen Apostelamt. Des verstorbenen Dr. Höflings Anschauungsweise, gegen welche Wucherers Schrift vor Allem gerichtet ist, ist nicht die streng lutherische. Aber indem Wucherer

1

The masthead for the first issue of *Lehre und Wehre*, published in January 1855 (courtesy Concordia Publishing House Library).

Another view of Walther's study, where many of his works were produced (courtesy Concordia Historical Institute).

C. H. R. Lange, Walther's seminary colleague and coeditor of *Lehre und Wehre,* 1861—64 (courtesy Concordia Publishing House Archives).

Walther's carriage, presently located at Concordia Historical Institute. An illustration of this carriage serves as the logo for this series.

Concordia Seminary in 1883, where Walther served as professor and president to the end of his life (courtesy Concordia Publishing House Archives).

Walther's bedroom, the scene of his death on May 7, 1887 (courtesy Concordia Historical Institute).

Scripture passages, Rev. 20, Ps. 67, Dan. 2 and 7, etc., if it contains such a teaching, since this teaching is *contrary* to the analogy of faith, namely *the article concerning the nature of the kingdom of Christ in the world, the general resurrection of the dead, the last day, and the return of Christ to judgment.* But although the synod declares every *designated kind* of chiliasm to be as false as it is destructive, it believes nevertheless that also a true Christian may fall into this error. The synod therefore regards it as its duty *not to deny at once the hand of brotherhood and church fellowship* to those who have fallen into this error, provided they are otherwise committed to the pure doctrine, do not seek to teach or to propagate their error, and are open to instruction. Yet the synod regards it equally as its duty to do all it can to lead such erring brethren back to the pure confession also in these points *(Proceedings, Ninth Convention of the Synod of Missouri, etc.,* 1857, pp. 25, 26, 42. Our translation).

Thus our synod has expressed itself on three matters: 1. what the chiliasm that must be rejected and condemned is;[7] 2. that the synod, following the practice of the whole Lutheran Church in its best days, will deny the hand of brotherhood and church fellowship to all who *persist* in this error; 3. but that only those are to be regarded as persistent, that is, stiff-necked chiliasts, with whom the church's available resources for turning them from their error to the truth have been exhausted and have proved fruitless.[15W]

Ehlers indeed concedes that "if chiliasts are in conflict with a genuine— not apparent—article of faith and refuse instruction and giving up their error, then church fellowship with them must be terminated." However, what he gives with one hand he takes back with the other, in part because he is not willing to acknowledge as *articles of faith* those with which "persistent chiliasts" openly come into conflict, in part because he appears not to see that chiliasts do *come into conflict* with indisputable doctrines of the Christian faith. From this we observe with profound sadness how dangerous it is not only to *hold* an error but also to fail to *hate* error with one's whole heart. This condition soon robs the eye of the keenness to distinguish accurately between truth and error.

Ehlers says that neither in Scripture nor in our church's confession does he find the article of a *general resurrection* of the dead on the last day, which crass chiliasts undeniably oppose with their so-called first resurrection. As for *Scripture,* first of all, we point only to John 6:39, 40, 44, 54, where in one discourse the Lord *four times* in succession promises all who believe in Him that He will raise them *"at the last day."* If anyone wants still clearer passages for our article of faith, we freely admit that there are none clearer. But we must add that people for whom such passages are not clear enough are not taken captive by the Bible at all but can deny with regard to *all* articles of the Christian faith that they are contained in the Bible. Ehlers cites Enoch, Elijah, and those who came forth from their graves already after Christ's resurrection (Matthew 27:52-53), but this is obviously an inappropriate reference. These are *genuine* individual *exceptions* which *establish* the rule rather than suspend it. However, in the assumption that either *all believers or at least all martyrs* will rise physically more than a thousand years before the general resurrection of the just and the unjust, we are not dealing with individual exceptions, but this is something obviously self-contradictory and it completely annuls the concept and doctrine of a general resurrection itself.

That this article is also contained in our *confession* only such a person is unable to *see*, we maintain, who has already taken the side of the opposing view so decidedly that he *overlooks* what is there. Article XVII of the Augsburg Confession clearly states: "It is also taught among us that our Lord Jesus Christ will return *on the last day* for judgment and will raise up *all the dead*, to give eternal life and everlasting joy to believers and the elect but to condemn ungodly men and the devil to hell and eternal punishment" [Tappert, p. 38]. In the appendix to his familiar edition of the symbolical books *Rechenberg* therefore cites the assumption of a particular resurrection as a *distinguishing characteristic* of the *crass chiliasts* condemned in Article XVII. He writes that Article XVII of the Augsburg Confession is directed *"against the crass chiliasts,* Anabaptists, Rosicrucians, Paracelsists, *who assume a particular resurrection of believers,* which they call the first resurrection, *preceding the general resurrection.*"[8] It is not necessary, however, to go to the Augsburg Confession. Already in the children's Bible, the precious Small *Catechism,* Luther teaches every Lutheran to "recite" and confess daily for himself and for all his brothers in the faith that *"on the last day He will raise up* ME *and* ALL *the dead."* No crass chiliast, who believes in a particular resurrection for the millennium, can make this confession without a Jesuitic mental reservation unless, oddly, he would be sure of being *excluded* from the millennium *himself!*

But why cite individual passages of our confession? From the beginning of the Christian church all believers and especially all holy martyrs, the crass chiliasts alone excepted, have to the present hour confessed unanimously with a loud voice in life and in death, in speeches, prayers, and hymns, the sure hope of their future resurrection on the last day. Hence there is *hardly an orthodox book of instruction, devotional book, sermon book, prayer book, and hymnbook that would not have to be altered in many places if it were true what the chiliasts dream about a particular resurrection before a still-to-be-awaited millennium and before the resurrection on the last day.*

The same applies to all the other distinguishing characteristics of crass chiliasm listed in our synodical resolution, namely that in part it contradicts the article *of the nature of Christ's kingdom in the world* as an invisible kingdom of faith and the cross; in part, the article *of the last day* as an event that may be awaited by Christians at every moment; in part, the article of *Christ's visible return* as an appearance that is to be expected only to execute judgment on the living and the dead.

Now, to be at peace and to pull at the same yoke with those who use their new pseudo-articles of faith, based on their private interpretation of prophetic passages, to overthrow or at least render uncertain and cause to teeter and totter *(wankend und schwankend)* those ancient articles of faith of the entire holy Christian church that are theoretically and practically so extremely important—this we do not want, this we cannot do. No, as much as our poor heart, especially in these last days of sore distress, would cherish peaceful fellowship with all who confess to be Christians and Lutherans, and as heavy, indeed as frightful, a cross it is for us to have to be separated from so many persons who are otherwise so lovable—God's truth and man's salvation based on it alone rank higher. Increasing the rifts and separations dare not deter us, for where there is no doctrinal unity, the rift and separation have already taken place, and that is the responsibility of the errorist, not the orthodox. What good is a large, externally united Lutheran Church on which the worm of spiritual disunity gnaws? Such a church we leave to the United [churches of the Union who combine Lutheran and Reformed teaching].

No matter if an ever larger number of those whom we heretofore counted among the loyal confessors of our Lutheran faith are engulfed by the current of the times and forsake the turret on our walls from which our fathers now resting in God battled also against "professed chiliasts," we cannot depart along with them. May they shift the one or the other stone in the wall of our good old confession to a position different from its original place, or even remove it altogether as unnecessary fill, in order to provide admission for more people and to put to shame the old gloomy prophets who can predict nothing but times that will get constantly worse—we cannot participate in such a deed and cooperate in finally turning into a Babel the church bequeathed to us, which came out of severe conflicts united in the faith. Others may venture one day to answer for it to the Lord of the church—we do not dare to do so.

Even Melanchthon's alterations in the Augsburg Confession seem like a much more honest deed to us than the current procedure of so many so-called "decided" Lutherans. Melanchthon laid hands only on the Augsburg Confession, which from his point of view he could easily regard

100

as his own work, and he at least honestly deleted what in the Augsburg Confession he regarded as opposed to his ideas of union. Now, however, people in fact want not only *an altered Augsburg Confession* but also *altered Catechisms, altered Smalcald Articles, an altered Formula of Concord.* And here they are not so honest as openly to *cross out* the words that do not fit in with the new faith, but they have rather agreed to *understand* the words in a way different from what, as everyone knows, they intended to say originally. And why?—In order that people who have long fallen away from the teaching of our church may retain the honor of loyalty and steadfastness, remain in our midst, and shed glory on our church.[16W]

May God preserve us from the nets of seduction in this evil age, nets that are woven ever more finely. Yes,

> In these last days of sore distress
> Grant us, dear Lord, true steadfastness,
> *That pure we keep, till life is spent,*
> *Thy holy Word and Sacrament.* Amen!

Foreword to the 1862 Volume

[Do we Lack Creative Activity?]

[First Part:] *Lehre und Wehre,* VIII, 1, Jan. 1862, pp. 1—6

From the beginning and from various quarters the charge has been raised (recently by Pastor Fengler of Loewenberg in Ehlers' *Kirchliches Zeitblatt* [Church Periodical], 1861, No. 7) against *Lehre und Wehre* and the Missouri Synod in general that they lack "creative activity," quote too much from old writers, and do not even make the old their own in a new form. It might therefore be an appropriate time for us to deal with this charge in some detail. As we are about to address ourselves to this matter in the current Foreword, we are not in any way moved to do so by a high opinion of the value of our periodical. On the contrary, no one can be more keenly aware than we ourselves of how insignificant the service is which we are rendering the church through it. However, since we also for our small part are called upon and desire to serve the church, and since we do not know of a better way to do it than we have done until now, we regard it as our duty to give an account, especially to our friends. So we ask these to consider worthy of their attention the following about the manner of our past, present, and (as long as God wills) also future theological activity.

First of all, we Missourians do not go along with the Montanistic, Anabaptistic, and Enthusiastic trend of our times, according to which nearly all theologians have adopted the attitude that the church, like a human being, grows not only in years but also in knowledge until it will have at last reached full maturity in the time just before Judgment Day. Furthermore, we do not by any means share the papistic idea of a gradual evolution of dogmas, an opinion that has made more and more inroads also in the Protestant church of our time.

On the contrary, instructed by Scripture and history, we share the belief of our fathers that the church, like the *moon,* has its phases, its waning and waxing, and even its eclipses; now in full bloom, now lying in the dust, buried beneath the debris of human teachings and abuses. The age of Moses, when all the nations were moved to exclaim with regard to the church, "Surely this nation is a wise and understanding people" (Deuteronomy 4:6), is always succeeded by the age of Eli, when "the word of the Lord was rare in those days; there was no frequent vision" (1 Samuel 3:1). The blessed times of David, when the Lord builds the walls of Jerusalem, are always followed by Elijah days, when the church's great desolation moves the few remaining faithful servants to lament, "The people of Israel have forsaken Thy covenant, thrown down Thy altars, and slain Thy prophets with the sword; and I, even I only, am left," so that God must console them by calling attention to His hidden church: "I will leave seven thousand in Israel, all the knees that have not bowed to Baal, and every mouth that has not kissed him" (1 Kings 19:14, 18). Periods in which the Word of God grows and the churches are strengthened in the faith (Acts 6:7; 16:5) alternate with periods of apostasy, when people turn their ears away from the truth and wander into myths (2 Thessalonians 2:3; 2 Timothy 4:4).

As necessary and important as we too consider the unremitting work of theologians to be, we do not on that account believe in a continuing organic growth of the church with regard to divine understanding, to be produced by the industry of the theologians. Rather we believe that a pure and profound understanding in matters of the Word of God is a gift of free divine grace and mercy which is bestowed on the church from time to time only by special visitations of divine grace. Here, too, the word applies: "To whom you give it, he has it *gratis.*" Pure doctrine and correct understanding are not a fruit of human free will. They are dependent neither on the presence nor the absence of learning and acumen. With all his industry man may well deal faithlessly with these supreme treasures of the church, but he cannot give them to himself. To bestow them is a royal prerogative of the Holy Spirit to whom also in this connection, indeed especially in this regard, the "where and when it pleases God" *(ubi et quando visum est)* of Augsburg Confession V applies. Now, when God gives the church an *Athanasius,* an *Augustine,* a *Huss,* days of great visitations of divine grace have dawned for the church, not only for the time that God fills such sanctified vessels, but for all time thereafter. Then the word is: ". . . buy while the market is at your door; gather in the harvest while there is sunshine and fair weather; make use of God's grace and word while it is there! For you should know that *God's word and grace is like a passing shower of rain* which does not return where it has once been" *(Luther's Works,* American Edition, Vol. 45, p. 352).

Such a time of gracious divine visitation was undoubtedly, above all, the age of the *Reformation.* There God at once gave by free grace what no theologians' industry of more than a thousand years had worked out and what it *could* not have worked out. There the apostolic age was renewed with the riches of its gifts. Immeasurable treasures of pure and profound divine knowledge were there brought to light out of the mine shaft of the divine Word. There the prophecy concerning the time of the New Testament was most gloriously fulfilled: "The earth shall be full of the knowledge of the Lord as the waters cover the sea" (Isaiah 11:9). There for once God demonstrated what a high degree of understanding there could be in a human being, even though illuminated mediately through the written Word, if it is His pleasure to fill that person with that knowledge. The time of midnight seemed already to have begun and nothing but the Lord's return to judgment loomed ahead when, behold! the prophecy of the prophet Zechariah still found fulfillment: "At evening time there shall be light" (Zechariah 14:7). The Antichrist's mystery of lawlessness seemed already to have become impenetrable, and thus the gates of death appeared to have prevailed against the church and to have deceived even the elect, when behold! the lawless one was unexpectedly revealed and slain with the breath of the Lord's mouth (2 Thessalonians 2:7-8). The church seemed already to have become a senile, barren old woman, but behold! by virtue of the divine promise she gave birth to an Isaac.

Just when the killing of Huss seemed to have silenced the voice of the last witness to the pure truth, behold! there occurred what the seer of the New Testament had already seen in a vision: "Then I saw another angel flying in midheaven (the church), with an *eternal* Gospel to proclaim to those who dwell on earth, *to every nation and tribe and tongue and people;* and he said with a loud voice, 'Fear God and give Him glory, *for the hour of His judgment has come;* and worship Him who made heaven and earth, the sea and the fountains of water' " (Revelation 14:6-7). It was not the temporal, transitory message of vain human doctrine that Luther proclaimed, but an *eternal* Gospel, the pure, clear, unalterable, and imperishable Word of the Most High. His calling was not only to give this bread of life to the little parish in Wittenberg, but *"to every nation and tribe and tongue and people,"* to bring back to them in its purity and unchanging form the Gospel which had previously been adulterated with everchanging error. Without a doubt Luther was God's last messenger to all nations before the day of *judgment.*

The time of the Lutheran reformation of the church was indeed a time of a great divine visitation of grace in restoring the divine teaching to apostolic purity and rekindling the heavenly light of true understanding in its pristine brilliance. Yet this time of visitation is by no means over. That Reformation with its great gifts was and is the great universal visitation upon the church "in these last times of this transitory world," as the princely confessors expressed it in the Preface to the *Book of Concord,* the "Christian, Reiterated, and Unanimous Confession" [Tappert, pp. 3 and

1]. We, too, are still in this time of visitation which, according to divine prophecy, will continue to the end of days.

How vividly the teachers of our church in the 16th and 17th centuries were aware of this time in which they were graciously visited by God through the rousing, endowment, and work of Luther! How humbly and frankly they all acknowledged themselves to be nothing but poor pupils of Luther, no matter how brilliant their own gifts and how blessed their own untiring labors! *Thereby they did not give glory to Luther* but to Him who out of fervent love for His devastated church showered on Luther a wealth of gifts as on no other teacher of the church since the time of the apostles. With what longing for pure understanding they all clung to Luther's lips after they had discovered how clear the Word of God became for them through Luther's words! How eagerly they waited for each new writing from Luther's pen and how zealously they read it! How gratefully they received Luther's teaching and how faithfully they reproduced it! They employed all their great gifts to disseminate in their own way what God had taught them through His servant Luther.

Both the Augsburg Confession and the Apology were authored by *Melanchthon,* but both of these incomparable confessions of the church contain nothing but *Luther's* theology. It is a fact that the real author of the Augsburg Confession was not Melanchthon but Luther, since the former only edited it on the basis of a writing of Luther's and gave it its final form. Also with regard to the Apology, its contents prove to be not perhaps only the equal result of Melanchthon's and Luther's Biblical studies, but a faithful epitome as well as an eloquent defense of the pure evangelical doctrine restored to the church by God through Luther. It was done, however, as by a man who had most clearly and vividly grasped Luther's theology and made it his own. In no document does Melanchthon appear as a pupil of Luther in such childlike loyalty as in the Apology, where he masterfully interprets and defends his teacher's teaching.

In the same relationship to Luther as also *Martin Chemnitz, John Gerhard,* and all the great teachers of our church down to the era of Pietism, except that with each new generation we see our teachers drawing from Luther in a more *indirect* way. In general, what else are Chemnitz' *Examen concilii Tridentini* [Examination of the Council of Trent], John Gerhard's *Loci theologici,* and all the immortal works of the best theologians of our church in its early days but golden structures erected with the gold of the doctrine God once permitted Luther to acquire? They did not regard it as their task to be "creatively" active but to recognize and make the most of the time of their visitation, to gather what God had strewn about with full hands, and to hold fast and preserve what they now had, so that no one might take their crown. And yet, what an active and fresh theological life developed in their midst! What labors, what searching in Scripture! What growth in understanding!

Consequently, before we can plan and undertake to become "creatively" active, we can at present only regard it as a holy obligation first of all to learn to know, appropriate, and share the treasures of doctrine and insight which God has bestowed by His grace during the nearly 2,000 years of the church's life, and particularly 300 years ago through the work of the Lutheran reformation of the church. If we did not want to do this, if we wanted to let spoil the blessings heaped up in the writings of Luther and his faithful disciples as in full store-houses, if we wanted to permit the rich supplies already amassed there to lie unused, and if we were only concerned about seeking new things, we would have to fear that the Lord would once more exclaim over us: "Would that even today you knew the things that make for peace! But now they are hid from your eyes . . . *because you did not know the time of your visitation"* (Luke 19:42, 44). What God revealed to Luther out of His Word 300 yeas ago was revealed and entrusted not only to him but to the whole church. It is a pound given to us all by the Lord with the command to "trade with these till I come" (Luke 19:13). Now if we wanted to keep this pound wrapped in the napkin of our libraries, we surely could not hope one day to hear the word: "Well done, good and faithful servant; you have been faithful over a little, I will set you over much" (Matthew 25:21). We would rather have to expect hearing the terrifying word: "You ought to have invested My money with the bankers, and at My coming I should have received what was My own with interest" (Matthew 25:27).

To let what has already been given the church lie unused, so that we ourselves might be "creatively" active, could be motivated on our part by nothing but dreadful ingratitude and arrogance. This would be to "despise prophesying" (1 Thessalonians 5:20) and for "the spirits of prophets" to refuse to be "subject to prophets" (1 Corinthians 14:32). If men like Melanchthon, Brenz, Rhegius, Chemnitz, John Gerhard wanted to be nothing but Luther's pupils and openly acknowledged that what they knew they owed to him next to Scripture, and had learned it from him, who are we to deny and conceal our place as pupils and strive to play the role of masters! "All things are yours," says the apostle, "whether Paul or Apollos or Cephas or the world" (1 Corinthians 3:21-22), and we may and must add, "whether Luther or Melanchthon, whether Chemnitz or Gerhard" and we should or would regard and treat this divinely given property as strange goods!? Or is it already truly ours if we have it only on our bookshelves? All gifts, the gift through the Spirit to utter wisdom and knowledge, the gift of prophecy, the gift of being able to distinguish between spirits, the gift of interpreting tongues, etc., gifts which God distributed so lavishly 300 and 200 years ago, all were given "for the common good" of the church in all places and all succeeding times (1 Corinthians 12:7-10)—and we should or would keep these gifts locked up unused!?

Or, while we should not seek anything different from what the orthodox church has already discovered, are we to seek it once again? Are we only to tread the same path our old teachers trod in the certain hope that we shall then arrive at the same goal and achieve the same results? Foolish thought! God does not give everything to everybody, nor does He at all times give the same things. One servant in the Lord's vineyard is given one gift, another a different one; one age is granted one visitation, another a different one. It is "one and the same Spirit, who apportions to each one individually *as He wills*" (1 Corinthians 12:11). It is therefore futile and even sacrilegious to attempt virtually to coerce God into repeating the gracious visitation which He granted the church 300 years ago, repeat it because people do not want to receive the gifts through God's chosen vessels whom He once endowed but, like them, want to obtain them as a fruit of their own searching. After God has graciously restored the precious treasure of pure doctrine to the church through Luther and his faithful followers, we must now either humbly permit this treasure to be transmitted to us through their service or we shall remain eternally deprived of it and fall from one error into another. God has made His church a body, which has not one member but many, and the eye cannot say to the hand, nor the hand to the eye, nor the head to the feet, "I have no need of you" [1 Corinthians 12:21]. Rather, God has so constituted His church that one member always needs the other and thus the whole can live only by a mutual exchange of gifts.

Curiously, Pastor Fengler discovers something sectarian in our childlike devotion to our faithful fathers and teachers. But this is precisely a distinguishing characteristic of a sect, that it breaks with the church of the past, severs continuity with it, despises the mediate preaching office, desires not to learn but to teach, not to be pupil but teacher, and to help the church by means of its new little discoveries! A sect does not promote reformation with Luther, who returned to the ancient church, but revolution with Carlstadt and Zwingli.

Conclusion: Vol. VIII, No. 2, Feb. 1862, pp. 33—42

Perhaps no one will deny that the church of the present must always appropriate and preserve as a precious deposit what God has already graciously granted the church of the past, its mother, in treasures of understanding and in elucidation of the content of Scripture. Now, has the church of our time already appropriated everything the church of the past has achieved by the grace of God?

It is, unfortunately, a fact that only a few even of those who in general want to participate in building the church are even *aware* of the classical literature of our church in its most blessed days, when its doctrine was most solidly grounded, most clearly developed, most cogently defended, and the opposing error was most powerfully disarmed and exposed. Much less have many *studied* these weighty documents, or at least the one or the other in each of the theological disciplines, that might serve as a representative of all, and *have made the contents their own.* People are content to have read this or that quotation, perhaps even torn out of its context, and then think they are in a position with their acumen to survey and criticize the whole doctrinal structure. Most newer theologians apparently regard it as their chief task to present everything in an elevated philosophical language and from a completely abstract perspective, so that even their most trivial thoughts and their most glaring paralogisms appear as high wisdom. As a result many think that if they know how to use scholarly phraseology they then belong to the oracles of the day, and especially the younger theologians loathe as worthless food [Numbers 21:5] the writings of our old teachers who, though very learned, were humble and sought only the edification of the church. Since these people quickly *grasp the words,* they think they have *known* all of that since long ago.

Another result is therefore that frequently rationalists like Carl Hase and Benedict Winer know our church's teaching better and present it more correctly than theologians who claim not only to report that teaching historically, as those men do, but also to transmit it as its *advocates.* How impudently are teachings now offered as doctrines of our church which our church in its symbols and in the writings of its best sons combatted might and main as antichristian errors! And with what unfeigned aversion are teachings rejected as thoroughly unlutheran, unchurchly, as fanatical, or even as papistic errors, when they are actually fundamental teachings of the Lutheran reformation of the church!

How much effort it will still cost to make the pure doctrine as it was unearthed 300 years ago the common property of even the leading theologians, at first just to be acquainted with it! What a change must take place before our Lutheran theologians and preachers in general will consider it worth their while to acquire at least the *works of Luther* and study them! What a dreadful sign of this time, although it has awakened to something better, that thousands of copies of the Erlangen Edition of Luther's works are getting moldy in the warehouse and the whole project has remained unfinished for lack of sales! In vain men like *Thomasius* write:

> For some time we have, quite rightly, begun again to go back to our older dogmaticians. But we will do well to become involved even more than formerly with *that man* in whose heart the blood of the evangelical faith pulsated most warmly and vigorously. *From Luther, in my opinion, we still have immeasurably much to gain for the revitalizing and invigorating of our dogmatics, of which it has recently been said that "it is beginning to turn somewhat cold" (Christi Person und Werk,* Part I, pp. v, vi).

In vain a man like *Rudelbach* testifies that *"Luther* recapitulates in himself more than half a millennium and at the same time shapes the development of subsequent generations" *(Zeitschrift* [Periodical], 1857, p. 381).

We are by no means blind to and ungrateful for the certainly not inconsiderable yield of the unremitting labors of our time also in the field of theology. We esteem highly what recent days have produced for a better knowledge of the holy languages, for illuminating the history of the church, for the solution of exegetical difficulties,[1w] etc. No one can with greater thankfulness and more heartfelt joy note and appropriate every new more profound grounding and further correct development of an old truth of Scripture than we ourselves. Nevertheless, we are mostly in a position to be horrified especially by the "creative activity" of our time. What is praised as a new discovery we usually find to be of a most dubious and suspicious character. In fact, only too often we are confronted with an old error in a new dress, a refurbished old heresy that was refuted and condemned by the church long ago. Or are the new and allegedly more correct presentations of the doctrines of inspiration, Christ's person, the effect of the sacraments, church and church polity, office and ordination, the last things, the intermediate state, etc.—are these anything else? We shall here let a man speak in whose publications we have otherwise found with joy many a nugget of precious truth, Professor Dr. *Kahnis,* who nevertheless writes:

[Editorial Note: Walther introduces a lengthy quotation from K. F. A. Kahnis, Der innere Gang des Deutschen Protestantismus *[The Inner Development of German Protestantism], 2nd ed., pp. 241 ff. Kahnis raises questions about a number of traditional Lutheran teachings, including inspiration, the sacraments, the Trinity, and the person of Christ. He thinks that the Lutheran presentation lacks depth and solid biblical foundation. Kahnis also attacks the teaching of man's total depravity and*

insists that man must be given some cooperative role in his salvation. Then Walther continues:]

So writes a man who himself pronounces the following judgment upon current theology:

Hand in hand with the dilettante complexity and mobility of our scholarship there is a lack of a sense of truth and human understanding, of logical energy, or originality in conception, of precision in presentation—a lack that surely belongs to the gloomy signs of the times. Our theology is about to enter the Alexandrian period (ibid., p. 247).

Here we are moved to exclaim: "If they do this when the wood is green, what will happen when it is dry?" [Luke 23:31]. If a Lutheran theologian of our time like *Kahnis* asserts that the old Lutheran theology is in need of a reformation with regard to the articles of inspiration, the Trinity, the person of Christ, the efficacy of the sacraments, original sin and free will, how much of the old Lutheran theology can we still expect to find in the writings of our modern theologians? At the most a few building blocks; the building itself has been demolished. Now, we want to rejoice heartily, and have always rejoiced heartily, wherever we find that an old building block of gold or silver or diamonds has been better prepared and more properly inserted by the modern theologians, but we can never live in the whole new structure with its partially ruined foundation and with its walls largely erected with wood, hay, and stubble. On the contrary, by God's preserving grace no one will persuade us to forsake the old building in which our soul has found security against God's wrath, judgment, and hell, and against the swirling winds of various and strange doctrines.

After Pastor Fengler in Ehlers' periodical criticized us Missourians for producing "relatively little of our own," for not "creating," he bursts forth in these words: *"Thank God that it is still better in Germany and also in our circles. . . .* Thank God. Recently a new periodical was established in our midst, and even the opponents will have to admit that most of its contents are worthwhile."

To this we respond by saying that we willingly concede to the authors in Germany, including some in the Lutheran Church of Prussia, that they are more learned and more intelligent writers, in whose literary productions more glorious gifts are mirrored than those we poor Missourians have received in our pitiful pioneering conditions. We neither seek to hide this from ourselves nor are we filled with envy as we become aware of how far we stand below Germany in this respect. Rather we highly esteem the great gifts which have been bestowed on the church of our fatherland and we rejoice over them as gifts that adorn the body of which we are members.

Nevertheless, we must ask: What is the *result* of the fact that the church of our fatherland is indeed not struck by the criticism of having produced "relatively little that is original" and of not having been "creative"? Even theological *schools* have barely maintained themselves; *there are as many theologies in Germany as there are theologians.* The church appears like an atomistic heap. Instead of the old unity of faith an unprecedented disunity prevails, a real Babylonian confusion of language and of faith.

Also the Lutheran Church of Prussia is only slightly different in this respect from the Lutheran territorial churches. This was glaringly in evidence in the controversies that recently erupted regarding church government and the teachings connected with it, to the astonishment of those who had not seen before that the Lutheran Church of Prussia was held together more by a united negation of the Prussian Union than by a positive oneness in Lutheran faith and doctrine. Even the new periodical of which Pastor Fengler speaks, although most of its contents are written with skill, vividness, and openness, by no means denies the conditions in the church body within which it was born. Alongside the church's pure doctrine much that is entirely new, original, and creatively produced is indeed being put forward. But in our opinion the Lutheran Church of Prussia should take to heart what Dr. Muenkel writes at the close of his report after having returned from that conference of Prussian Lutherans in Berlin as a former member of the conferring committee: *"It* [the church] *least of all has the task of undertaking progress and new formulations in doctrine;* every significant attempt of this kind threatens it also with the danger of schism." Would to God the Prussian Lutheran Church had to a greater extent followed our method—forgive us this statement which only *sounds* arrogant—and immersed itself in the writings of our old and true teachers, especially Luther, and published what it found there. In that case that church would undoubtedly have prospered differently and would not now stand at the edge of an abyss that threatens to devour it. Indeed, if that church is not willing first to learn humbly from our fathers in the faith, and only then teach and become creatively active, its fate is sealed. It will finally disappear like a drop in the ocean of the great new church which will finally lay exclusive claim to the old Lutheran name (as the Roman Church usurped the catholic name, the United Church the evangelical, and the rationalistic church the Protestant) and expel the old genuinely Lutheran Church as a "sect."

Be that as it may, we Missourians are conscious of no other *calling* than to bring forth anew the treasures of our old truly reformed church after these have long reposed uselessly as dead capital in our inherited libraries (where a century-long vandalism has not already destroyed them as worthless waste paper), to make these treasures our own through serious and unremitting study with fervent prayer for enlightened eyes from above, and then to serve the church with the talents thus recovered. If our learned, intelligent, creative age regards this as lowly work, as an insignificant menial service—so be it! Then allow us lowly Missourians to perform this most modest service for the church. We desire no greater glory. We do not even consider ourselves worthy of doing even this service for the church. We most humbly thank God that by His great grace He has hitherto counted us worthy of it and has also blessed it—if it served a purpose, we could cite many testimonies—both here and in Germany far beyond what we may ask or think [Ephesians 3:20].

But, Pastor Fengler will respond, we are not so much criticizing you for reproducing only the old Lutheran doctrine as we are for "failing to publish even the old in a new way," and nearly always letting the fathers speak for themselves through a mass of citations.

The following may serve as our reply.

It is unfortunately a matter of common experience that within our church a large number of writers are now claiming to put forth from within themselves *nothing but the old*—only in a new dress, in clearer, more accurate, and more profound development, more suited to the needs and demands of our time, provided with more correct, in fact with the newly discovered only correct "Scripture proof." But under the guise of this claim they are introducing a completely *new doctrine,* a completely new *religion* into the church. With some this may stem from self-deception, but with others it is obviously the use of a pious fraud. The latter regard the Lutheran Church as a beautiful, old, solid Gothic structure that can weather the storms of time; therefore in their opinion it would be a shame to raze it and erect one in the new style, less solid and not yet resting on the popular consciousness. Therefore they regard it as most prudent to keep as much as possible of the old walls and rafters, the old name, the old ceremonies, the old ornaments, the old endowments. Only a better doctrine, a system in which all branches of learning are reconciled, something therefore that must at last be palatable also to a philosophically trained world—this shall henceforth sound forth from the pulpit of the venerable cathedral. We do not want to be confused with this class of theologians. We are serious when we say that we regard the doctrine of the old Lutheran Church as the doctrine of the true church and that we desire to offer no other. One way of demonstrating this is to let our fathers speak for themselves so frequently.

Furthermore, there is at present a dreadful confusion, lack of clarity, and ignorance of what is really Lutheran. For that reason we, on our part, who are constantly being eyed with great suspicion as wretched dilettantes, would be acting most unwisely if, for the purpose of restoring to dominance the true *Lutheran* teaching (for which a certain pious regard still widely prevails among theologians and even more among the common people), we would present this teaching exclusively in our own words and arrogantly refuse to let our authorities and teachers speak for themselves. Even if we could present the pure Lutheran doctrine more adequately and convincingly than our fathers—something we cannot do—we are firmly convinced that our testimony would do more to discredit Lutheran teaching than recommend it and promote its acceptance. Our age makes much of having finally emancipated itself from dependence on human authorities, but it is only too evident that now more than ever the big question is *who* is saying something. A theological celebrity can confidently write things that would be ridiculed as nonsense if they had come from the pen of a lesser light; those strange lines are thought to contain some profound truth. Examples are odious. Who are *we* to dare to hope for a hearing in such a time as this, as we must and want to get people to acknowledge again as Lutheran doctrine what theologians as well as others often no longer regard as Lutheran!

Add to this the fact that we are dealing with opponents who claim to be strictly Lutheran, who constantly pursue us with their anathemas and excommunications as enemies of the Lutheran Church and doctrine, at times as papists and at times as United [combining Lutheran and Reformed teaching] and fanatics; opponents who in their insistence on Lutheran orthodoxy believe and teach the very opposite of what Luther and his faithful followers believed and taught and therefore wretchedly deceive and seduce the people under the false guise of old Lutheranism. If we do not want to stand idly by as Lutheran people are deceived and seduced under a Lutheran mask to regard crypto-papists as pillars of Lutheranism and the old pure evangelical Lutheran teaching that we confess as fanatical rubbish, what else can we do but show black on white from the writings of Luther and his co-workers and disciples themselves what those men of God, to whom our opponents hypocritically erect tombs (yes, tombs!), actually taught? If the opponents deceive the unwitting people with all kinds of tricks by means of which they themselves keep on torturing the most lucid testimonies of a Luther, a Chemnitz, a Gerhard, and others until they say the opposite of what these men said, how much easier it would be for our opponents to make us appear before the people as anti-Lutheran heretics, if we would deduce everything from Scripture only in our own manner so as not to be suspected of parroting

(Nachbeterei) or, as Pastor Fengler puts it, of simply "reciting all manner of entirely correct, excellent statements of faith"!

If in this situation we had not raised the fathers of our church from the dead and had not let them speak for us, a confusion would long ago have arisen among the people in which even the most honorable would often have been deceived by the pseudo-Lutherans and we with our pure genuine Lutheran teaching would have been shunned as apostates by thousands who now sincerely believe and cheerfully confess as we do. The blessing that has accompanied our testimony in this country is great, be it said loudly to the glory of God, but we shall never forget that a chief cause of this blessing by the grace of God has been just this practice of ours, that we have placed not ourselves but our teachers at the podium, teachers who, thank God, still enjoy the confidence of thousands upon thousands that they were faithful stewards of the mysteries of God, the kind of confidence extended at present to no living theologian.

It is true what Pastor Fengler writes, that "the ancients must become part of our flesh and blood" and our confession must come "from our innermost being where faith dwells." But we know that this is the case with us. We believe that already the manner of documenting a doctrine with citations as we have been doing shows that we have not looked up these citations in indexes but that we have appropriated and grasped the whole of the old teaching in a living way, that it is our very own possession, the jewel of our heart's faith, for which we have not only gladly taken upon ourselves all the ignominy poured out on us but we are also ready to make even greater sacrifices. Whoever thinks it is possible to cite in this way without having mastered the whole doctrine and bearing it in one's heart, just let him imitate us without doing this.

Incidentally, the more than 17 volumes of our *Lutheraner,* which has dealt largely also with expressed non-Lutherans, may themselves testify whether by the grace of God we know how to prove and uphold Lutheran teaching from the Bible and to nullify the opposing error over against those who acknowledge no Lutheran authority and for whom the question is not whether something is Lutheran but whether what is Lutheran is Biblical.

On this matter we would never have said a word if Pastor Fengler's arrogantly judgmental attacks in the Ehlers periodical had not compelled us to do so.[2W] What we have achieved as in some sense our possession we ourselves regard as nothing alongside the grace God has given us to be helpful in bringing Luther and his greatest pupils back from the dead and reinstating them as teachers of our time.

Opening Address at the Convention of the General Synod of Missouri, Ohio, and Other States, at Trinity Lutheran Church, St. Louis, Mo., Oct. 31, 1866[1w]

Lehre und Wehre, XIII, 1, Jan. 1867, pp. 1—8

In the name of the Holy Blessed Trinity, God the Father, God the Son, and God the Holy Spirit. Amen.

Venerable and beloved fathers and brothers in the Lord!

Twenty years ago 16 preachers met in the city of Ft. Wayne, Ind., for the purpose of drafting a constitution for the projected Synod of Missouri, Ohio, and other States. They acted on the conviction granted them by God's grace that the Evangelical Lutheran Church of the Unaltered Augsburg Confession is the true visible church of God on earth and that, consequently, also the doctrine deposited in that church's official Confessions is pure, like "silver refined in a furnace on the ground, purified seven times" [Psalm 12:6]. They were convinced that Luther was not only a witness to this or that important truth but the angel prophesied in the Word of God, bearing the eternal Gospel, flying in midheaven [Revelation 14:6], the *Reformer* of the church, chosen and aroused and called by God Himself, and that the reformation of the church successfully achieved by his service was a genuine reformation, a true renewal of the first apostolic church.

Therefore these men determined not to produce anything new, but in all things, in doctrine and practice, to make the church of the Reformation their model. Having come to a clear understanding of pure Scripture teaching and thus to a firm, immovable ground of faith through the public Confessions of the Evangelical Lutheran Church as well as through the private writings of Luther and his faithful co-workers and successors, they were deterred neither by the alleged new discoveries of the scholars of their old homeland in the area of doctrine, nor by the adverse conditions of this our new fatherland, from vigorously working toward the building of a church in America just as, nearly 350 years ago, it rose from the rubble of a thousand years as a result of the Lutheran Reformation of the church. However weak and unworthy they felt in every respect for so great and difficult a task, it was precisely this awareness of hereby not following their own wisdom and shrewdness and not seeking their own glory, but of walking in the footsteps of servants of God sealed by God Himself and seeking only the glory of God and the salvation of souls—this was what made them strong and confident.

When our synod came into being, it committed itself before friend and foe not only to all the Symbols of the old Evangelical Lutheran Church, openly and without reservation, and adopted as its motto, "God's Word and Luther's doctrine pure shall to eternity endure," and thus joyfully began its work—but it also undertook really to act in accordance with those symbols and its motto, in teaching and defense, in structure and practice. But immediately loud and intensive objections arose from the most diverse quarters and in the most diverse ways.

Because we declared the church in which the doctrine of the Unaltered Augsburg Confession is really in vogue to be the true visible church of God on earth, and all other churchly associations to be false churches and sects, we were accused of harboring an overtly papistic view of the church. Because we expressed the conviction that the Confessions of the Evangelical Lutheran Church are pure and without any error in the faith, and that every servant of our church is solemnly pledged to teach in accordance with them for the duration of his service, we were accused of placing human writings alongside, nay, over the Word of God and of introducing an intolerable tyranny of conscience. Because we acknowledged Luther as God's chosen vessel for a genuine reformation of the church and affirmed that the pure doctrine of our church and the correct understanding of its Confessions are to be drawn, next to the Word of God, especially from his writings, we were accused of deifying Luther and ascribing to him the infallibility of a pope. But because we also protested loudly and solemnly against those erring Lutherans who called the visible Evangelical Lutheran Church the one holy Christian church outside of which there is no help and salvation, and because for that reason we frankly conceded that the church of the believers and those being saved lies concealed also outside the visible Evangelical Lutheran Church, even among the sects and even under the rule of the Roman Antichrist, we were accused from the other side of being unionists at bottom. However, because we not only opposed every error in the faith conflicting with the Word of God as endangering souls but also renounced every kind of syncretism and every external church union without inner unity of faith and confession, and even withdrew from all

116

associations of those of various beliefs formed for a joint extension of the kingdom of God, we were accused by others of pharisaic intolerance, contentiousness and heresy hunting, narrowmindedness and lack of love and zeal for the work of the Lord. Because we followed Luther and the church of the Reformation in ascribing to the office of the ministry no other and no further power than that of the Word, and to believing Christians the full dignity of the spiritual priesthood, we were accused of delivering and surrendering the dignity and power of the holy ministry to the caprice of the rude masses and the holy Christian faith to the decision of majority votes. But because we were concerned at the same time to lay the foundation of an evangelical church order and discipline, rejected the temporary hiring of preachers and insisted on a proper call, retained the practice of announcing for Communion, and introduced the use of the binding key against stiff-necked impenitents and those erring in the faith, we were accused from the other side of papistic usurpation of power, priest rule, and fanaticism. Because we followed Luther and the old Lutheran Church in refusing to bind our conscience to any human church order, freely chose an order in line with our new circumstances in this country, and in general insisted on our freedom in all matters neither commanded nor forbidden by God, that is, in all so-called indifferent things, we were accused by one group of opposition to all discipline and order, of libertarian fraud and an itch for novelty. But because we refused at the same time to label as sinful the retention of certain old and edifying customs and ceremonies, which confess our faith against error, we were accused by another group of being on the road to Rome. Because we affirmed the original equality and autonomy of every church and parish and recognized no church's sovereignty over another, and no synod's over an individual congregation, we were accused of a separatistic lust for independence. But because we ourselves established a synod with boards of control and circuit counselors, we were accused of harboring hierarchical plans against the freedom of congregations. Because we followed Luther and the church of the Reformation in making the doctrine of justification through faith alone without any works of the Law the constant focus of our teaching and in refusing to have anything to do with so-called new measures to achieve so-called religious revivals and to accept any other means of grace than God's Word and the holy sacraments, and in always insisting first of all on pure doctrine as the chief thing, we were accused of being enemies of a living Christianity, of antinomianism, of reliance on a so-called dead orthodoxy, and of lifeless insistence on formulas. But because we preached at the same time that true faith exists only in a penitent heart and purifies, renews, and regenerates it, we were

117

accused of promoting a pietistic-legalistic Christianity. Because we condemned the new gospel of these last days which proclaims inborn inalienable human rights and universal liberty and equality in civil affairs as an attack on God's order among fallen human beings, we were accused of sanctioning tyranny and injustice. Finally, because we refused to have anything to do with a so-called progressive development, or rather with an alleged improvement or reformation of our church's teaching, such as the scholars within the church, especially in our old fatherland, are now promoting with the admixture of philosophy, and because we ourselves also acknowledged that we are not minded to seek and to establish anything new in doctrine or practice but to keep what we have, we were accused of an arrogant smugness and of being enemies of theological scholarship and progress, of lacking spirit and creative power, and of having a theology that is nothing but a dead mechanical learning and parrotlike repetition of the obsolete.

Consequently, a quick and certain demise of our synod or, at best, a wretched existence without blessing and influence was predicted. Our synod was regarded as a tree that may have been capable of greening, flowering, and bearing fruit in the 16th century, but one that was bound to wither quickly when transplanted to the alien soil of the 19th century. Nothing could be expected of our synod but disaster, disturbance of the former peace, confusion of consciences, contention, strife, and schism.

But no matter how vehemently attempts were made from all sides to force us off the position we had taken, we would not permit anything to make us waver but moved confidently forward on our chosen path with eyes fixed firmly on the model of the church of the Reformation and impervious to all attacks from the right or the left.

And what was the result? Has the prediction of our opponents been fulfilled? No; not only is our synod still here after 19 years, but through its service thousands of immortal souls have already been led to Christ. Of these, some have already fallen asleep with a joyful confession of His name and are now celebrating their triumph before the throne of God, while others are still living and confessing in word and deed that they have come to the truth and through it have received God's grace and a new and firm heart. Not only has a host of individual souls, known only to God, been saved through our service, but all storms that have buffeted us have served only to cause this frail sprig of our synod, ever more united in doctrine and practice, to grow into a tree ever more deeply and firmly rooted, with branches spread ever more widely.

As for whether we have exerted influence also on the outside, let those bear witness who at the beginning loudly objected precisely to what they themselves now affirm, or what they now strive to obtain. Instead of shunning us as the church's destroyers as they did earlier, they now extend their hand for fraternal union. Even beyond the confines of the Lutheran name our new witness to the old truth has stultified many a dangerous error and gained courageous defenders for many a precious truth. Yes, I dare to say it: The founding and growth of our synod has here undeniably ushered in the time of a newly awakening Lutheran life of faith and a victorious battle of the old Lutheran truth against error and encroaching ruin.

How now? Am I saying this in order to give ourselves the glory for all of this? Woe unto me if that were the reason! Then I would be struck with the curse of Him who said: "My glory I give to no other"[Isaiah 42:8]. For, in truth, not to us, not to us belongs the glory for the blessing that has accompanied our synod's existence in this country. On the contrary, this blessing is a monument to the free grace of the great and wonderful God who dwells aloft in His sanctuary and has regard for the lowly. This blessing is a new seal on the word: "I will have mercy on whom I have mercy, and I will have compassion on whom I have compassion. So it depends not upon man's will or exertion, but upon God's mercy"[Romans 9:15-16]. Indeed, that blessing is another concrete demonstration of the Holy Spirit's statement: "Not many of you were wise according to worldly standards, not many were powerful, not many were of noble birth; but God chose what is foolish in the world to shame the wise, God chose what is weak in the world to shame the strong, God chose what is low and despised in the world, even things that are not, to bring to nothing things that are, so that no human being might boast in the presence of God"[1 Corinthians 1:26-29].

Yes, my brothers, in view of our synod's history we today join David in exclaiming from the bottom of our hearts: "Not to us, O Lord, not to us, but to Thy name give glory, for the sake of Thy steadfast love and Thy faithfulness!"[Psalm 115:1]. For not we, not we, but the Lord alone is the Creator of all the blessings that have hitherto rested upon our synod.

But I ask you, what was the *way* by which the Lord caused us to share in this blessing and deigned us worthy of it? It was none other than this: Here we established nothing new or original but inquired about the former paths and walked on the good old way; we sat as pupils at the feet of Luther and other orthodox and devout teachers already triumphing in heaven, and we followed in their footsteps; we took the church of the Reformation as our model and its pure Confessions as our banner, our guiding star, and our protecting wall. If you will, we have made the attempt to determine whether the doctrine of the 16th century could be used for the salvation of souls also in our 19th century, whether the tree of our old Lutheran Church, which for centuries produced such glorious fruits for the welfare of millions, might still demonstrate its pristine vitality and fruitfulness—and behold! our hope was not put to shame. Even though the time of our synod's existence is not as great a visitation of grace as was the time of the Lutheran reformation of the church, the old doctrine has now again demonstrated its old and eternally new power; thousands of souls have been led thereby to faith and through faith to salvation, and a church has come into being that is united in faith and confession and aglow with love and good works.

Therefore, my brothers, I am today compelled to call out to you: Do not forget, we do not owe our blessings to our wisdom, much less to our worthiness and zeal, but by God's grace to this fact alone that, despairing of our wisdom and will and ability, we returned as obedient children of the old Lutheran Church to this mother of ours, that is, to its doctrine and practice. Thus, this was the hidden cause of all our overt successes, this the secret ground of our unity until now, this the armor in which we did not succumb to the great host of our opponents, in spite of being so poor and weak in all things.

What do we now want to do and what must we do, my brothers? Shall we strike out on a new path from today on? Has the time perhaps arrived in which we have come of age and have become the peers of the church in our time that searches for what is new, so that we must now think of removing the stigma of being without creative power?

God forbid! Our situation would indeed be tragic if we had based and continued to base our faith on Luther and on the church bearing his name. But we have never done this, and by God's grace have no intention of doing it, until finally we shall see what we believe. It is true, we have been sons and pupils of none other than Luther and the church bearing his name, but only in the sense that we allowed ourselves to be led by them into Scripture, this one fountain of Israel, this exclusive norm of faith and life, and this sole judge in all questions regarding the heavenly teaching. Hence we never stayed put with Luther and his faithful successors. If we had done so, we could for that very reason not be their pupils, for they themselves taught us something entirely different. On the contrary, like the Beroeans we daily searched the Scriptures to see if these things that they taught us were so [Acts 17:11] and, having joyfully come to the living, divine conviction that this was the case, we felt like those Samaritans who said to the woman who had led them to Christ: "It is no longer because of your words that we believe, for we heard for ourselves, and we know that this is indeed the Savior of the world" [John 4:42].

Blessed are we if we continue in this sense! The moment we are ashamed to be mere pupils and seek the glory of being masters and creating something new, and want to do homage to progress and reform the Reformation—from that moment the Lord will depart from us with His blessing and then show us in His wrath what was the cause of our former blessing, namely nothing but our desire to be nothing ourselves except preservers of what has been entrusted to us Lutherans.

Let us permit nothing to entice us away from our secure fortress. Let us remain under the old flag under which the Lord of the church has led us to victory through many a fierce battle. Let us remain at the fountains opened for us by our fathers, from which we have drawn truth, certainty, grace, comfort, life, and strength, and from which we have refreshed many a thirsty soul. Let us continue to do without the honor of ourselves being the angel who has rekindled and restored to the church the bright star of the eternal Gospel; let us rather join the great chorus of those who only followed the angel flying in midheaven and participated in the psalm of victory already begun: "Fallen, fallen is Babylon the great! Here is a call for the endurance of the saints, those who keep the commandments of God and the faith of Jesus" [Revelation 18:2; 14:12].

Let other churches have the fame of not being the children but the fathers of the church of the past; let their's be the glory of not having inherited the truth but of having done independent research and having acquired the truth for themselves; let them have the zeal to transform the church of the Reformation in accordance with the demands of a new and more enlightened age, to enrich it with newly discovered truths, to guide it toward a nobler consummation, to reconcile it with the spirit of the times, and thus to speed ahead of us and leave us far behind: We will stay on our good old path! On this day (Oct. 31) 349 years ago Luther made his motto not "Forward!" but "Backward!" namely by returning to the apostolic church. Even so, let us this day, on the anniversary of our Lutheran Zion, pledge to each other: We want to return to Luther and with him to the church of the apostles and prophets, to their doctrine and practice.

In this new age and new shelter opened to our church in this country we will continue to take seriously the truth that the Evangelical Lutheran Church of the Unaltered Augsburg Confession is the true visible church of God on earth. For just as there is only one sun that has through all the ages shone in both the West and the East, so there is only one truth; and just as the one old sun still has the same power today as in millennia past to draw pleasant fruits from the earth, so the same truth will produce the fruit of the one holy apostolic-catholic Christian church of the elect, today as it has for hundreds and thousands of years. Amen.

121

Foreword to the 1875 Volume
Are We Guilty of Despising Scholarship?

[First Part:] *Lehre und Wehre,* XXI, 1, Jan. 1875, pp. 1—13

The various reproaches directed at us Lutherans in America, especially of the Missouri Synod, are concentrated in two chief criticisms: 1. Exclusiveness and a polemic corresponding to it in form and content; 2. contempt of scholarship, coupled with a mind closed to the intellectual movements of our time, particularly their progress. The first criticism has been dealt with repeatedly in these pages and evaluated from all angles. This has not so far been the case with regard to the second criticism. For that reason we beg your indulgence for coming to grips with it in our current Foreword.

So we are supposed to be *despisers of scholarship.* We could be quite brief in our rebuttal of this charge by simply calling attention to certain companions in suffering; men who, though unquestionably not despisers of learning, nevertheless had to hear the same charge as soon as they dared to attack prominent leaders of modern so-called theological science. When Dr. Kliefoth wrote a thorough and critical review of Dr. v. Hofmann's *Schriftbeweis* [Scriptural Proof], what kind of an answer did the former receive? Dr. Kliefoth reports: "As Dr. v. Hofmann's entire reply appears to be intended for such as have not read my essay, those people may at once get it black on white right in the first three pages that v. Hofmann as bearer and representative of learning was attacked by me, an *idiotic despiser* of learning, because he was neither appreciated nor understood. Too bad that none of it is true" *(Kirchliche Zeitschrift* [Church Periodical], ed. Dr. Kliefoth and Dr. Mejer, VI, 244). Furthermore, when Dr. Muenkel had reported in his *Neues Zeitblatt* [New Periodical] on Dr. Kahnis' *Lutherische Dogmatik,* published in 1861, exposing the apostasy from the truth that was being perpetrated and made evident in this work, Kahnis responded the next year in a document intended to offer his defense, *Zeugnis von den Grundwahrheiten des Protestantismus* [Witness to the Basic Truths of Protestantism]. He said:

> I can't imagine that Pastor Muenkel, who claims to be a doctor of theology (!), knows so little of theology that he doesn't know that there

are difficulties that must be discussed (!). Of course, such investigations are not meant for the common people. But who brings them to the common people? Sheets such as those published by Pastor Muenkel. Hence it is he, *this tattle-tale between scholarship and common people, who does not really fit in with either circle,* he is the one who confuses the people. Not I. If Pastor Muenkel can't stand the high altitudes where there are avalanches and rock slides, let him stay in Lueneburg Heath with its creatures, raise bees and cultivate asparagus.

Dr. Philippi had a quite similar experience when he attacked Dr. v. Hofmann's false teaching on reconciliation and justification. In the *Erlanger Zeitschrift* (1856, No. 3) the latter retorted: "I am well aware that not only in the Roman church but also in our church there are many who see interpretation of Scripture not as an interpretation of the whole in the strength of the church's faith, but as the *repetition of the traditional exegesis* of individual passages." With these words Dr. v. Hofmann obviously meant to brand his thoroughly learned opponent as an unscholarly theologian dealing only with a repristination of old material and simply parroting what the ancients have said.

From these examples it should have become clear that in Germany they are quite generous with the charge of being unscholarly, and quick to raise it as soon as alleged results of "scholarly research" are not immediately accepted, even in defiance of the old teaching of the Bible. It would seem that it behooved particularly us American theologians—if the gentlemen in the land of learning will permit us this predicate—to defend ourselves specifically against the charge leveled at us so often and from so many quarters that we are despisers of scholarship.

We will indeed concede to our opponents in advance that we are not a church body within which the field of learning is or can be cultivated as it is on the soil of the church in our old homeland. It would be utterly ridiculous for us to make that claim. But if we give up all claim to the honor of having achieved anything of merit in the *promotion* of learning, we most emphatically reject the charge that we are *despisers* of learning. On the contrary, we will be surpassed by no one in the world in the true esteem of genuine learning. For that reason we have throughout our existence nurtured it most zealously with all the resources at our command (limited as they are), and this under the most trying circumstances.

We are keenly aware of the incomparable importance (except for the Word of God) of learning, not only for the temporal welfare of mankind but also for the eternal welfare of the world, for church and theology, and we know what irretrievable damage contempt of this noble gift of God has repeatedly done in the past and must necessarily do. There is no room in our midst for the spirit of Carlstadt, the Anabaptists, and others who despise learning as something useless, even dangerous and carnal, and boast of direct communications from the "Spirit" instead. We know full well not only that all branches of knowledge can enter and be drawn into the service of sacred theology, but also that without many of them, particularly without thorough acquaintance with the original languages of Holy Scripture, without knowledge of secular and sacred history, history of religion and church history, without knowledge of classical antiquity, as of Biblical and ecclesiastical antiquity, etc., a thorough and relatively comprehensive understanding of Scripture and thus the development and preservation of pure Biblical teaching is impossible. We do not forget what indescribably valuable treasures in understanding and experience the Christian church has stored up through 18 centuries down to the present day in writings of the most diverse languages, or at least in a form which is completely foreign to the reader who has not had a scholarly education. All of these treasures would be lost to the church of the present without scholarly learning.

We are alive to the fact that only through many years of general scholarly training, beginning in one's youth, can one become a fully equipped theologian and only in this way acquire that trained mental acumen, that state of mind, that intellectual capacity which is simply indispensable for one who is able to demonstrate and defend the divine truth against all kinds of deniers, not only himself able to detect every perversion of the truth and every arising antiscriptural error and perceive it both in its scope and destructiveness but also to reveal this to others and convince them, able to resolve the linguistic, historical, and logical difficulties and apparent contradictions in Scripture, to come to the aid of honest people assailed by all manner of doubts, to respond to all objections, no matter how plausible, of the enemies of the truth, to penetrate and expose all false conclusions, no matter how well concealed, in short, to clear the muddy water of the opposition's sophistry and to defeat the enemy, if possible, with his own weapons. We are not of the opinion that the church should flee into the desert, isolate itself for self-preservation, seal itself off from the unbelieving world, let the enemies have free rein, give up the antireligious educated (who can be reached with the Gospel only in a certain form) and abandon them, and address itself only to the uneducated masses. By no means. We regard it as our sacred obligation to "become all things to all men so that we might by all means save some" [1 Corinthians 9:22]. We fully agree with Melanchthon, who once wrote: "An unscholarly theology is an Iliad filled with evils" *(Corpus Reformatorum,* XI, 278).[1w]

How could we call ourselves *Lutherans,* or even *Christians,* if we despised learning? We read how the Holy Spirit calls attention to the fact that "Moses was instructed in all the wisdom of the Egyptians"[Acts 7:22], that "Solomon's wisdom surpassed the wisdom of all the people of the east, and all the wisdom of Egypt," that "he spoke of trees, from the cedar that is in Lebanon to the hyssop that grows out of the wall; he spoke also of beasts, and of birds, and of reptiles, and of fish"[1 Kings 4:30,33]. Not only that, but the Holy Spirit, through a miraculous condescension in His instruments, the inspired holy men of God like (in addition to the ones mentioned) an Isaiah, a Luke, a Paul, consecrated learning and drew it into His service and especially through the same achieved great things. Nor are we blind to the hint that is there for all Christian theologians in the fact that Paul did not disdain to cite Epimenides, the philosophical poet of antiquity (Titus 1:12), and even a dramatist like Menander (1 Corinthians 15:33) in his letters to Christians, and his countryman, the pagan astronomer and poet Aratus, in his address to the cultured pagan audience of Athens (Acts 17:28). We are convinced that in "the wealth of the nations" (Isaiah 61:6) promised as a possession to the church of the New Testament the good arts and sciences of the heathen are undoubtedly included.[2W]

The entire history of the church bears witness to this. As long as and wherever the Christian church flourished, it always and everywhere proved itself to be a friend and cultivator of all good arts and sciences, gave its future servants a scholarly preparatory training, and did not disdain to permit its gifted youths at its schools of higher learning[3W] to be trained by the standard products of even pagan art and science. In this way the church really came into its promised inheritance, "the wealth of the nations." How much this benefited the church was recognized so clearly by Julian the Apostate that he forbade the Christians to conduct schools of literature and explain the classics to their pupils. With the slackening of zeal for searching the Scriptures and for pure doctrine in the Christian church, there was also a waning of interest in art and learning. How, then, could we even call ourselves Christians if we were so blinded as to despise or even only belittle any good art or science?

Still less would we be entitled to call ourselves *Lutherans.* We would have to be struck with blindness not to notice that "the age of the restoration of the sciences" not only chronologically immediately preceded the Reformation of the church, but that this time sequence was an act of divine providence. For God so guided the course of world history by His miraculous intervention that before the appearance of the man through whom God again wanted to place the light of pure saving knowledge on a lampstand, so that it might "give light to all in the house" [Matthew

5:15], there was a revival of the knowledge of the two original Biblical languages as well as of other languages and of a variety of good arts and sciences. We would have to be struck with blindness to fail to see not only what a glorious aid the reawakened learning was for achieving the work of reformation, but also that without that learning that work would have been impossible, unless God had chosen to suspend His method of ruling His church through mediately called and enlightened servants and had decided again to give His church inspired prophets and apostles immediately called and equipped and certified with extraordinary miraculous gifts.

If we wanted to call ourselves Lutherans while despising art and science, we would read our verdict of condemnation even in the Symbols of our church. In the article of the Apology of the Augsburg Confession dealing with confession and satisfaction we read:

> It is ridiculous and quite childish for knowledgeable people to apply the proverb of Solomon: "Know well the condition of your flocks" (Prov. 27:23), to the subject of confession or absolution.... Here "know" must mean to hear confessions, and "cattle" or "sheep" must mean people. "Stable," we think, means a school in which there are such doctors and orators. *But it serves them right to make such crude mistakes in grammar for thus despising Holy Scripture and all fine arts* (Apology, XII, 106, German paraphrase, cf. *Concordia Triglot,* p. 283; Latin: "The interpretation surely is a neat one, worthy of these men who despise grammar," Tappert, p. 197).

Later in the same article it says: "Our opponents are paying the penalty for their neglect of grammar when they explain 'judge' (1 Cor. 11:31) as 'to make a pilgrimage to St. James dressed in armor or to perform similar works' " (Apology, XII, 163; Tappert, p. 208).

But if we listened to *Luther* on the significance of fine arts and sciences, we could not possibly call ourselves by his name if we harbored the spirit of contempt for these good gifts of God. A few pertinent short utterances of Luther might be cited here. Commenting on Isaiah 14:12: "How are you fallen from heaven, O Day Star, Son of Dawn!" Luther writes: "Because the people did not understand rhetoric, they took this to refer to the fall of the angel Lucifer, although it is only figurative decoration. For that reason this highly significant error of the whole papacy in referring this text to the fall of the angels should move us *to study the learned sciences and rhetoric as things that are extremely necessary for a theologian as he deals with Holy Scripture"* (from the German in the St. Louis Edition, VI, 258).

In his exposition of "the glorious mandate" of Christ, 1537, he writes:

"The unlearned, such as the Anabaptists, who want to be moved by the 'Spirit,' openly assert: 'I am not permitted to know either Hebrew, or Latin, or Greek, for I have a Spirit who teaches me. What do I care about the arts, grammar, dialectics, and other things? All of it is superfluous and unnecessary.' This is what they say, and these poor people do not see in Paul's writings and in many places, *that the church must have the languages and arts.* May God forgive them their blasphemy!" (from the German in the Walch Edition, IX, 2703).[1]

As early as 1523 Luther had written to the poet Eobanus Hessus:

Do not worry that we Germans are becoming more barbarous than we ever have been, or that our theology causes a decline of learning. Certain people are often afraid when there is nothing to fear. *I myself am convinced that without the knowledge of the studies, pure theology can by no means exist,* as has been the case until now: when the studies were miserably ruined and prostrate [theology] declined and lay neglected. I realize there has never been a great revelation of God's Word unless God has first prepared the way by the rise and the flourishing of languages and learning, as though these were forerunners, a sort of [John the] Baptist. Certainly I do not intend that young people should give up poetry and rhetoric. I certainly wish there would be a tremendous number of poets and orators, since I realize that through these studies, as through nothing else, people are wonderfully equipped for grasping the sacred truths, as well as for handling them skillfully and successfully. . . . [As] Christ lives, I am often angry even with myself, that [these] times and ways of living do not give me leisure for an occasional reading of poets and orators. Once I [even] bought an edition of Homer in order to become a Greek *(Luther's Works,* American Edition, Vol. 49, p. 34).

Furthermore, in his preface to Johann Walther's spiritual songs, 1524, Luther wrote:

These songs were arranged in four parts to give the young—who should at any rate be trained in music and other fine arts—something to wean them away from love ballads and carnal songs and to teach them something of value in their place, thus combining the good with the pleasing, as is proper for youth. Nor am I of the opinion that the gospel should destroy and blight all the arts, as some of the pseudo-religious claim. But I would like to see all the arts, especially music, used in the service of Him who gave and made them. I therefore pray that every pious Christian would be pleased with this and lend his help if God has given him like or greater gifts (*Luther's Works,* American Edition, Vol. 53, p. 316).

In the same year Luther wrote *An Open Letter to the Councilmen of All Cities of Germany, Urging Them to Establish and Maintain Christian Schools.* In this booklet, short but one of the most powerful and blessed of

Luther's writings, this man of God writes:[4W] [*Editorial note: Here Walther introduces a lengthy quotation of about five printed pages, in which Luther is critical of "universities and monasteries" "as they have been in the past" and hopes that they might be "converted into Christian schools." He pleads for the teaching of languages for the sake of receiving and preserving the Gospel. To people who ask, "What is the use of teaching Latin, Greek, and Hebrew, and the other liberal arts?" Luther replies that Germans already have the reputation of being "beasts and wild animals."[5W] He goes on to say that languages and the arts are of great benefit "both for the understanding of Holy Scripture and the conduct of temporal government." "Although the Gospel came and still comes to us through the Holy Spirit alone, we cannot deny that it came through the medium of languages, was spread abroad by that means, and must be preserved by the same means." "In proportion then as we value the Gospel, let us zealously hold to the languages." "And let us be sure of this: We will not long preserve the Gospel without the languages." This, says Luther, is borne out by experience. Even great teachers of the past, like St. Augustine, were severely hampered by their ignorance of the Biblical languages. A preacher who does not know the languages may "know and teach Christ, lead a holy life, and preach to others. But when it comes to interpreting Scripture, and working with it on your own, and disputing with those who cite it incorrectly, he is unequal to the task; that cannot be done without languages. Now there must always be such prophets in the Christian church who can dig into Scripture, expound it, and carry on disputations. A saintly life and right doctrine are not enough." The languages are also necessary for judging doctrine, says Luther. The entire tract is printed in the American Edition of Luther's Works, Vol. 45, pp. 347—78. The German text is in the St. Louis Edition, X, 458—85. Walther continues:*]

In this way Luther expresses himself on the necessity of studying the languages. With regard to the need for acquiring competence in other branches of learning, Luther emphasizes a thorough study of history, dialectic or logic, rhetoric, poetics, and mathematics (See *Luther's Works*, American Edition, Vol. 16, p. 3; Vol. 44, pp. 200 ff.; Vol. 40, pp. 314—20).

How highly Luther regarded all arts and sciences may also be discerned from his great esteem for men of his time who distinguished themselves by their learning, men like Reuchlin and Erasmus, though they did not support the pure Gospel and even, like Erasmus, opposed it and promoted their own glory.[6W] In 1518 Luther called *Reuchlin* his "most worthy and most honored teacher," a "hero," who in response to the groaning church's plea "joined so many heroes of learning," a "most welcome instrument of God's counsel for all who love pure theology," and whose "cause he had supported at all times with his hopes and prayers" (Walch Edition, XXI, 606 ff.). As late as 1537 Luther referred to Reuchlin as "that precious man."

In his book *On the Bondage of the Will,* directed against *Erasmus* in 1525, in which he rather clearly presents Erasmus as a secret mocker of religion and a disciple of Epicurus, Luther nevertheless states at the outset: "Those who think very highly of Erasmus and not so highly of me are not really so much against me; for I myself think very highly of Erasmus and accord him great honor. I also know that Erasmus is a great and valuable man, and I probably know it better than those crude asses, priests, monks, and papists, who know it only by hearsay. I know very well that God has given Erasmus outstanding gifts above anyone else in teaching, arts, eloquence, experience, in Latin and Greek, in writing and speaking" (Walch Edition XVIII, 2051; cf. *Luther's Works,* American Edition, Vol. 33, p. 15).

In view of this we ask: Who can have Luther's spirit and still despise art and learning? That Luther's spirit also in this respect continued to animate not only this or that Lutheran theologian but the whole Lutheran church needs no proof. Even a very limited acquaintance with the immortal works of our theologians from the golden age of our church will reveal that these men were "heroes of learning" as much as they were heroes of faith. As one reads their writings on methodology, in which they show students the way to acquire theological competence, one will soon discover that the demands they make on young theologians with a view to thorough and genuine learning were at least as great as those made on young theologians in our day. Not to mention the fact that in 1598 Dr. Daniel Hofmann of Helmstaedt had to recant publicly and solemnly just for having asserted that philosophy was already *per se* a work of the flesh and was therefore of no salutary use.[7 w]

Now, when we American Lutherans affirm that Luther's and our whole orthodox church's attitude toward learning as we have just described it is our own attitude, our opponents nevertheless undoubtedly will not absolve us of the charge that we despise learning. Concerning the reason for this we will, God willing, write in the next number of this periodical.

Continuation: Vol. XXI, No. 2, Feb. 1875, pp. 33—42

As firmly as we Lutherans in America reject the charge against us that we are guilty of a barbarous contempt of learning, we do indeed uphold certain principles because of which people will perhaps nevertheless think that they cannot absolve us of this charge. And far be it from us to abandon those principles or to deny them, perhaps for the sake of salvaging for ourselves a reputation for scholarship. On the contrary, we affirm those principles freely and openly also at this opportunity. We will cheerfully leave it up to those who are of the truth to judge whether these principles do in fact involve a contempt of learning.

In the first place, we confess that no matter how much we think of learning, we do not rank it above the truth of Scripture, nor even as its equal, but immeasurably below it. Hence we indeed say frankly and openly with Luther: "It is better for learning to be destroyed rather than religion, if learning refuses to be a servant and desires to tread Christ under foot" (Letter to Amsdorf, 28 June, 1534; St. Louis Edition, XXIb, 1912). A single little passage of Scripture means incomparably more to us and is an immeasurably greater treasure for us than all the wisdom of this world. If we needed human consolation here, we might take comfort even from a *Kahnis,* who himself declared in his better days: "Things would be better in the church if its servants would pursue *truth first* and *then learning" (Die Lehre vom Abendmahle* [The Doctrine of the Lord's Supper], Leipzig, 1851, p. 176).

We admit furthermore that, as highly as we regard the benefit which the church and theology can derive from all good arts and sciences when these are used in true fear of God and in humility and are thus truly placed into the service of the church and of theology, we at the same time consider nothing more dangerous and destructive than a use of scholarship in the church without that fear of God and that humility. Here, too, we join our Luther in saying: "He who without danger wishes to philosophize by using Aristotle, must first become thoroughly foolish in Christ" (Heidelberg Disputation, 1518, Thesis 29; *Luther's Works,* American Edition, Vol. 31, p. 41). But why cite *Luther?* He only repeated what the holy *apostle* said to the Corinthians: "If any one among you thinks he is wise in this age, *let him become a fool* that he may become wise" [1 Corinthians 3:18]; or to the Colossians: "See to it that no one makes a prey of you by philosophy and empty deceit, according to human tradition, according to the elemental spirits of the universe, and not according to Christ" [Colossians 2:8]. And have not all centuries of church history down to the present hour confirmed as undeniable truth what *Tertullian* wrote: "*The philosophers are the patriarchs of the heretics"? (Lib: advers. Hermog.* [Books Against Hermogenes], ch. 8) Even those who openly despised learning nevertheless made use of it to turn the divine truth of Scripture into a lie; as, to cite just one example, Francis de Sales, founder of a mystical order of nuns, did not blush to call learning the "eighth sacrament of the hierarchy" (see Herzog, *Realencyklopädie,* in the article "French Reformation," p. 527).

We admit further that as necessary as we consider learning to be, especially the study of languages, logic, rhetoric, and history, for searching the content of Scripture, we nevertheless reject any learning that, instead of being handmaid and pupil, wants to assume the role of mistress and teacher instead of merely helping to discover the truth contained in Scripture presumes to sit in judgment, and instead of submitting to Scripture's correction desires to correct Scripture, instead of remaining in its sphere attempts to elevate the laws that happen to obtain in its field to universal ones and impose them also upon Scripture. We regard such a transfer of rules from one discipline to another *(metabasis eis allo genos)* to be as idolatrous as it is unscholarly. We agree fully with *Melanchthon* when he wrote: "Just as it would be madness to say that one could judge Christian doctrine by the rules of the cobbler's trade, so they err who ascribe to *philosophy* the competence to judge doctrine" *Scholia in epist. ad Col.* [Notes on the Epistle to the Colossians], p. 68. (Cited in C. Schmidt, *Melanchthon's Leben* [Melanchthon's Life], Elberfeld, 1861, p. 700).

However confidently scholarship may publish the results of its research as absolutely sure truths, we do not regard such scholarship, but rather Scripture, as infallible. If the results of scientific research contradict clear Scripture, we are therefore *a priori* certain that they are nothing but certain error, even if we cannot demonstrate the error as such in any other way than by an appeal to Scripture. At all events Holy Scripture stands firm for us, no matter how great the conflict may be in which we will become involved with the results of "science" because of this attitude. Whenever we must choose between science and Scripture, we will say with Christ our Lord: "Scripture cannot be broken" (John 10:35) and with the holy apostle: "We take every thought captive to obey Christ" (2 Corinthians 10:5).

No matter if it is claimed that it is, of course, not *natural* reason, but only *regenerate* and *enlightened* reason that is entitled to this honor, we will not let this deceive us; for through enlightenment reason does not receive its own light, next to Scripture, but its enlightenment is precisely this, that through the operation of the Holy Spirit the Word of the prophets and apostles has become its only light in matters of faith. What *John Gerhard* once said to the Reformed in response to their appeal to regenerated and enlightened reason for the right to abandon the clear wording of Scripture if that contradicted the principles of their own

131

reason,—this is also our conviction to the present day. He wrote [in the latter part of the long quotation which follows]:

> Even if . . . a person's reason has been regenerated, to the extent that it desires to argue against articles of faith on the basis of its own principles it is no longer regenerated, because regenerate reason argues on the basis of the principles of the Word. One who argues against the mysteries of faith on the basis of the principles of reason does not do so as a Christian but as a person who is misusing philosophy. Hence, just as one who is born of God does not sin (1 John 3:9), namely *to the extent that* he is such and to the extent that he retains the grace of regeneration, but if he desires to follow the lusts of the flesh he sins and becomes subject to death (Rom. 8:13), so reborn reason does not oppose articles of faith, namely *to the extent that* it is such and to the extent that it follows the leading of the Word; but if it wants to attack the Word of God on the basis of its own principles, it errs and is no longer reborn *(Loci theologici,* On the Interpretation of Scripture, par. 175—77).

As decisively as we renounce a scholarship that presumes to correct and reject articles of faith because they are absurdities according to its principles, so we also abhor that scholarship that pretends to be Christian and yet, whether from unbelief or from a desire to safeguard its scientific reputation, approaches matters of Biblical introduction (isagogics) and criticism not with the presupposition that the written bases on which the church of Christ stands are immovable, but rather as a skeptic and makes it depend on the results of its researches whether those bases were sand or rock—and therefore declares one foundation stone after another to be unsure or even rejects them, altogether. We do not regard a scholarship as Christian, but rather as *pagan,* that first asks whether the foundation of the apostles and prophets may not perhaps, at least in part, be a false foundation. Of such scholarship there should be no trace in the church except insofar as it is to be combatted and overcome. But a scholarship that aims at, or results in, undermining the ground on which Christianity stands and rests throughout its existence we regard as nothing else than as a weapon of the *devil,* and all who use it as servants of the devil. A Biblical criticism and introduction (isagogics) that defeats the enemies of Scripture with their own weapons we esteem very highly; but if these disciplines, in the interest of scholarship, make the least concession to the enemies in opposition to the foundation upon which the church stands, we will tread them underfoot as traitors.

We do not wait for scholarship to secure our foundation for us. We already have it, and *before* all scientific investigation or testing it stands as firm as our God who laid it. No matter what scholarship may unearth, it will neither give us faith nor deprive us of faith. We stand on a rock which

132

we know cannot be overcome even by the gates of hell, let alone by human learning, and therefore we laugh at all enemies and their scientific battering rams and demolition engines with which they surge in insane rage against the rock that towers sky high above the stormy waters of the world. For thus says the Lord: "Every one who falls on that stone will be broken to pieces; but when it falls on any one it will crush him" (Luke 20:18).

We admit further, that as highly as we rate the value of scholarship as an *instrument,* we do not expect from it any growth of our Christian theology as to its *content.* On the contrary, we reject everything whereby scholarship seeks to enrich our theology in this respect as under all circumstances a dangerous gift of the Greeks, no matter whether scientific learning seeks to enrich us from Scripture or from its own achievements. First of all, with regard to matters of our faith we consider Holy Scripture so clear that we do not harbor the faintest hope that the newer and greater scientific aids will disclose to us, or have already disclosed, a new article of faith that was hitherto unknown to the church or concealed from it. We do not believe in a growth in understanding on the part of the church that results from a gradual evolution of dogmas. Rather we believe that the church of the first century was already in possession of all those dogmas that are really Biblical dogmas. We do not view the apostolic church as the church in its infancy that only gradually matures to adult stature through the work of scientifically trained theologians; we are, rather, firmly convinced that with regard to the clarity and purity of its understanding the church resembles the moon, waning and again waxing, and at times experiencing tragic eclipses. We do not agree with the skeptic of Rotterdam [Erasmus], who expected the resurgence of learning to lead also to the rise of a light that had not previously illumined the church. On the contrary, we side with *Luther,* who in his book, *The Bondage of the Will* opposed this maze of error with the following words:

[*Editorial note: In the long quotation which follows, from* Luther's Works, *American Edition, Vol. 33, pp. 25—26, Luther defends the clarity of Scripture even though there are, of course, difficult passages. Walther continues:*]

As earnestly, therefore, as we protest against every enrichment of the church with alleged new articles of faith produced by scientific scholarship from *Scripture,* we self-evidently protest even more loudly, in the second place, when scholarship wants to endow the church out of *its own store.* For as unquestionable as we hold the value, indeed the necessity, of a *formal* or *organic* use of the philosophical sciences in theology to be, to the same degree we regard as reprehensible their *real* or *material* use in the doctrine of the Christian faith.[8w] We do not acknowledge reason, science or scientific method as the formal principle of theology; that is and will remain for us Holy Scripture alone and none other. We say with Isaiah: "To the teaching and to the testimony!" (Isaiah 8:20) and with Paul: "A little leaven" (of human teaching) "leavens the whole lump" (Galatians 5:9). We want a Christianity that has been neither purified nor supplemented by 19th-century scholarship. Here our guiding star is the great word of the rock-man: "Whoever speaks" (namely in the church), "as one who utters oracles of God" (1 Peter 4:11). Hence God's Word and nothing but God's Word is to be preached to the church as the doctrine of faith. The structure of Christian theology should be built on the eternal foundation, Christ, only with the gold, silver, and precious stones of the truths revealed by God through His holy prophets and apostles and recorded in Holy Scripture, and there should be nothing of the wood, hay, and stubble of human opinions, and certainly no such food for the fire dare be foisted on the structure of truth as a part of its foundation. Therefore no tradition cheers our heart more than the one of *Clement of Alexandria*, who reports that Peter is supposed to have said on his own behalf and in the name of all the other apostles: "We say nothing without Scripture" (*Stromata*, ed. Sylburg, Cologne, 1688, fol. 678). For that reason we agree fully with the old erudite Luebeck theologian *August Pfeiffer*, who defined theology thus: "Positive theology is nothing else than *Holy Scripture* distributed among certain areas of doctrine in strict order and according to a clear method; hence not one member, however small, is permitted to be in that body of doctrine that is not drawn from and supported by Scripture correctly understood" (*Thesaurus hermeneut*, Prolegom., p. 5). We agree equally with *John Gerhard* when he writes: "The only principle of theology is the Word of God; *therefore what is not revealed in the Word of God is not theological*" *(Loci theologici*, On Creation, Par. 3). By the way, we renounce not only such additions of science to theology as directly contradict Biblical truth but, in short, *everything* that is supposed to supplement our Biblical theology; for God forbids not only *opposing* anything to His Word but, with equal finality, *adding* anything (Deuteronomy 12:32), and He threatens those who commit this sin with nothing less than eternal damnation (Revelation 22:18).

We admit further, that as much as we delight in a convincing proof of reason for articles of faith that have a mixed character, we nevertheless regard that theology as false and not Christian that bases the truth and certainty of any article of faith on scientific demonstration instead of the Word of God. Rather, we are convinced that only he is a true theologian who can say with Paul: "My speech and my message were not in plausible words of wisdom, but in demonstration of the Spirit and power, that your faith might not rest in the wisdom of men but in the power of God" (1 Corinthians 2:4-5). We are in complete agreement with the old Leipzig theologian *Huelsemann,* who writes: "It is here (between us Lutherans and the Calvinists) not a question regarding a secondary and so to speak superfluous class of proofs, when either the truth has already been sufficiently documented or error has been sufficiently refuted through the divinely revealed testimonies, whether it is *then* useful or permissible to demonstrate the truth or falsity of theological dogmas for good measure also from the judgment of human senses or innate reason. But the question concerns the proximate principle which *determines* man's judgment *(Calvinismus irreconciliabilis,* pp. 58 f.).

Still more inimical to the nature of Christian theology is the attempt to provide rational proof *a posteriori* even for *pure* articles of faith, or to claim that these have been newly discovered by way of philosophical speculation, hence even to demonstrate them *a priori.* However great the service that this appears to render Christian theology, we are nevertheless certain that such alleged demonstrations not only are nothing but a deception but also that, instead of *explaining and proving* the mysteries of faith, they *alter and completely destroy* them in their substance, and only *thereby* produce the *appearance* of a demonstration and reproduction of the mysteries of the Christian faith. All such apologetic we loathe with our whole heart, for it presupposes that there is something even more certain than the Word of God, from which "more certain something" the mysterious content of revelation can be deduced by way of discursive reasoning. But of God's mysteries His Word itself tells us that they were "kept secret for long ages but [are] now disclosed and through the prophetic writings [are] made known to all nations, according to the command of the eternal God"(Romans 16:25-26). They are the content of a message which is "folly" to human reason, beyond natural man's comprehension; in fact, they are a light which *God* commanded to shine "out of *darkness"*(1 Corinthians 1:21; 2:14; 2 Corinthians 4:6).

There is one more thing we must concede here, something that really follows from what has been said. As absolutely certain as we are that between Christian theology and *true* science, science in the abstract, there neither is nor can be a real contradiction, we by no means regard it as either a theologian's task or as possible, ever to reconcile our Biblical theology and science, as it exists concretely, with each other. The charge leveled against us that we do not on our part seek to lead the present unbelieving generation back to faith by demonstrating to the world the harmony of the Christian faith and science—this charge is correct. However, we do not consider it a reproach but rather an honor which by God's grace we never want to be taken from us. For we are firmly assured that also the present apostate world cannot be helped by the lie that the revealed divine truth is in perfect accord with the wisdom of this world, but solely (if it will not stubbornly reject it) by hearing the preaching of the divine folly, the old, unchanged Gospel, of which Paul and the history of the church of all times and of every individual Christian testify that it is "the power of God for salvation to every one who has faith, to the Jew first and also to the Greek" [Romans 1:16]. A person who has been won for Christianity through the demonstration that Christianity can bear the closest scrutiny of science has not yet been won, and his faith is not yet faith.

Where Christ, leaving this earth and returning to the Father, disclosed His last will to His disciples, there beyond question we will find expressed what the sum and substance of our holy religion is and what the precise instructions are which His servants have received for conquering the world for Christ's kingdom. And what does the Lord say? "Go into all the world and preach the Gospel to the whole creation. He who believes and is baptized will be saved; but he who does not believe will be condemned" (Mark 16:15-16). Please observe, there is nothing here to suggest that Christ's servants are to provide scientific answers to the world for its questions: "How can this be?" [John 3:9] or "How shall I know this?" [Luke 1:18]. No, as "ambassadors for Christ" [2 Corinthians 5:20], in the name of the great God, they are to testify "of repentance to God and of faith in our Lord Jesus Christ" [Acts 20:21]. Having done that, they have discharged their task toward the world, and as many as are ordained to eternal life will come to faith (Acts 13:48).

Let them disparage such a theology in this scientific age. No matter. This is the theology of the prophets and apostles, with which we hope to remain until our death! So help us God. Amen.

Conclusion: Vol. XXI, No. 3, March 1875, pp. 65—80

As we indicated already at the beginning, the second chief accusation against us Lutherans in America, namely, that we are despisers of scholarship, contains the added charge *that we have insulated ourselves from the modern intellectual currents in theology, especially from its progress.*

If this is meant to assert, in the first place, that we here are in a state of theological stagnation, that our theology is nothing but the act of mechanically receiving the theology of our fathers into our mind and memory, a dead repristination of that theology, a slavish subjection to the doctrinal decisions of the 17th-century dogmaticians, or at least of Luther or of our church as expressed in its Symbols and other public pronouncements, so that with us the "he said it"[2] takes the place of Scripture proof—all we can do is say to our accusers, Come and see! Make the rounds in our fellowship from parish to parish and from church to church and see whether a so-called dead orthodoxism prevails there, and not rather a lively knowledge gained by experience and matured through inner conflicts. Visit our pastoral conferences, which are held regularly between our annual synodical conventions, and see whether they manifest that mercenary spirit which looks upon the office as a job to make a living (a spirit which we unfortunately had occasion to observe all too often in the land of learning), or rather an active theological life and the concern to learn how a servant of Christ "ought to behave in the household of God, which is the church of the living God" [1 Timothy 3:15]. Attend the sessions of our synodical conventions and see whether there is a "swearing by the words of the master" *(Jurare in verba magistri)* or not rather the attitude of Luther: "Unless I am convinced by the testimonies of Holy Scripture or evident, clear, and manifest grounds and reasons, I am neither able nor willing to recant."

The United-Reformed Krummacher, after only a brief glance at our Missouri Synod, accused it of the inconsistency that "with regard to doctrine it affirms a version of the formal principle that very often has been called Reformed 'Biblicism' " *(Deutsches Leben in Nordamerica: Reiseeindruecke von H. Krummacher* [German Life in North America: Travel Observations by H. Krummacher], Neusalz on the Oder, 1874, pp. 103 f.). In our opinion a United-Reformed theologian could hardly have paid us a greater compliment; for if our characterization as faithfully adhering to the Scripture principle, a claim which the Reformed Church incorrectly makes for itself, is factual and truthful, we are true Protestants, true Lutherans.

Now, it is indeed a fact that our publications have hitherto been marked by a constant documentation of our statements through testimonies drawn from the older orthodox teachers of our church. This has indeed created the impression that our theology is doctrinal traditionalism without independence and merely a dead repristination. But we were driven to proceed in just this way solely by the circumstances in which we found ourselves from the beginning and still find ourselves.

Unfortunately we did not, like our fathers, enjoy the inexpressible blessing of being surrounded by a cloud of witnesses within our church in whose company we could do battle against its enemies. On the contrary, the very people who share the Lutheran name with us were our most vehement opponents, who attempted to dispute our claim that our teaching is that of the Evangelical Lutheran Church. When we Lutherans in America again unfurled the good old banner of our church and again

137

gathered around it in closed ranks, while all around us Zwinglianism, enthusiasm, and rationalism sailed under the Lutheran flag, it was immediately said: Another new sect! Some said, You are on the way to Rome! Others, You are Unionists! Still others, You are Separatists! And still others, You are Pietists, Enthusiasts, Donatists, Calvinists!—who can name all the sects that are supposed to have been revived and renewed through us? In short, we were said to be everything but what we claimed to be—confessors of the teaching of the Reformation, *Lutherans.*

What then could we do and what did we have to do to avoid being labeled a sect? As long as they disputed our character of being true Lutherans, we had to continue to summon the precious Confession and the old unquestionably faithful teachers of our church to bear witness in our behalf. We believe we have done it in such a way that anyone who wanted to see had to see that we did not follow those faithful teachers of our church blindly, but rather in living conviction, that we are not their mindless imitators and adherents but their sons, so that we have always been able to say: "I believe, and so I speak" [cf. 2 Corinthians 4:13]. It is true, the Confession and its confessors were our leaders, but we allowed ourselves to be led by them into Scripture, so that at all times and in all points we could finally say: "It is no longer because of your words that we believe, but we ourselves have read and come to know that your teaching is God's truth" [cf. John 4:42]. As incomparably valuable especially the pure Confession of our church has been to us, we have never subjected ourselves to it as to a law of doctrine imposed on us, but we have rather accepted it with joyful thanks to God for His inexpressible grace solely because in it we discovered our own confession. Furthermore, our American Lutheran church had to fight many an arduous battle with the proud sects in our country, whom we self-evidently could not oppose with the witness of our fathers, and one who has witnessed these battles knows that the written Word of God, also in our weak hands, proved a victorious weapon.

By the way, those who label our theology the theology of the 17th century do not know us. As much as we cherish the immense work produced by the great Lutheran dogmaticians of that period, it is not really they to whom we returned but above all to our precious *Book of Concord* and to Luther, whom we have recognized as the man whom God chose as the Moses of His church in the New Testament to lead out of bondage the church caught in the slavery of Antichrist, following the guidance of the cloudy and fiery pillars of the pure-as-gold Word of God. The dogmatic works of that time—no matter how immeasurably rich the treasures of knowledge and experience stored in them, so that we learn from them day and night with joy and pleasure—are nevertheless neither our Bible nor

138

our Confession. On the contrary, even in them we already observe an occasional muddying of the stream that gushed crystal-clear in the 16th century.

But perhaps we are being reproached not so much for giving no evidence of theological life at all as for insulating ourselves from every contact with *modern* theology. However, also with regard to this charge we emphatically deny that it has any validity. As a matter of fact, we in America suffer from nothing so little as theological indolence also with regard to the latest in theology. We are deeply concerned with all aspects of this theology and pursue its development with the keenest interest. We spend considerable sums of money to acquire the most valuable of the new theological literature in all its various branches. In spite of our circumstances, in which a purely practical activity occupies our attention much more than elsewhere, we do not fail in the short time allotted to us to devote ourselves also to the more significant phenomena in the field of theological literature. We try to acquire an exact knowledge even of what is being written at present in *opposition* to Christian truth, and we do not keep these attacks with their specious apparatus from our students, because we are convinced that one who has gained a thorough and lively knowledge of the truth thereby possesses the sure protection against being infected by even the most attractive error. Nor are we at all blind to the fact that also the recent theological studies have produced and continue to produce an equally rich and valuable benefit for the church in many areas. Every genuine gain produced by this scholarship is hailed with great joy wherever we find it, and we exploit it to the limit.

To be sure, it is to be feared that even all of these public statements will not suffice to purge us in the eyes of our accusers of that charge which we regard as the most far-reaching one, namely the accusation that we insulate ourselves from the undeniable and magnificent *progress,* as is alleged, *of even the newer Lutheran theology in the field of doctrine.* And, in fact, this is really the point where we heartily plead guilty.

We do not deny that from the heretics that have from time to time arisen in its midst the church has derived the great benefit of learning to give expression to what it believes in ever more precise and unequivocal terms. For example, orthodox teachers speak of the person of Christ with far greater precision after the victorious battles with Arians, Semi-Arians, Nestorians, and Eutychians; much more accurately of free will after the Pelagian and Semi-Pelagian controversies; much more clearly of justification, of the church, ministry, and church authority after the great Reformation conflict with the papacy; much more incisively of the means of grace of the Word and the holy sacraments after the attacks of

Zwinglianism, Calvinism, Anabaptism, and related enthusiasms. How true and applicable also to all other orthodox teachers of the churches, therefore, the word of *Luther* regarding the sects that arose in his time:

Everything must work for our good and must benefit us in a variety of ways. In the first place, we are trained thereby to be the more zealous in studying and keeping the Word of God, and so become steadily more sure of the truth. For if there were not such sects through which the devil has thus aroused us, we would become too lazy; we would sleep and snore ourselves to death. Both faith and Word would become dull and rusty in our midst until everything would be ruined. But now such sects are our whetstone and polisher that sharpen and polish our faith and teaching, so that they sparkle smooth and clear like a mirror (Preface to *The Teaching and Secret of the Anabaptists Refuted from Holy Scripture*, St. Louis Edition, XIV, 307 f.).

If it were this fruit of the conflicts the church has had to wage at all times and must still wage that people have in mind when they speak of further development and progress in doctrine, we would wholeheartedly admit that there indeed has been, and still is, further development and progress in doctrine within the church. We ourselves owe it in large measure to our opponents (with no thanks from them) that we believe we have gained in clarity of understanding and in definiteness and precision of expression.

But, unfortunately, this is not what people today mean by further development and progress in doctrine. Not a greater definiteness in presenting the old doctrine, not an ampler documentation of it from Scripture, not a clinching argument that had not been used before to show that the newly surfacing doctrines were refuted long ago by the old, sure, immovable, permanently valid teaching—on the contrary, what they have in mind is entirely new doctrine, not further development but alteration, not demonstration but correction, not defense but dissolution, destruction, abandonment, and alleged refutation of the old doctrine, not only of one or the other subordinate teaching but the basic teachings of our church, indeed, a demolition of its foundation. This is what is ballyhooed to us, even within our Lutheran Church, as further development and progress, and this is what we are asked to acknowledge as development and progress in doctrine.

It is as though the spokesmen also within the church of our time that calls itself Lutheran, with very few exceptions, had tacitly agreed to divide the different chapters of our Lutheran doctrinal structure among themselves, so that each one would make it his business to ruin one of the doctrines, until they were all either deleted from Lutheran dogmatics or substantially reshaped, resulting in a completely new Christian religion in harmony with the alleged results of scientific research and acceptable to our progressive age. The antitheses between the Lutheran and old Reformed doctrine shrink by comparison with the antitheses between the neo-Lutheran and original Lutheran teaching into something that could be reconciled far more easily. These are no exaggerations, but it is unfortunately an undeniable fact that can be corroborated by way of induction; and if God grants us life and strength, we promise to corroborate it thus in this periodical during the current year.

To support our claim that we are not standing alone in our judgment on the so-called doctrinal progress of the more recent theology and that our judgment does not spring from American Lutheran lack of scholarship and narrowmindedness, we shall content ourselves for the present with offering a few testimonies that have become audible from within the theological world of Germany.

[*Editorial note: Walther brings extensive citations (11 printed pages) from a large number of German Lutheran theological books and periodicals. While appreciating the positive contributions of modern theological scholarship, the authors are highly critical of attempts at reshaping the church's teaching and consider such attempts a dismal failure. By way of contrast, they express admiration for "the grandeur and profundity of those systems in which for centuries our fathers deposited their most exalted perceptions and in which complete and able men gave expression to their religious thought." Some were appalled to observe that "hardly a single doctrine is left that has not been subjected to extensive remodeling, addition, and deletion." In fact, the alleged "further development" of Lutheran doctrine "sweeps out the most essential elements of that doctrine as rubbish." Walther continues:*]

In conclusion, I cite a judgment on the *language* of modern theology, as expressed by Dr. Muenkel in the Foreword of *Neues Zeitblatt* [New Periodical], 1866. He writes:

In addition, theologians use a language of their own as soon as they want to amount to something. Some use a very *involved* language that is impossible to penetrate, others a *high-flown* style that loses itself in a fog of scientific terms and foreign expressions and is apparently designed to conceal ordinary everyday thoughts. If the church was at pains to employ uniform speech, the modern theologian takes that as an indication of not having kept pace. Or, *some use the church's terms like counterfeiters* and make them say the very opposite of what they mean and thus increase the confusion. For nowadays when two people write, teach, and preach about the same matter in the same terms, we cannot be sure that both of them are not bitter opponents with regard to the same matter.

Let this suffice, first of all, to demonstrate that the judgment of Lutherans in America concerning the alleged doctrinal progress of which modern Lutheran theology boasts is not a specifically American judgment, but one passed in Germany even by men of learning and adopted also by us. No less, however, does this serve to demonstrate that we surely have sufficient grounds for refusing to become involved with such progress and such further development, since both—as Dr. Carl Scheele says so truly—are nothing but the "accursed heritage of an inebriated scholarship,"[9w] namely of that philosophy which attempts to solve the riddle of the world by way of speculation.

But in order that the uninitiated reader need not rely on someone else's judgment, we shall devote a special article to demonstrating by means of the very words of our modern Lutheran theologians that their alleged progress in the saving doctrine is nothing but an open apostasy from Lutheran truth. The reader will then gain the conviction that the cited judgments on the more recent theology, far from being too harsh, have not gone even halfway in describing the desolation wrought by that theology.

Foreword to the 1877 Volume
[On the 300th Anniversary of the Formula of Concord]

[First Part:] *Lehre und Wehre,* XXIII, 1, Jan. 1877, pp. 1—5

The year 1877 is a jubilee year for our precious Evangelical Lutheran Church: the third centenary of its Formula of Concord.[1] It was on May 29, 1577, shortly before Pentecost, that the six designated Lutheran theologians in Bergen Cloister, near Magdeburg, subscribed the so-called Formula of Concord that had finally been completed with the help of God and thus made a beginning of its solemn acceptance as a Confession of the church. The six theologians were *Martin Chemnitz,* superintendent in Brunswick, *Jacob Andreae,* professor of theology, chancellor, and provost at Tuebingen, *Nicholas Selnecker,* superintendent in Leipzig, *David Chytraeus,* professor of theology and superintendent in Rostock, *Andrew Musculus,* general superintendent of the Mark Brandenburg and principal professor of theology in Frankfurt on the Oder, and *Christopher Koerner,* professor of theology at the same place and general superintendent of Electoral Brandenburg. They subscribed the Formula with the following words:

> Therefore, in the presence of God and of all Christendom among both our contemporaries and our posterity, we wish to have testified that the present explanation of all the foregoing controverted articles here explained, and none other, is our teaching, belief, and confession in which by God's grace we shall appear with intrepid hearts before the judgment seat of Jesus Christ and for which we shall give an account. Nor shall we speak or write anything, privately or publicly, contrary to this confession, but we intend through God's grace to abide by it. In view of this we have advisedly, in the fear and invocation of God, subscribed our signatures with our own hands (Solid Declaration, XII, 40; Tappert, p. 636).[1W]

To be sure, the jubilee in remembrance of the reception of the Formula of Concord as one of our church's Confessions has been celebrated in different years. Most frequently the observance was set for the year '80, since in that year not only did the Formula of Concord appear in print for the first time as a part of the whole *Book of*

143

Concord, namely in folio at Dresden, 1580, but also the 50th anniversary of the Augsburg Confession could be combined with it. Where the latter occurred, June 25 was chosen as the jubilee date, all the more because Lutheran people were generally acquainted with the Augsburg Confession, while all too often they unfortunately knew very little about the Formula of Concord. Yet the specific divine deed which is above all to be remembered in an anniversary celebration of the Formula of Concord is, in our opinion, not so much its appearance in print, nor its official acceptance by many thousands of high and low estate, important as both of these are otherwise, but rather the gift of this document through the gracious illumination of the Holy Spirit. This divine bestowal occurred at the moment when those enlightened theologians with invocation and in the name of the great God affixed their signatures to this precious document, now happily accomplished by the grace of God, and then presented it to the church as their Confession. Since it is stated at the close of the Epitome that it was "done at Bergen, May 29, 1577," we think that 1877 is also the proper year and May 29 the proper day for observing a God-honoring and God-blest anniversary celebration to thank Him for this great gift.

For that reason this highly important event was commemorated by means of a very festive "festival of thanksgiving and jubilee" on May 30, 1677, in the Cloister Church at Bergen, where the Formula of Concord was completed and first subscribed 100 years before. As J. N. Anton *(Geschichte der Concordienformel* [History of the Formula of Concord], Leipzig, 1779, II, 152 ff.) relates, the abbot of Cloister Bergen, Dr. Sebastian Goebel, "to that end published, several days in advance, a short Latin notice, in which he publicly announced his plans and invited the right reverend cathedral chapter, plus other spiritual and temporal dignitaries, and especially all the church and school personnel in Magdeburg." In this program it says, among other things:

> For us to ignore this extremely great blessing which divine goodness has granted our churches through so many and so great princes and so famous and upright men by means of so many meetings, so much effort and work and even greater expense, on the occasion of this centennial at this place, where a century ago, a few days before Pentecost, the Book [Formula] of Concord was brought to completion—I say, to pass over this event in silence would be highly disgraceful for us cloister residents already because all of us, abbot and conventuals of this widely known cloister, ought to be devoted to the study of Holy Scripture and the nurture of sacred theology.

[*Editorial note: The quotation continues by mentioning the good example of two princes who observed the anniversaries of the Swabian-*

Saxon Formula and the Torgau Book, earlier stages in the Formula's development.[2 W]

But is the writing and inclusion of the Formula of Concord as one of our church's Confessions really an occasion worthy to be commemorated in anniversary celebrations even in our day? We answer: Certainly and truly! In the first place, because it is, after all, a Symbol, quite apart from its significance as constituting, so to say, the capstone of the lofty confessional structure of our precious Evangelical Lutheran Church.

As the Formula of Concord says, the Symbols of an orthodox church are a "summary formula and pattern, unanimously approved, in which the summarized doctrine commonly confessed by the churches of the pure Christian religion is drawn together out of the Word of God," or a summary form of teaching that is based "not on mere private writings, but on such books as had been written, approved, and accepted in the name of those churches which confessed the same doctrine and religion" (Solid Declaration, Rule and Norm, 1; Tappert, p. 503). As imperishable treasures more precious than all the world's gold we regard already the masterful presentations of doctrine and its convincing support from the Word of God, as well as the penetrating exposures and thorough refutations of dangerous errors arising in the church, as contained in the private writings of some especially gifted and enlightened teachers of the church and left to posterity. How much greater is the treasure, a treasure beyond words, contained in the declarations on behalf of the truth and in opposition to error in important questions regarding the heavenly teaching which an entire orthodox church has publicly issued and put into writing for all future ages! Woe to a church that has inherited a pure confession of doctrine from an earlier orthodox church as the victory spoils of severe conflicts, as the gold of truth refined seven times in the furnace of violent trials, as a fruit of rich visitations of grace—and then discards this legacy as old-fashioned rubble, as worthless dross, as unripe sour grapes, or at least allows it to gather dust without use!

It is, of course, true that a church's Symbols are not, as has sometimes been claimed, absolutely necessary or perhaps even to be regarded as supplements to an insufficient canon but, as orthodox teachers of our church have always claimed and attested, only hypothetically necessary through a so-called necessity of expedience created by circumstances (cf. Carpzov, *Isagog.*, p. 5). Nevertheless, next to God's written Word the Confessions of the orthodox church are the most precious writings given to it by the grace of God. These documents are the possession of the church at a later time and therefore truly deserve to be celebrated by the church at the completion of another century since the Lord gave it this treasure—

celebrated by jointly and publicly giving ardent and humble thanks to the Lord for this gift and its gracious preservation.

But as to why the Evangelical Lutheran Church also in this year has great reason to celebrate especially because of its Formula of Concord—concerning this allow us to speak in the next number of this periodical.

Continuation: Vol. XXIII, No. 2, Feb. 1877, pp. 33—54

Aside from the fact that the Formula of Concord is one of the official Confessions of our orthodox Evangelical Lutheran Church, and therefore in it we Lutherans hear not the voice of a private individual but indisputably the voice of our dear church itself with regard to the most important articles of the Christian faith, there are mainly three more reasons that should move us to celebrate a festival of thanksgiving and jubilee in the current year to commemorate that Confession given to us by God 300 years ago: I. Its glorious character; II. the great blessing it once brought to our church; III. the current state of our church, in which we cannot sufficiently thank God that we possess not only the other Confessions of the church but also in particular this Symbol, the Formula of Concord.

I

Regarding the *character* of the Formula of Concord, it is distinguished not only (A) by a salutary calm objectivity, and even gentleness, as well as firmness, but also (B) by an equally remarkable clarity, precision, and thoroughness, as well as simplicity.

A

The enemies of pure doctrine have, indeed, continually decreed the Formula of Concord so vehemently, as a horrible product of orthodoxistic fanatics and heartless zealots whose mouth is full of cursing and bitterness, that it stands in ill repute even with many who are otherwise sincerely devoted to pure doctrine—if they have not themselves read the document. It is, of course, true that in it all falsifications of the Word of God are decisively condemned without respect of persons, even of such widely esteemed and revered men as Melanchthon and Flacius. However, not only is the Formula of Concord free of all personal invective, but—in order to spare those who favorably interpreted erroneous statements of their revered teachers and exonerated them of blame, and in order not to destroy the benefit that had hitherto accrued, and could well continue to accrue, to the church from many writings also of those men who in a time of nearly general confusion had fallen into serious error—the Formula of

146

Concord even declined to mention by name those whose errors it refutes and rejects. Thus neither Melanchthon nor Flacius nor, to proceed impartially, George Major, John Agricola, Francis Stancarus, Andrew Osiander, Paul Eber, John Pfeffinger, Nicholas von Amsdorf, John Stoessel, and others, are mentioned as errorists by name. To be sure, neither are the writings of Melanchthon and Flacius recommended, however splendid their content. Of all private writings, only those of Luther are recommended as pure, and reference is made to them only for further elaboration of the respective doctrines as being in accord with the Word of God.[3W]

When the Formula of Concord appeared, it was for that very reason severely criticized from two directions. Apart from those who were Calvinists under cover of the Lutheran name (such as several Wittenberg and Leipzig theologians, and the men of Lower Hessia or Hessen-Cassel, and those of Anhalt[4W]), the admirers of Melanchthon, even those who did not dare to defend his errors, on the one side accused the Formula of Concord of being *too strict* because it not only sidetracked the *Corpus doctrinae Philippicum*[2] and failed to honor him as Luther's co-worker, but also rejected and condemned statements made by Melanchthon that were clearly recognizable as his errors, even though his name was not mentioned. Some went so far as to *refuse to subscribe the Formula of Concord* and even exerted all their influence to thwart its introduction into the churches of their province. Others did not go beyond expressing their *disapproval* in this respect.

Belonging to the *first class* of Philippists was Paul von Eitzen, general superintendent of Holstein, who succeeded in barring acceptance of the Formula of Concord in his territory during his lifetime. In 1581 he wrote to Jacob Runge, general superintendent in Wolgast: "As far as my humble self is concerned, I assure you in the name and in the face of our Lord Jesus Christ and by invocation of the same: Even though the whole world should subscribe the book of the so-called discordant concord, I will never sign it, so help me God's grace!" (J. H. Balthasar, *Historie des Torgischen Buchs* [History of the Torgau Book], Greifswald and Leipzig, 1741, I, 17).[3] Another of this first class of Philippists was Jacob Runge, who prevented the acceptance of the Formula of Concord in Pomerania, and Maurice Heling, preacher at St. Sebaldus in Nuernberg,[5W] who did the same in his city, etc.

The *second class* of genuinely Lutheran admirers of Melanchthon, unhappy that Melanchthon was more or less pilloried by the Formula of Concord, yet still *accepting* it, consisted mainly of the people of the electoral Palatinate (although Elector Louis, Count Palatine on the Rhine,

147

was the first among the princes to sign the Preface to the *Book of Concord,* cf. Anton, I, 244). To placate these and other true Lutherans who shared their views, Luther's pamphlets on marriage and on Baptism *(Trau-buechlein, Taufbuechlein)* were deleted and the following words were inserted in the Preface to the whole *Book of Concord:* " . . . inasmuch as we never understood or accepted[6W] the second edition [the Variata] in any other sense than that of the first Augsburg Confession as it was submitted. Nor do we want to have rejected or condemned any other profitable writings of Master Philip *Melanchthon* or of [John] Brenz, Urban Rhegius, [John Bugenhagen] of Pomerania, and others in *so far as (quatenus) they are in agreement with the norm incorporated in the* [*Formula of*] *Concord"* (Tappert, pp. 9 f.). Balthasar writes:

> When the men of Rostock read this, they wrote . . . to their prince: "We are also very happy to see that the name of Philip Melanchthon, as the principal teacher of our church next to Dr. Luther, is explicitly mentioned in the Preface. This was much and often referred to in the deliberations but could not be carried out, even when nearly half of the critiques received, and especially the Palatinate, Hessia, Anhalt, Holstein, Pomerania, and others requested this in particular, and the most vehement and hateful hue and cry was therefore stirred up by some against this work because the name and writings of the highly deserving man Philip were ignored. For that reason we are happy to see in this statement inserted in the Preface at Heidelberg that through insistent pressure on the part of the Elector Palatinate this venomous calumny [against Melanchthon] is being counteracted to some extent" *(Hist. des Torgau Buches* [History of the Torgau Book], II, 59).

However, as Balthasar adds, while the passionate partisans of Melanchthon, who sought to put a favorable construction on all of his writings, "were not yet satisfied with that, since Melanchthon's *Corpus doctrinae* was not to be the norm, but rather his writings were to be subjected to another norm, especially the *Book of Concord,* and thus clearly be made suspect"—others accused the Formula of Concord of the opposite, namely of being *too lenient* and forebearing, even lax. *Heshusius,* for example, had written to Chemnitz even before the Formula of Concord appeared: "In our opinion the church's welfare demands that in this formula the originators and supporters of falsifications, Illyricus [Flacius], Philip, Pfeffinger, Osiander, Major, Calvin, Peter Martyr, Philip's letter to the people in the Palatinate,[7W] *be mentioned by name* and at least indicated to the church and to posterity, so that young people reading those books might be on guard against the errors conflicting with the Formula of Concord." Further:

This is about the sum of our observations, with the plea that the decision about abolishing the Meissen [or Philippist] *Corpus doctrinae* (so that it not be a doctrinal norm) and about the rejection of those false reports (I mean the *Acta synodica* and their ilk) be published and made known to the whole church. . . . If the names of Philip, Pfeffinger, and Major could be omitted without detriment to the church, we would be entirely in favor of that. Nor do we anticipate any pleasure or profit, if with mention of the name it is explicitly stated that Philip's views on free will and on the Lord's Supper conflict with the Word of God. But since we see that there are extremely important and urgent reasons, and we have the examples of the apostles of Christ and the ancient church, we humbly request that there be concern for the young people who read Philip's writings with immature judgment and for posterity (Balthasar, II, 57).[8W]

Yet when the Formula of Concord was published, Heshusius as well as all the Helmstaedt theologians at once subscribed voluntarily and even joyfully. To the cheerful and confident general formula of subscription he added: "I, Tilemann Heshusius, doctor of theology, subscribe with heart and mouth and hand and pray God with all my heart that He would suppress all falsifications and by His Holy Spirit promote and establish the work of salutary concord" *(Concordia concors*, pp. 1197 f.). In fact, when in the following year, 1578, a forged letter was printed under the name of Heshusius, attacking the Formula of Concord, he issued a reply in self-defense wherein among other things, it says:

I ask you, enemy of God, treacherous forger of the letter, tell me, what error did you find in the Formula? Do not mumble in your beard; do not whisper out of the dust like the sorcerers; but speak up freely and clearly: what errors are there in the Bergen Book and the Formula of Concord (improved on the basis of the Torgau Book)? Name the errors. Cite chapter and verse. Which words express them? Which passages from God's Word will refute the errors, so that we may desist from them and be on our guard against them? . . . As for what I, Tilemann Heshusius, think of the Formula of Concord revised at Cloister Bergen, I will say clearly and correctly in this publication before all of Christendom that I am unable to find any error or false teaching in the Formula of Concord; on the contrary, what I read there is sound, pure, salutary, and truthful doctrine which agrees with the writings of the prophets and apostles and is drawn from the fountain of Israel. . . . It never occurred to me to compose this unchristian, ungodly writing against the Formula of Concord. A spiteful, false, godless, evil man and, in my opinion, a brazen Calvinist liar . . . has treacherously concocted this writing and circulated it under my name, no doubt aiming to prevent the salutary, Christian, and most necessary work of concord, and also to create the suspicion that I am opposed to all Christian unity. . . . I have subscribed the Formula of Concord not only with my hand but also with my heart, and the *Book of Concord* is so well grounded in God's Word that all the Calvinists and schismatics will be unable to do it any harm *(Concordia concors,* pp. 91, 589).

However, quite beyond comprehension, Heshusius and the other Helmstaedt theologians, Daniel Hoffmann and Basilius Sattler, adopted a completely different attitude toward the *Book of Concord* after it was published.[9W] Among other things he charged that the printed text did not agree with the one subscribed by him but was extensively altered. He persisted in this accusation even after Chemnitz had shown him convincingly that the changes could in part be traced to copyists and printers and in part were quite unessential and harmless. Furthermore, Heshusius now also accused the Formula of laxity because those who had fostered the errors condemned by it were *not mentioned by name.* He also claimed that the explanation given in the Preface about the "condemnations" occurring in the Formula had *weakened the cause of doctrinal discipline.* However, Chemnitz and his co-workers allowed neither the objections of those for whom the Formula of Concord was too strict, nor of those who found it to be too lenient and too lax, to divert them from their course.[10W]

With regard to the latter objection Chemnitz, Selnecker, and Koerner thoroughly vindicated their procedures at the colloquy of Quedlinburg in 1583 and received the approval of all other theologians present (with the exception of the above-mentioned men of Helmstaedt).

[*Editorial note: Walther cites the proceedings of the colloquy at considerable length* (Concordia concors, pp. 1068—75). *Chemnitz and others point out that they were not opposed to mentioning false teachers by name if circumstances required it, but they saw no need for this procedure in the Formula of Concord. As precedents they appealed to the apostolic council, (Acts 15), to councils of the early church, as well as the Wittenberg Concord of 1536. In the Preface to the* Book of Concord *the authors had offered the following explanation: "With reference to the condemnations, censures, and rejections of false and adulterated doctrine, especially in the article concerning the Lord's Supper, these have to be set forth expressly and distinctly in this explanation and thorough settlement of the controverted articles. . . . However, it is not our purpose and intention to mean thereby those persons who err ingenuously and who do not blaspheme the truth of the divine Word, and far less do we mean entire churches inside or outside the Holy Empire of the German Nation. On the contrary, we mean specifically to condemn only false and seductive doctrines and their stiff-necked proponents and blasphemers" (Tappert, p.*

11). In answer to the charge that these words weakened doctrinal discipline it was stated that a distinction must be made between stiff-necked ringleaders and those led astray by them, just as St. Paul in his dealings with the Corinthians and the Galatians distinguished between false apostles and their victims. Walther continues:]

Hence we cannot sufficiently thank God that in its *character* our precious Formula of Concord constitutes a Confession that is marked by an equally salutary calm, objectivity, even gentleness, as well as firmness, and thus pursues the true golden mean.

B

In this respect the Formula is also distinguished by an admirable *clarity, precision, and thoroughness, as well as simplicity.*

That the Formula of Concord does not suffer from lack of clarity and precision needs no proof. The chief criticism of its opponents is that its definitions are too minute, too subtle, too hair-splitting, which in fact criticizes nothing but its incomparable clarity and precision. But without these properties the writing of a Formula of Concord for the purpose of doing away with the previous unspeakable confusion in doctrine would have been empty juggling, an "Interim," an instrument of union *(Henoticon)* like that of Emperor Zeno, which would only have promoted hypocrisy and increased the confusion. Blessed rather be those precious men of God who by the Holy Spirit's illumination bequeathed to us a Confession that is so clear and so precise with regard to such highly important articles!

To be sure, recent theologians take a different view. For example, Dr. F. H. R. Frank, in his *Theologie der Concordienformel* [Theology of the Formula of Concord], says of the article on the election of grace [Article XI] that the Formula's type of teaching "in this point suffers from a lack of scientific scholarship because of its inconsistency." But God be eternally praised that our precious Formula of Concord suffers from this alleged scientific shortcoming, for it is nothing but a refusal to do what the moderns attempt, namely to solve the mystery of predestination synergistically, that is to say, to destroy it. On the contrary, the Formula's authors were bent on faithfully preserving this mystery.

As for *thoroughness,* probably no churchly Symbol has ever been drawn up in so thorough, careful, and conscientious a fashion as our dear Formula of Concord. True, already Paul von Eitzen tried to disparage it by claiming that it was composed *by a few arrogant individuals* and imposed on others. As his fourth reason for rejecting the Formula of Concord ("even though this might entail noose, sword, fire, and water!") he advanced the following: "Because Jacob Andreae and his theological cohorts have the nerve by means of the new confession to introduce this dangerous process, unknown in the old true Christian church, as a corrupting example; namely, that *six theologians,* in part infected with enthusiasm, in part consciously conniving at it, meet now here, now there, and as dictators of faith shape and reshape their book and then present it everywhere as if by plenary authority and without synodical action, which they fear, and demand that every theologian, preacher, and schoolmaster subscribe it" *(Concordia concors,* pp. 385, 381). Andreae did not think it worth the effort to defend himself against this attack in Eitzen's thoroughly mendacious libel. He simply explained that all this "had already been discussed in the Preface of the electors and princes that was to be attached to the *Book of Concord,* so that it was not necessary to waste any further words on this matter" (p. 394).

But when the Helmstaedt theologians, long after they had subscribed the Formula of Concord with the assurance of great willingness and with holy protestations, subsequently did an about-face and raised the same criticisms, and the matter was brought up at the Quedlinburg convention in 1583, the attending counselors of both Electoral Saxony and Brandenburg responded as follows:

Everyone knows that although in Bergen only a few theologians were employed, the entire document was revised and edited on the basis of critiques that had been received and then sent out once more to the estates and their theologians to read it again for good measure and to examine how and in what manner the appointed theologians dealt with it, and if they discovered some further shortcoming, to report it frankly and hold back nothing, so that this work might be defended in such a way that none of the theologians who were asked to review it would have any reason to complain. By God's grace they were found to be well satisfied and attested their agreement clearly by their own subscription. And, to be sure, such a frequently repeated revision and reexamination of the Christian *Book of Concord* is a far greater task than if a general synod had been convened for one meeting, to which every ruler would send two or three theologians to help examine and approve the book in the name of all the rest. In that case there would have been only one such synod to examine this work, while by our procedure there were as many synods as there are rulers to whom the book was sent and who had their theologians soberly and maturely weigh and evaluate it by the Word of God. As is clear from church history, from the beginning of Christianity *no other book or matter of religion was dealt with so thoroughly.* Accordingly, the theologians who reviewed it on the basis of the critiques did not take the decisive action themselves but submitted it to the theologians of all the estates for a final revision; and their critiques had the last word *(Concordia concors, pp. 1127 f.).*

This is the actual and undeniable truth. It is well known that the Formula of Concord did not come into being in this way, that those six theologians came together by order of their princes at Cloister Bergen and drew up this confession in a few days, and that then the princes commanded or urged the servants of the church in their lands to subscribe it! The origin and eventual acceptance of the Formula of Concord followed an entirely different course.

[*Editorial note: At this point Walther launches into a lengthy review of the history of the Formula of Concord, detailing the many attempts between 1568 and 1576 to produce a document that would restore concord to the Lutheran Church. After repeated false starts and failures and an incalculable amount of effort by theologians with the support of their princes, the path to peace was at last established. The main steps were literary efforts by Jacob Andreae ("Six Sermons"), approved by his region (Swabia) after recasting in the form of articles. These were then sent to North Germany (Lower Saxony), where they were extensively revised and rewritten, and returned to Andreae as the "Swabian-Saxon Concord." This document, together with another proposal, the so-called "Maulbronn Formula," was assigned to a number of theologians meeting in Torgau to produce one document, the so-called "Torgau Book," the immediate forerunner of the so-called "Bergen Book," the final version of the Formula of Concord, which was subscribed by its authors on May 29, 1577.[4] Walther concludes his historical review with the following paragraph, quoted from Anton (I, 260):*]

"No writing in the entire world can be found which before its public appearance went through so many hands and was so often and so exactly and carefully scrutinized, and improved and corrected with such great diligence, also in respect to the words and expressions, as the Formula of Concord of the Evangelical Lutheran Church."

A final criticism of the Formula of Concord is that it is *a confession only for theologians, not for Christians in general.* It is, of course, true that this writing offers not only "milk" but also "solid food" [cf. Hebrews 5:12] and that in its doctrinal definitions it goes beyond the substance of the Catechism. However, in view of the cleverly planned doctrinal falsifications which it opposed, this was a matter of absolute necessity and should therefore not be censured but highly commended.[11w]

Nevertheless, the Formula of Concord is composed in *such simple* words that the unlearned Christian who has some knowledge of Scripture and is well grounded in his Catechism may understand it quite well. The

Swabian-Saxon formula still contained many technical theological terms and various Latin phrases and citations. But all this had already been dropped from the Torgau Book on the advice of Andreae, so that the layman might also be able to understand, examine, and accept this confession. Hence we can say, "Take and read!" also to every *layperson*, to everyone who is no longer one of those "children" who must still be taught "the first principles of God's Word" and are therefore "tossed to and fro and carried about with every wind of doctrine" [Ephesians 4:14]. Such a mature person will confess that he, too, understands the Formula of Concord very well.

Conclusion: Vol. XXIII, No. 3, March 1877, pp. 65—76

II

That our Evangelical Lutheran Church has been greatly blessed by the writing of the Formula of Concord is something that all its friends know and joyfully acknowledge and even all its enemies must admit, though with resentment and anger.

Before the adoption of this confession the German Lutheran church, to which the eyes of all Lutherans outside of Germany were directed as to the Lutheran mother church, was split and torn into almost countless parties. Philippists, Majorists, Flacians, Synergists, Osiandrists, Standcarists, Adiaphorists, Antinomians, Crypto-Calvinists, etc., occupied a large number of its pulpits and academic chairs, even claimed to be the only genuine Lutherans, and either were the leading spokesmen in our Lutheran Church or at least kept it in constant turmoil. The confusion was so great that even Elector August—who could honestly say that "if he knew he still had a single Calvinistic vein in his body, he would have it torn out"—was deceived and deluded by his Crypto-Calvinist counselors and theologians so that he deposed the most faithful teachers of Lutheran doctrine as "Flacians," drove them and their families into misery, and put fanatical Calvinists, who paraded in the sheep's clothing of the Lutheran name, in their place.

The confusion was so great that in 1561 at the Naumburg "day of princes" the Altered Augsburg Confession of 1540 was solemnly acknowledged and subscribed also by genuinely Lutheran princes and recommended as one that was "a little more fully and thoroughly formulated and expanded and augmented on the basis of Holy Scripture" *(Hist. motuum,* III, 203). In most Lutheran territorial churches there was high regard for the *Corpus doctrinae Philippicum,* though permeated with various errors; in fact, in some territories, notably electoral Saxony, it was the officially designated collection of confessions. Whoever refused to be pledged to these was dismissed from office and banished. Everywhere Calvinists were infiltrating Lutheran churches and threatening to devour them completely.

This was especially the case in electoral Saxony. They had gained complete control of Wittenberg University and by deceit and treachery completely won the pious elector, cast a spell over him, and made him their willing tool. They believed they had reached their goal, namely of banishing Luther's teaching from the Lutheran Church and having Melanchthon's union theology acknowledged and established in its place. Already all enemies of our church were gloating that its demise was only a question of time.

It was then that by the production of the Formula of Concord the unspeakable confusion was suddenly, almost magically,[12w] brought to an end, and the Lutheran church of Germany was saved from destruction. Countless Lutherans, loyal yet weak and wavering and in great danger of being caught by the whirlpool and dragged down to ruin, were enlightened, strengthened, and plucked out of all danger. The orthodox members and servants of our church were rallied around a common banner, and true peace, true agreement, true union, in short, a true *Concordia* was established while the enemies lost heart. Noteworthy are the comments of Struve on this point in his *Pfaelzische Kirchen-Historie* [Church History of the Palatinate]:

> When Count Palatine John Casimir, an ardent Calvinist, noticed how the Formula of Concord would *strike a heavy blow against the Reformed churches and their confessions,* he dispatched emissaries or letters to Queen Elizabeth of England, the princes of Conde, and the French, Hungarian, Polish, Bohemian, Swiss, and Dutch churches, requesting them to send several theologians along with some politicians to the Fall Fair in Frankfurt, 1577, who might, invoking divine guidance, deliberate on what was needed *to preserve the Reformed religion.* At the appointed time Daniel Roger represented the queen of England through his substitute, Robert Beal. There were also delegates from the French, Polish, Hungarian, Dutch, and other churches. The congress was opened on Sept. 27, and Wenceslas Zuleger, chief counselor of the Court Palatine and an ardent Calvinist, pictured *the danger to the Reformed churches* if their teachings would be condemned in the Formula of Concord.
>
> It was resolved, first, to send a delegation to the Evangelical princes to argue against publishing the Formula of Concord. It was resolved, secondly, "to supply the need of *formulating a common confession of all Reformed churches.* The queen was to send a theologian from England to start the project. Meanwhile Z. Ursinus and H. Zanchi were commissioned to draft such a confession and then send it to R. Gualther

in Zuerich and Th. Beza in Geneva for review and revision. Thereupon the confession should be sent to all churches and, upon their approval, be published in the name of all." However, though all necessary steps were taken, the common confession, as Struve observes, *"did not become a reality"* (pp. 361 f.).

Thus the Formula of Concord barred entrance of the Reformed into the Lutheran Church and shouted an energetic "Halt!" to the Reformed war of conquest and triumphal parade through Lutheran territories. Henceforth, instead of the Lutheran Church, the Reformed had to assume the role of those churches in Germany whose existence was threatened. No wonder that a Reformed theologian, Rudolph Hospinian, wrote a book in opposition to the Formula of Concord and published it under the title *Concordia discors*. It is one of the most libelous books ever printed, as Leonard Hutter shows in his *Concordia concors*. He does it so convincingly that to the very end the reader cannot get over his astonishment at the bold liar, forger, and blasphemer.

To be sure, the Formula of Concord never became a *universal* confession of all Lutheran churches inside and outside Germany. However, those so-called Lutheran territorial churches that declined to adopt it did so, in part, because they had already become Calvinized, such as Lower Hessia, Anhalt, and Bremen, and therefore soon withdrew from the Lutheran Church and identified themselves as Reformed, a step of great blessing to the Lutheran Church; in part, they adopted the Formula of Concord later on, as in Holstein, Pomerania, Zweibruecken, Krain, Carinthia, and Styria, as well as in Sweden;[13w] in part, even in all those Lutheran churches in which by governmental force its canonical authority was circumvented or later repealed, the Formula was esteemed as a pure Confession of Lutheranism.

A special blessing bestowed by God on our church at that time through the Formula of Concord is that it provides *an authentic catalog of the generally accepted Symbols of our church.* Before the Formula of Concord there were a large number of *corpora doctrinae* [collections of Symbols] in the various Lutheran territorial churches, among which the so-called *Corpus doctrinae Philippicum* or *Misnicum* enjoyed especially high prestige. As indicated, it was precisely this collection of allegedly Lutheran Symbols that contained not only all of Melanchthon's errors but also a type of teaching by means of which, as Anton correctly notes, "a variety of errors of Papists, Calvinists, Adiaphorists, and other errorists could be maintained" (I, 49). Consequently, the loyal Lutheran preachers in the small principalities of Reuss and Schoenburg in the year 1567, that dreadful time when the Crypto-Calvinists tried to impose the Melanchthon collection on the churches by force, stated in their glorious confession:

Thirdly, we commit ourselves with honest mouth and heart to the old, true, unmoved Augsburg Confession . . . which the Adiaphorists later altered in many places in word and substance, mutilated, misinterpreted, and falsified, included in Philip Melanchthon's *Corpus doctrinae* in 1560, and published. . . . This version became like a buskin, a clog, a sandal, and a Polish boot for both shanks, or a cloak and changeling, whereby the Adiaphorists, Sacramentarians, Antinomians, new Synergists, and the like cover, adorn, defend, and establish their errors and falsifications under the guise and name of the true Augsburg Confession. Thus they pretend that they, too, are committed to the Augsburg Confession, *only so that* under its shadow they might enjoy the general *imperial peace* against the hail and rain, and might all the more easily and safely sell, promote, and spread their errors disguised as friends. Yet at bottom they are the greatest and worst perverters of the truth of the correct, first, and original Augsburg Confession, men about whom we can fittingly complain as Christ did in John 13:18: "He who ate My bread has lifted his heel against Me" (Confession-Schrift [Confessional Writing], 3rd ed., Gera, 1699, pp. 22 ff.).

Melanchthon's *Corpus doctrinae,* as assembled by his son-in-law Caspar Peucer, contains the Altered Augsburg Confession, Melanchthon's *Loci* of 1553, the Examination of Candidates for Ordination, but *not* the Apology, nor the Smalcald Articles, nor Luther's Catechisms. That this dangerous book was crowded out of our church by the Formula of Concord is a divine blessing that cannot be praised enough. Woe to us Lutherans if the plan to make Melanchthon's *Corpus* the norm for our church had succeeded! The Lutheran Church would have turned into a Melanchthonian church, and the latter into a Calvinistic one, and the heritage of the Reformation would have been lost forever already in the 16th century.

But equally important is also the commitment expressed in the Formula of Concord to the original Symbols, which are therefore included in the *Book of Concord.* The documents were selected with great care, being limited to those to which no Lutheran can object without coming under suspicion. On March 14 [1577] Chemnitz, Andreae, and Selnecker reported on this matter to the elector of Saxony: "With regard to the documents which contain the ground and explanation of our Christian faith and confession, since we commit ourselves, first of all, to the prophetic and apostolic writings, the three Symbols, the Augsburg Confession, Apology, Smalcald Articles, and both of Luther's Catechisms, there is (praise God!) unanimity among the most noble and honorable electors, princes, counts, and cities (imperial cities), as among their theologians—not excluding even Holstein and Anhalt" *(Concordia concors*, p. 432). For when the Formula of Concord was subscribed by 86 imperial estates (51 princes and 35 imperial cities) and between 8,000 and 9,000 servants of church and school, those earlier confessions at the same time were accorded such a general, solemn, and public confirmation as they had not enjoyed before. Hence in the course of time all other documents, including pure particular confessions, receded more and more into the background and finally lost their official significance. Thus the Formula of Concord produced a unity and solidarity of confession in the genuine Lutheran Church such as no other church possesses, quite apart from the truth of the contents.

The church of Reuss is a fine example of a territorial church that ackowledged the Formula of Concord as a pure Symbol, *even though without formal subscription.* In the Preface to the third edition of its *Confession-Schrift,* 1599, the authors say:

> We know of no other divine, heavenly, saving truth than that which God graciously brought to light from the prophetic and apostolic writings through His chosen instrument, Dr. Martin Luther. This heavenly deposit, which we are duty-bound to observe and preserve, we earnestly and sincerely believe is faithfully comprehended and repeated in the oft-mentioned *Book of Concord* and has been vindicated and preserved against many corruptions (against which our confession obviously fought even before the Formula was written). Therefore, instead of repeating our subscription to this book, we cite again the judgment of the man of God, Luther, upon the unalloyed Augsburg Confession in calling it "the last trumpet before Judgment Day." . . . Consequently we acknowledge all, whether near or far, who have earnestly and sincerely subscribed the Christian *Book of Concord* and believe and teach accordingly in thesis and antithesis, as our beloved brothers and co-confessors in the Lord. As such we will laud and love them, praise and honor them, pray for them, rejoice with them when they prosper and weep with them when they weep. It is our friendly and brotherly prayer that all of them would in turn acknowledge us in the same way, be concerned about us, and in these gloomy times include us in their intercessions. . . . Beyond this, we declare explicitly and frankly that by God's grace (thanks and praise be to Him!) we have never sided, nor will we ever side, with those who have gratuitously and wilfully suggested or might yet suggest that something has been patched on the Formula of Concord or changed in it in a dangerous way (as the men of Helmstaedt later alleged). We say without hesitation that we will regard with suspicion these and all others, no matter how exalted or important, who secretly or openly oppose this salutary and useful book, and expect

nothing good of them. We state furthermore that such people not only do not edify the church of God but in many ways offend it, deeply grieve it, and even wretchedly destroy it in many places, and for this they will have to give account on the great day of the Lord (Preface, f, 4, b).

Thus even those true Lutherans who for various reasons declined to subscribe the Formula of Concord nevertheless committed themselves to it. So Rudelbach writes:

> The Formula of Concord was a work of peace that could thus expect and receive approval most of all in places where the conflict had vitally touched many members or entire churches. It must, therefore, not surprise us that those at greater distance, among whom either this controversy did not achieve such importance and wide distribution or who even believed that the quarrels would be increased by the Formula (this was true principally in Denmark,[14W] although especially there the Philippist position with its characteristic wavering had taken deep root through the efforts of the famous Nicholas Hemming) rejected adoption of the Formula in this sense, *while in no way denying the doctrinal purity of this document*. In the church of Strasbourg they went one step farther and adopted the Formula of Concord to the extent that all candidates for ordination were examined on the basis of the Formula and were directed to it, without requiring its acceptance in the formal oath of office *(Historisch-kritische Einleitung in die Augsburgische Confession* [Historical-Critical Introduction to the Augsburg Confession], Dresden, 1841, p. 209).

Therefore Lutherans in whose churches the Formula of Concord has normative authority have always been willing to acknowledge also those churches as genuinely Lutheran which regarded the doctrine of the Formula as in accord with the Word of God, even though they did not give it symbolical status. In an equal measure, however, they refused to recognize as truly Lutheran those churches that were ready to accept the Augsburg Confession as a pure confession but not the Formula of Concord.

Least of all were those who were willing to be pledged to the earlier Symbols but not to the Formula considered fit for the ministry in a church that includes that document among its Confessions. Such men were rejected either as muddleheaded in doctrine or as hypocrites who follow the old Crypto-Calvinists in electoral Saxony and accept the Augsburg Confession as a cloak but refuse the Formula of Concord because it unmasks their apostasy from the Augsburg Confession. They want to subscribe the Augsburg Confession in the spirit of Calvin in Strasbourg, who in true Jesuitical fashion later sought to harmonize his subscription with other statements of his by writing to Martin Schalling, 1557: "Nor do

I reject the Augsburg Confession, which I once willingly and gladly subscribed in the sense in which its author himself explained it" *(Letters,* ed. by Beza, Lausanne, 1576, p. 390). But to make such hypocritical subscriptions impossible was one of the many important reasons why the Evangelical Lutheran Church of the Unaltered Augsburg Confession drew up the Formula of Concord and requested those who desired to assume office in one of its parishes to subscribe it as a test of their sincere commitment to the Augsburg Confession. Accordingly the introduction to the Formula of Concord (Solid Declaration) states:

> Although the Christian doctrine set forth in this [Augsburg] Confession
> has remained practically unchallenged—except for the charges of the
> papists—it can nevertheless not be denied that some theologians did
> depart from it in several important and significant articles, either
> because they failed to grasp their true meaning or because they did not
> abide by them. Some, while boasting of and benefiting from their
> adherence to the Augsburg Confession, even dared to give a false
> interpretation to these articles. This caused serious and dangerous
> schisms in the true Evangelical churches. . . . For that reason necessity
> requires that such controverted articles be explained on the basis of
> God's Word and of approved writings in such a way that anybody with
> Christian intelligence can see which opinion in the controverted issues
> agrees with the Word of God and the Christian Augsburg Confession,
> and so that well-meaning Christians who are really concerned about the
> truth may know how to guard and protect themselves against the errors
> and corruptions that have invaded our midst (Tappert, pp. 502 f.).

Consequently, when in 1580 some Wittenbergers stated that they were ready to subscribe the first part of the *Book of Concord,* namely the Augsburg Confession, Apology, Smalcald Articles, and Luther's Catechisms, but not the Formula of Concord, the elector informed them:

> Since they agree with the first part of the Christian *Book of Concord,*
> they cannot, *to the extent that they are really serious about it,* refuse to
> subscribe the explanation of the controverted articles, inasmuch as *this
> is geared to the books of the preceding part.* It is sufficiently safeguarded
> in the Preface to the Christian *Book of Concord* that the just-mentioned
> explanation *offers nothing new* but only sheds light, in a correct
> Christian understanding and unanimity, on the *misunderstandings* that
> have occurred with regard to the controverted articles. Dresden, Jan. 3,
> 1581 (cited in Carpzov, *Isagoge,* pp. 20 f.).

Even the anything but rigorous Henry von Seelen, rector of the Luebeck *Gymnasium,* said of the Calvinists in his anniversary address of 1730: "Let them consider whether by opposing the Formula of Concord they are not at the same time attacking the Augsburg Confession, since the latter is the *basis* of the former, and the former does *not dissent* from the latter" *(Bibliothec. Lubec.,* IX, 377).

At one time, when the Duchy of Magdeburg intended to refrain in the Diploma of Vocation from further mention of the Formula of Concord as one of the Symbols, the abbot of Cloister Bergen, Sebastian Goebel, making use of the occasion of the first centennial of the *Book of Concord,* wrote to the deputies of the ducal estates on Aug. 24, 1680, requesting "that the Formula of Concord not be omitted in the Diplomas of Vocation." As the last reason for his request he stated "that those who live in the Duchy of Magdeburg would not have to let themselves be regarded as half-Lutherans by their coreligionists" *(Neue Beitraege von alten und neuen theologischen Sachen* [New Articles about Old and New Theological Matters], Leipzig, 1755, p. 44).

III

Finally, while the great benefit that came to our church 300 years ago through the appearance of the Formula of Concord is a blessing which we may enjoy in our time just as did our fathers, the state of our church *at present* is such that we Lutherans in this our day have a particular reason to praise God for our cherished Formula of Concord. Now that 300 years have elapsed since it was written, we have every reason to join in a public celebration to commemorate this great mercy bestowed on our church and to render due thanks to God for preserving this treasure for 300 years.

What a flood of abuse the modern Lutherans, who are to the last hair like the Crypto-Calvinist Lutherans in the days before the Formula of Concord, are now loosing upon those who desire to remain faithful to the old Unaltered Augsburg Confession and not give up one iota of it! How much different would be their behavior if 300 years ago those who remained true to the teaching of the Augsburg Confession had not closed ranks and for all time demonstrated and recorded its proper meaning by means of a "general, pure, correct, and definitive restatement and exposition of a number of articles of the Augsburg Confession"! [Title of the Solid Declaration; Tappert, p. 501]. How would our Philippists, Synergists, Majorists, Adiaphorists, and Interimists (i.e., Unionists and Syncretists), Crypto-Calvinists and Crypto-papists act today against Lutherans who remained faithful, if there had been no Formula of Concord, if the Philippists with their *Corpus doctrinae,* their Altered Augsburg Confession, and their Calvinizing and Pelagianizing dogmatics *(Loci)* had gained control in our church, while Luther and his teaching and practice had been proscribed! Now they have a bad conscience maligning the true sons of the Reformation as disturbers and destroyers of the

161

Lutheran Church and as sectarians. What would they do if the authentic witness of our church that they are the apostates, disturbers, and destroyers would not stare them in the face and confront their conscience through the cherished Formula of Concord?

We do not have the space to mention everything for which we should be thankful to the Formula of Concord in our time. But we cannot refrain from calling the following to your attention:

1. None of the trend-setting so-called Lutheran theologians of our time are correct in their position on the doctrine of the inspired Word of God and the principle of theology or Christian doctrine. These have already been judged by our church in the opening statements of the Formula of Concord.

2. People want to be Lutheran nowadays although they eliminate everything from the Confessions that they no longer believe. This they have done by resorting to the mendacious theory that nothing in the Symbols is binding except what is explicitly stated as confession and what is explicitly labeled as the decision in doctrinal controversies. The so-called incidental statements and the content of the lines of argument are not binding, they say, still less the inferences that could be drawn from the explanations offered in the Symbols. The Formula of Concord is a concrete testimony of our church in opposition to this, since in it the proofs are derived from the total context of the earlier Symbols, the clear inferences flowing from their explanation are fixed as the correct teaching of our church, and what logically follows as its opposite is condemned as anti-Lutheran false teaching.

3. Some would like to see certain "different trends" and so-called "open questions" recognized within our church, also in Biblical articles of faith. They claim that the demand for agreement in all articles of faith is orthodoxistic extremism and requires something that is impossible in view of the way human nature is constituted. Such a course is said to thwart all unity and necessarily lead to endless splintering. The Formula of Concord is the concrete counter witness to this view. In Article X it asks churches not to condemn each other because of a difference in ceremonies, "as long as they are otherwise agreed in doctrine and *in all its articles* and are also agreed concerning the right use of the holy sacraments"[Solid Declaration, X, 31, Tappert, p. 616]. The Formula of Concord owes its own origin to the insight that in a true church there can be no "different trends" and "open questions" in the teachings of faith, and its introduction into the church is practical proof that this demand is not stretching the concept of church unity too far and does not necessarily lead to splintering, but is rather the only way to true unity.

162

4. It is an illusion for modern Lutheranism to allege that it permits doctrinal differences only within the limits of the Confessions. What it means to say is that any departure must be tolerated in those who are formally committed to the Symbols of our church and who claim to be operating on their basis. The Formula of Concord anticipated this wretched juggling act, for it aimed at excluding from the fellowship of the orthodox those who acknowledged the earlier Symbols but, "while boasting of and benefiting from their adherence to the Augsburg Confession, even dared to give a false interpretation to these articles" [Solid Declaration, Introduction, Tappert, p. 502]. The Formula of Concord anticipated the unionistic theory of modern Lutherans which proposes to regard as a true Lutheran, with whom one should have church, pulpit, and altar fellowship, anyone who accepts some so-called specifically or distinctively Lutheran teachings, such as the presence of the body and blood in the Lord's Supper, even though he might harbor all kinds of papistic, Calvinistic, Arian, or Pelagian, and even pantheistic errors or theosophical fantasies. The Philippists, Synergists, Majorists, and Crypto-Calvinists also claimed to be good Lutherans and in part were better Lutherans than most modern Lutheran theologians. But by means of the Formula of Concord faithful Lutherans have forever rejected church fellowship with such "false brethren," even though they call themselves Lutheran and pretend or really believe that they want to make their peculiar teachings valid only within the confines of the Confessions.

5. Modern Lutheranism often makes a display of great indignation against the government's external union of administration and cultus, even though there is continued inner disunity in faith and doctrine. At the same time, under the cloak of the Lutheran name they carry on the most frightful unionism in their own house with false teachers of every sort, even with such as blaspheme Christ and His Word. Against this pestilence of our time the Formula of Concord, and especially its golden Article X, offers a preservative, bequeathed to us by our fathers, for which we cannot ever sufficiently thank and praise God.

Though much more could be said on this subject, this shall suffice for now. May it help us Lutherans, in this year of remembering the 300th anniversary of the true concord achieved in our church by the grace of God and in genuine gratitude for the preservation of this precious charter to the present hour, to celebrate a fitting jubilee with sincere and joyful thanks. And may God strengthen us both in our general service to the church and in the editing of this theological monthly, so that we may prove ourselves to be faithful confessors of our *Concordia,* ready to subscribe it even with our blood, if that should be necessary.

Foreword to the 1882 Volume
[The Only Source of Doctrine]

[First Part:] *Lehre und Wehre*, XXVIII, 1, Jan. 1882, pp. 1—6

When Lutherans appeal to the fathers in support of a dogma apart from, or even in opposition to, Scripture, they are guilty of a glaring apostasy from the supreme principle of true Protestantism, the Reformation, and thus our Evangelical Lutheran church.

A principal factor in the unspeakable corruption of the church just before the Reformation was, among others, the fact that Scripture was not permitted to be the only fountain from which all saving truth must be drawn, nor the only rule and norm according to which all teachers and teachings must be judged and evaluated, and therefore also not the only judge in all doctrinal controversies. On the contrary, the alleged teaching of the church was derived chiefly from the writings of the fathers, even the writings of the church's teachers in the Middle Ages, the so-called scholastics, and people wanted to judge and settle all doctrinal controversies on that basis. Refusal to submit unconditionally to the opinion of a church father or an esteemed scholastic was taken as a sure sign of suspicion of heresy, if not of being an outright heretic.

As the seeds of nearly all evils that gradually infiltrated the Roman church go back to early times, so also this *erroneous principle of doctrine.* Already at the time of Athanasius [296—373] and Augustine [354—430], and even of Justin Martyr [100—166], false teachers not infrequently appealed to expressions or teachings of earlier recognized orthodox teachers in an attempt to put the stamp of orthodoxy on their heterodoxies. At that time, however, orthodox teachers still unanimously and decisively rejected any attempt to bind them by the authority of noninspired human teachers, even the best of them. They sought, wherever possible and where conscience allowed, either to give an acceptable interpretation to inappropriate statements of acknowledged orthodox writers to which heretics appealed, or at least to excuse what was incorrect in their writings, or they firmly and boldly rejected and condemned what was obviously wrong and could not be explained in a good sense. At the same time they did not on that account hereticize those of whom they were convinced that those writers had not wantonly, consciously, and willfully followed their own reason and forsaken the "pattern of . . . sound words" [2 Timothy 1:13] but only because of (even great) human weakness had departed from God's clear Word.

[*Editorial note: In support of his thesis Walther cites Martin Chemnitz, who in turn cites the ancient fathers Justin, Athanasius, Augustine, and Basil. See Chemnitz,* Examination of the Council of Trent, *(St. Louis: Concordia Publishing House, 1971), Concerning Traditions, pp. 217—307. Walther continues:*]

The dear church fathers also refused to be bound by the prestige of *contemporary* teachers of the church, and they declined even more to bind the consciences of others by their *own* writings and utterances.

When Jerome felt highly offended because Augustine refused to agree with him on a certain point and criticized and refuted his assertions, *Augustine* answered:

> I confess to your love that I have learned to show this reverence and honor *exclusively* to those books of the Scriptures that are called *canonical,* so that I believe most firmly that none of the authors erred in any way when he wrote. And when I do run into something in these writings that seems to be contrary to the truth, I have no doubt that either the manuscript is faulty or the translator has not captured the meaning, or I myself have not understood it. Other books I read in this way that, however distinguished in piety and learning they may be, I do not regard something as true simply because it was their belief, but because they were able to convince me, either by those canonical authors or by plausible reason, that it does not conflict with the truth. Nor do I believe, my brother, that you think differently; in fact, I am sure that you do not want your books to be read like those of the prophets and apostles. With regard to them, it is godless to doubt that they are without error (Letter XIX [or, by another numbering, LXXXII] to Jerome).

As rigidly as Augustine distinguished between the writings of other fathers and those of the prophets and apostles, he differentiated with equal firmness between *his own* writings and those of the prophets and apostles.

[*Editorial note: Augustine refers to his own past mistakes and his growth in understanding, but he admits that he is still short of perfection. However, he points out that there is a difference between being wrong but willing to be corrected and stubbornly defending one's errors. Walther continues:*]

In the ancient church, therefore, it was not the teachers of the church, but only the *false teachers and heretics* who tried to justify their false teaching from the writings of acknowledged orthodox fathers, in part by appealing to inappropriate expressions used by the fathers or to the

165

obviously wrong ones that had found their way into their writings. Subsequently, however, under the rule of the papacy, the opposite practice was observed. Instead of deriving, supporting, and defending the church's teaching from Holy Scripture as their only source, as well as evaluating and judging every teaching and writing exclusively by the written Word of God, and deciding doctrinal controversies on that basis, it was not so much the heretics as *the church's teachers* who presented the so-called doctrine of the church mostly on the basis of statements of the fathers instead of Scripture. These teachers put the fathers' writings *on a par* with Scripture, and even *above* it, in practice, if not in theory. A case in point are the *sentences* of Peter Lombard in the 12th century, which in this respect exerted an even greater influence on the character of the papal church than the even more highly esteemed Thomas Aquinas with his *Summary of All Theology.*

It was only the Reformation of the church through Luther that uncovered this abomination and by the grace and the help of God cleanses the church of it.

We will speak of this in the next issue.

Continuation: Vol. XXVIII, No. 2, Feb. 1882, pp. 49—57

If the day when Luther publicly proclaimed his *95 Theses* against the abomination of the papal indulgences is, in a sense, the birthday of the work of Reformation, its conception may be thought to be the day in 1503 when Luther for the first time held a complete Bible in his hands.[1w] Without doubt Luther had learned from his pious parents and teachers even in his early youth that the Bible is a book that contains God's own Word, and this must have made a deep impression on the bright, inquisitive, and God-fearing lad. However, when he quite unexpectedly saw a complete Bible for the first time, not only was his heart overjoyed at the discovery of this incomparable treasure, but from henceforth the Bible more than ever became the only source of infallible truth from which he drew and the ultimate touchstone by which he tested everything he read or heard elsewhere. Herein he was confirmed no little by what he heard as a student in Erfurt from the mouth of his revered professor Jodocus Trutvetter. For later on (1518), when that teacher reproved Luther for ignoring the decisions of the scholastics and being so free in his judgments, Luther answered: "If you will permit the boldness of your pupil and obedient servant, this is my opinion. I learned it first from you that one must believe only the canonical (or divinely inspired) books and test all others, as St. Augustine, yes, also Paul and John teach" (St. Louis Edition, XV, 413). When he entered the monastery, his chief aim was to devote himself to undisturbed searching of the Scriptures and thus to become ever more firmly grounded in the saving truth, and so to find the right way to eternal life. And even though his superiors tried to divert him from that purpose by assigning to him all kinds of menial tasks, he used every spare hour to strengthen and refresh his soul through Scripture as the true fountain of truth and genuine comfort. Junius writes: "Although Luther felt his assigned chores, especially the beggar's bag, to be a real burden, he did not complain, but amid all trials continued in prayer and, whenever time allowed, read all the more eagerly in his precious Latin Bible, bound in red leather. He became so well versed in it that he could find everything in a moment" *(Compendium Seckendorfianum,* 1755, I, 39). Therefore the counsel of another former teacher, Bartholomew von Usingen, made no impression on him: "Brother Martin, what is the Bible! You should read the old teachers. They have extracted the juice of truth from the Bible." Luther himself reported this in his Table Talk (St. Louis Edition, XXII, 26).

Even though Holy Scripture had long been the supreme authority for Luther in all matters, it is remarkable how hard it was for him to free himself from the authority of the Roman church and the pope and how long it took him to achieve a breakthrough in this respect. After he had published his *95 Theses,* he wrote:

Many good men thought very highly of my Theses, but it was impossible for me to acknowledge them as limbs of the church, gifted with the Holy Spirit. I looked up to the pope, the cardinals, bishops, theologians, jurists, monks, and priests and expected the Spirit from them. For I had so eagerly devoured and guzzled their teaching (if I may speak thus) that I was quite drunk with it and did not know whether I was awake or asleep. And when I had overcome all arguments (that lay in my way) by means of the Scriptures, I was finally able, by the grace of Christ, yet with extreme fear and difficulty, to surmount this one argument, namely, that one must listen to the *church.* . . . As I was thus awaiting the verdict of the church and the Holy Spirit, I was ordered to keep still, and custom was appealed to. Since I was intimidated by the prestige of the name of the church (which every Christian should honor and hold in high esteem), I yielded and promised Cardinal Cajetan at Augsburg to remain silent, humbly requesting him to impose silence also on the hue and cry of my opponents. However, he not only denied this request[2W] but threatened that unless I recanted he would condemn all that I had ever taught (*Preface to Luther's Theses Against Indulgences,* 1538, St. Louis Edition, XIV, 453).

At that time Luther offered to remain silent obviously not because he was unsure of his teaching from Scripture, but because he did not yet fully

167

see through the contradiction of the alleged church's command to be silent in opposition to Scripture. Therefore he continues: "However, I had already taught the Catechism with the result that many people had improved their lives; therefore I knew that I could not allow it to be condemned, for to do so would be to deny Christ. Thus necessity compelled me to attempt extreme measures and be prepared for anything" (ibid., 454).[1] As much as Luther in 1518 was still captive in his conscience to the authority of the Roman church and the pope, the "Catechism," that is, the *Bible,* of which it is a short summary, had priority. Hence he was ready to keep still but never to recant. Therefore also no error he had not yet overcome at that time harmed him. Having the Bible as God's infallible Word in his heart, he was more and more liberated from error after error, year by year, yes, day by day.

To be sure, at the Leipzig Debate in 1519 Luther dealt with quotations from the church fathers, of whose writings Dr. Eck had a truly stupendous knowledge and with which he deluged Luther. The latter demonstrated to the admiration of the audience that he was equally conversant with those writings. Yet, however respectfully he expressed his opinions on the church fathers, he declared:

> I am greatly surprised that the honorable doctor has undertaken to prove the divine right (of the pope) and that to this day he does not cite a syllable from *Scripture* for this purpose, but only expressions and acts of the *fathers,* and indeed such as contradict one another. . . . As proof he offers the words: "You are Peter and on this rock I will build my church," which Augustine is said to have interpreted as saying, "on this rock, that is, on Peter," and did not retract this interpretation. I answer: is that to me? If he wants to argue with me, let him first bring into harmony the expressions that contradict this. For it is certain that Augustine frequently interpreted the rock as referring to Christ, and perhaps barely once as referring to Peter. Therefore he is more with me than against me. *But even if Augustine and all the fathers took the rock to mean Peter, I, as one individual, will oppose them* by authority of the *apostle* (that is, by divine right), saying: "No other foundation can any one lay than that which is laid, which is Jesus Christ" (1 Corinthians 3:11), and by the authority of Peter, who in 1 Peter 2:4 ff. calls Christ the "living stone" and "cornerstone" and teaches that on this foundation we should be "built into a spiritual house" (St. Louis Edition, XV, 938 ff.).[2]

As is well known, Luther took the same position two years later when the great moment of decision finally came for him at Worms, whether to renounce his doctrine and the work which God had begun through him, or to prefer being expelled as an accursed heretic and condemned insurrectionist by world and church, that is, the organization which then bore the name of church. Luther chose the latter. After he had solemnly and at length stated his reasons before emperor and empire why he could not recant any of his writings with a clear conscience, he added: "Therefore, I ask by the mercy of God, may your serene majesty, most illustrious lordships, or anyone at all who is able, either high or low, bear witness, expose my errors, overthrowing them by the writings of the prophets and the evangelists. Once I have been taught I shall be quite ready to renounce every error, and I shall be the first to cast my books into the fire" (*Luther's Works,* American Edition, Vol. 32, p. 111). When Luther was then requested to answer concisely whether or not he would recant, he gave his eternally memorable reply: "Unless I am convinced by the testimony of the Scripture or by clear reason[3W] (for I do not trust either in the pope or in councils alone, since it is well known that they have often erred and contradicted themselves), I am bound by the Scriptures I have quoted and my conscience is captive to the Word of God. I cannot and will not retract anything, since it is neither safe nor right to go against conscience. I cannot do otherwise, here I stand, may God help me, Amen" *(Luther's Works,* American Edition, Vol. 32, pp. 112f.).

If Luther according to this, was unwilling to have his conscience bound by the decrees of entire councils but would submit only to the Word of God, he was even less inclined to subject himself without condition to the opinions of individual fathers as expressed in their private writings.

In the days that followed, a number of attempts were made in private discussions with Luther to persuade him to back down and simply and unconditionally leave the judgment on his writings to the emperor and the empire. Luther replied that he would willingly do and endure everything if only they would abide by the authority of Scripture and let it be *master and judge;* otherwise he would agree to nothing. When they kept after him, he said plainly that he would not let human beings judge God's Word. Finally they sought that he should at least submit his cause to the judgment of some future council. He agreed with the proviso that they show him the parts taken from his books to be submitted to the council, and that they judge them by the testimony of Scripture and that the contrary doctrine be presented and proved with the same witness. When Luther was informed that the emperor would now "proceed" against him, he replied:

First of all to his most serene majesty, to the prince electors, the princes, and the rest of the imperial estates, I give most humble thanks for a favorable and kind audience and for the safe-conduct which has been kept and is to be kept. For I have desired nothing in all this except a reformation according to holy Scripture, and this I have urgently demanded. Otherwise I will endure all things for his imperial majesty and the empire: life and death, fame and infamy, reserving nothing at all for myself except only the right to confess and testify to the Word of the Lord. *(Luther's Works,* American Edition, Vol. 32, pp. 118—123).

This attitude toward the written Word of God as the only source of saving truth over against all human writings, even of the best fathers or authors of the church, remained Luther's until his death.

[*Editorial note: To demonstrate Luther's unchanged posture, Walther cites Luther's* The Misuse of the Mass, *1521* (Luther's Works, *Vol. 36, pp. 135—37); part 1 of his Church Postil, 1522 (Walch Edition, XI, 2538); a sermon for the day of St. James the Apostle, 1522 (St. Louis Edition, XI, 2333); a sermon for the Third Sunday After Epiphany, 1524 (St. Louis Edition, XI, 487). In all these passages Luther rejects the authority of the church and the fathers as normative for faith. Scripture alone is normative. Walther continues:*]

Unfortunately the space allotted to this periodical does not permit reprinting the great passage from Luther's precious book *On the Councils and the Church,* 1539 (*Luther's Works,* American Edition, Vol. 41, pp. 14 ff.). To it we therefore refer our esteemed readers, of whom at least the Lutheran preachers have Luther's works (or should have them, even if they would have to go without meat for a whole year to acquire them).

In the next issue we intend to show that what Luther wrote about this matter in his personal writings through which he became the Reformer of the church, was also carried into our public Confessions. Finally we will permit ourselves to make the application to our present circumstances.

Conclusion: Vol. XXVIII, No. 3, March 1882, pp. 97—108

In the primary confession of our Evangelical Lutheran Church, the Unaltered Augsburg Confession, there is no separate article which designates the Holy Scriptures of the Old and New Testaments as the only principle of knowledge with regard to Christian truth and, hence, the only critical principle according to which all that claims to be Christian truth, whether spoken or written, must be judged. However, from beginning to end this is assumed in the Augsburg Confession and applied without further ado. Long ago the Roman church had in practice put tradition on a par with Scripture but had not yet defined this dogmatically. As is known, this was done at the Council of Trent after Luther's reformation of the church. Already in the Preface of the Augsburg Confession, directed to the emperor, the confessing princes and imperial cities declare in the name of our church: "Wherefore, in dutiful obedience to Your Imperial Majesty, we offer and present a confession of our pastors' and preachers' teaching and of our own faith, setting forth how and in what manner, on the basis of the Holy Scriptures, these things are preached, taught, communicated, and embraced in our lands, principalities, dominions, cities, and territories" (Preface, Augsburg Confession, 8; Tappert, p. 25).

Thus the confessors will have nothing to do with any "foundation" of their faith and teaching other than the written Word of God. To be sure, in the confession itself there are references to the church and the old teachers in addition to Holy Scriptures, but only as *witnesses,* not as sources and judges. On the contrary, the last article asks, ". . . why does the divine Scripture so frequently forbid the making and keeping of human regulations? Why does it call them doctrines of the devil? Is it possible that the Holy Spirit warned against them for nothing?" (Augsburg Confession, XXVIII, 49; Tappert, p. 89). Indeed, the closing statement of the confession reads: "In keeping with the summons, we have desired to present the above articles as a declaration of our confession and the teaching of our preachers. If anyone should consider that it is lacking in some respect, we are ready to present further information on the basis of the divine Holy Scripture" (Augsburg Confession, Conclusion, 6-7; Tappert, pp. 95 f.).

Nowhere do the Lutherans promise to prove their teaching by the writings of the fathers and councils. When the confession had been read, even such a fanatical papal partisan as Duke William of Bavaria said to Dr. Eck: "What was described to me as Luther's teaching is quite different from what I heard affirmed in their confession. You assured me that their teaching can be refuted." Eck replied: "I can do it with the church fathers, but not with Scripture." Whereupon Duke William turned away angrily with the remark: "It seems, then, that the Lutherans are sitting in the Scriptures and we outside!" (St. Louis Edition, XVI, 880; cf. E. G. Schwiebert, *Luther and His Times* [St. Louis: Concordia Publishing House, 1950], p. 730). Later on, Elector Joachim of Brandenburg read the Imperial Recess containing the emperor's decision. In threatening terms it commanded the protesting estates to accept his verdict, since their teaching had long been recognized by many Christian councils as heretical and unchristian. Chancellor Brueck replied in the name of the Protestants: "The Confession which their electoral and princely graces and others had presented at the beginning of the Diet . . . is so well founded on the divine Holy Scripture and the holy Gospel . . . that the gates of hell cannot stand or endure against it, as against God's Word and the holy Gospel" (St. Louis Edition XVI, 1547; cf. Theo. Graebner, *The Story of the Augsburg Confession.* [St. Louis: Concordia Publishing House, 1929], p. 200).

The more stubbornly the papists continued to insist on their doctrinal traditions without and contrary to Scripture, the more it was necessary for our church to express itself publicly and officially. This was done. The so-called Smalcald Articles, composed in response to Pope Paul III's summons to a council at Mantua, express our church's ultimatum to the papists:

> The papists here adduce passages from Augustine and some of the Fathers who are said to have written about purgatory. They suppose that we do not understand for what purpose and to what end the authors wrote these passages. St. Augustine does not write that there is a purgatory, nor does he cite any passage of the Scriptures that would constrain him to adopt such an opinion. He leaves it undecided whether or not there is a purgatory and merely mentions that his mother asked that she be remembered at the altar or sacrament. Now, this is nothing but a human opinion of certain individuals and cannot establish an article of faith. That is the prerogative of God alone. But our papists make use of such human opinions to make men believe their shameful, blasphemous, accursed traffic in Masses which are offered for souls in purgatory, etc. They can never demonstrate these things from Augustine. Only when they have abolished their traffic in purgatorial Masses (which St. Augustine never dreamed of) shall we be ready to discuss with them whether statements of St. Augustine are to be accepted when they are without the support of the Scriptures and whether the dead are to be commemorated in the sacrament. It will not do to make articles of faith out of the holy Fathers' words or works. Otherwise what they ate, how they dressed, and what kind of houses they lived in would have to become articles of faith—as has happened in the case of relics. This means that *the Word of God shall establish articles of faith and no one else, not even an angel* (Smalcald Articles, Part II, Article II, 13-15; Tappert, p. 295).

Yet after Luther's death our church was even more urgently called upon once for all to renounce turning for proof of the truth of a teaching not only to God's clear written Word but also to statements of human teachers, old or new, be they ever so pious, and looking upon these statements as deciding doctrine and binding consciences. So-called Philippism made this necessary. As is known, after Luther's death Philip Melanchthon was accorded such high esteem in our church that, in part, even upright men were deterred in their understanding as well as their confession of the truth and, in part, impure spirits sought to smuggle horrible heresies into our church under the aegis of the "teacher of Germany"[Melanchthon was called *Praeceptor Germaniae*]. This they did by claiming that their teachings were those of our Confessions, as was incontrovertibly evident from the writings of their principal author, the great Mélanchthon.[3] Consequently our church was in extreme danger of losing the treasure of the pure apostolic doctrine that had been regained through the Reformation. Our church escaped this danger only through an endeavor such as the writing and adoption of the Formula of Concord. In it the doctrine of the Reformation contained in the Augsburg Confession is reiterated, not according to the interpretation of this or that prominent teacher but, as the Formula of Concord explicitly states: "... we abide by the plain, clear, and pure meaning of its words" (Solid Declaration, Introduction, 4; Tappert, p. 502). In it also all private writings, including those of Melanchthon, are denied the authority of being the voice of our church, and the position of being the true norm of what must be believed is ascribed exclusively to the Holy Scriptures.

Thus the Epitome of the Formula of Concord begins with these words: "We believe, teach, and confess that the prophetic and apostolic writings of the Old and New Testaments are the only rule and norm according to which all doctrines and teachers alike must be appraised and judged, as it is written in Ps. 119:105, 'Thy word is a lamp to my feet and a light to my path.' And St. Paul says in Gal. 1:8, 'Even if an angel from heaven should preach to you a gospel contrary to that which we preached to you, let him be accursed'" (Rule and Norm, 1; Tappert, p. 464). In the Solid Declaration this is expressed as follows: "We pledge ourselves to the prophetic and apostolic writings of the Old and New Testaments as the pure and clear fountain of Israel, which is the only true norm according to which all teachers and teachings are to be judged and evaluated" (Rule and Norm, 3; Tappert, pp. 503 f.).

Not content with acknowledging Holy Scripture as the doctrinal norm, the Formula of Concord adds the following antithesis in order to indicate the scope of its affirmation: "Other writings of ancient and modern teachers, *whatever their names,* should not be put on a par with Holy Scripture. Every single one of them should be subordinated to the Scriptures and should be received in no other way and no further than as witnesses to the fashion in which the doctrine of the prophets and apostles was preserved in post-apostolic times" (Epitome, Rule and Norm, 2; Tappert, pp. 464 f.). The history of the Formula of Concord shows that the *"modern* teachers, whatever their names" has reference particularly to Melanchthon. After listing the official confessions of our church, the Epitome continues: "In this way the distinction between the Holy Scripture of the Old and New Testaments and all other writings is maintained, and Holy Scripture remains the only judge, rule, and norm according to which as the only touchstone all doctrines should and must be understood and judged as good or evil, right or wrong" (ibid., 7; Tappert, p. 465).

After the outbreak of serious doctrinal controversies in our church at that time the question was not only in general, "What is truth?" but also specifically, "What is Lutheran? What is the teaching of the Augsburg Confession?" The Philippists wanted at least the last question answered on the basis of Melanchthon's writings. However, the Formula of Concord states right at the beginning that the "doctrine commonly confessed by the churches of the pure Christian religion is drawn together out of the Word of God." It must be based *"not on* mere *private writings,* but on such books as had been written, approved, and accepted in the name of those churches which confessed the same doctrine and religion" (Solid Declaration, Rule and Norm, 1; Tappert, p. 503). Furthermore, with regard to the correct *understanding* of these official confessional writings of our church, the Formula of Concord also refuses to countenance the scheme of the Philippists to seek this understanding in Melanchthon's private writings, although he had been the literary author of the primary creed of our church. In the Introduction to its Solid Declaration the Formula of Concord declares: "Herewith we again whole-heartedly subscribe this Christian and thoroughly scriptural Augsburg Confession, and we abide by the plain, clear, and pure meaning of its words" (Par. 4; Tappert, p. 502).

More than that! The Formula of Concord does indeed say that it is "appealing to . . . extensive statements in [Luther's] doctrinal and polemical writings" (Solid Declaration, Rule and Norm, 9; Tappert, p. 505), and who would dare to call himself Lutheran without wanting to acknowledge Luther as God's highly enlightened instrument and one equipped above all others for the task of rediscovering the pure apostolic teaching? Yet even with regard to *Luther* the Formula of Concord remains true to its principle and therefore adds the words: ". . . but in the necessary and Christian terms and manner in which he himself refers to them in the Preface to the Latin edition of his collected works [cf. *Luther's Works,* American Edition, Vol. 34, pp. 327—38]. Here he expressly asserts by way of distinction that the Word of God is and should remain the sole rule and norm of all doctrine, and that no human being's writings dare be put on a par with it, but that everything must be subjected to it" (Solid Declaration, Rule and Norm, 9; Tappert, p. 505).

Finally the Formula of Concord testifies in the presence of all of Christendom: "We therefore declare our adherence to the first, unaltered Augsburg Confession . . . not because this confession was prepared by our theologians but because it is taken from the Word of God and solidly and well grounded therein" (ibid., 5; Tappert, p. 504). For that reason the Formula of Concord affirms that while this confession and all others accepted by our church are and shall remain a norm of doctrine within our church, they are not to be the primary norm but only secondary, one that does not of itself become obligatory but only in its demonstrated complete agreement with the written Word of God. The Formula of Concord expresses this with the following words: "Our intention was only to have a single, universally accepted, certain, and common form of doctrine which all our Evangelical churches subscribe and from which and according to which, *because it is drawn from the Word of God,* all other writings are to be approved and accepted, judged and regulated" (ibid., 10; Tappert, p. 506).

But far from throwing out the baby with the bath water, the Formula states at once: "This, of course, does not mean that other good, useful, and pure books, such as interpretations of the Holy Scriptures, refutations of errors, and expositions of doctrinal articles, should be rejected. If they are in accord with the aforementioned pattern of doctrine they are to be accepted and used as helpful expositions and explanations" (ibid.). In fact, the Preface to the whole *Book of Concord* calls even the writings of Melanchthon, along with those of Brenz, Urban Rhegius, Bugenhagen, and others, "profitable writings," which are not to be "rejected or condemned" "in so far as they are in agreement with the norm incorporated in the [Formula of] Concord" (Tappert, pp. 9 f.).

There can be no doubt that our dear Evangelical Lutheran Church stands on a foundation which even the gates of hell shall not overcome, the unshakable eternal foundation of the Word of apostles and prophets, with Jesus Christ as the Cornerstone. The cited paragraphs from our church's Confessions deal the death blow to every human authority in matters of faith and doctrine within our church. Thereby the church has publicly and solemnly guaranteed each of its members complete freedom of conscience. As such, a Lutheran is subjected in his conscience to no man, no angel, in short, no creature, but only to Christ and His Word. It is just this that makes it the most glorious church fellowship within all of Christendom on earth. To it therefore applies also in these last days what the Lord once said to the church at Philadelphia: "Hold fast what you have, so that no one may seize your crown" (Revelation 3:11).

Down to most recent times no church body that seriously claimed to be a part or branch of the Evangelical Lutheran Church of the Unaltered Augsburg Confession has thought of shaking that foundation. Only our America has most recently acquired the tragic distinction of being the first country to harbor such a church. Within the Evangelical Lutheran Synodical Conference, as is well-known, a controversy on the doctrine of predestination has erupted within the past two years. In this controversy

175

one of the parties not only desires to base the truth of its teaching primarily on the private writings of a number of Lutheran dogmaticians and calls its opponents heretical for dissenting from certain statements of these dogmaticians,[4W] but it also attempts to interpret and understand our church's official confession in the light of these private opinions. This marks a return to those days when the fanatical Philippists sought to have the Augsburg Confession interpreted and understood in line with Melanchthon's *Loci*, his *Examination of Candidates for Ordination*, etc., and put the label of Flacians on those Lutherans who did not want to surrender the hard-won principle of their church.

It has become all too evident that the leaders of this post-Lutheran movement are guided by quite different motives than concern for the preservation of what they regard as doctrinal purity. It is also clear that the crowd being deceived by them and following them has only "a zeal for God" that "is not enlightened" [Romans 10:2] and was so easily captured only because it hereby found occasion to cast off what had long been an oppressive burden, and to do so even under the guise of zeal for pure doctrine. Whatever the motives that initiated the present battle against loyal confessors of our *Book of Concord* as against Calvinists (!)—it is and remains a fact that a whole church body was not only seduced into adopting a thoroughly un-Lutheran principle, but now also puts it into practice by hereticizing its opponents and excluding them from church fellowship. We must therefore in all seriousness preserve the supreme doctrinal treasure and deepest foundation of our church by means of instruction and defense, witness and reproof.

At its last convention, in Wheeling, W. Va., September 1881, the General Ev. Lutheran Synod of Ohio and Other States defined its "position in the" (controverted) "doctrine of predestination" as follows:

> Herewith we again (?!) acknowledge the doctrine of predestination as contained in the Formula of Concord *and also as always taught by and large in agreement therewith by the teachers of our church;* specifically, we regard as in accord with Scripture and the Confessions, and therefore as genuinely Lutheran, the teaching of our fathers that ordaining the elect to eternal life was done *in view of faith,* that is, in view of the merits of Christ *apprehended by faith.* Therefore be it
>
> *Resolved,* That as in the past (?!) so also in the future the doctrine here again affirmed by us is the *only one entitled to be presented* in our institutions, schools, publications, and churchs (*Proceedings of the 25th Special Convention,* etc., p. 39).[5W]

This resolution of a whole church body, consisting of both laymen and clergy, is without parallel in the history not only of the Lutheran

Church, but also of the so-called Protestant church in general. Only the papal church has achieved something similar. Bear in mind that according to that document not only all attending preachers, of whom a considerable number have not even read the chief writings of the so-called "teachers of our church," but also the cherished laymen have been seduced into acknowledging a doctrine "as always taught by and large . . . by the teachers of our church"! Surely no unsuspecting, innocent group of people belonging to our church have ever been more irresponsibly abused by their leaders and seduced into denying their old-Protestant ground of faith and even acknowledging something of which they could not even know what it was! A more offensive papism could hardly be introduced within the Lutheran Church.

Here we are vividly reminded of that papistic legend with which Luther once confronted the Crypto-Zwinglians who said to the Lutherans, "It is enough for you to believe in the body *that Christ has in mind.*"Luther relates the story told by papists: "On the bridge at Prague a doctor (theologian) asked a collier, for whom he felt sorry as for a poor layman, 'My good man, tell me, what do you believe?' The collier answered, 'I believe what the church believes.' The doctor: 'And what does the church believe?' The collier: 'What I believe.' Subsequently, when the doctor was on his deathbed, he was assailed so violently in his faith by the devil that he could stay nowhere nor have any rest until he said, 'I believe what the *collier* believes'" (St. Louis Edition, XVII, 2013). Even so, a poor Ohio Synod layman, when asked, "What do you believe about predestination in addition to what is in the Formula of Concord?" must now answer, "I believe about it the same as this doctrine has by and large[6w] always been treated by the teachers of our church." If he is then asked, "How has this doctrine by and large always been treated by the teachers?" he must answer, "Just as our Ohio Synod treats it." But if he is finally asked, "How do you know this?" he must say, if he wants to be honest, "I know it because our professors say so."—May God have mercy on a synod that calls itself Lutheran and implants this kind of faith and confession in its members!

We bring our preface to the current volume of this theological periodical to a close with the declaration that with God's gracious assistance we will continue to cling inviolably to the Scripture principle of our beloved church in doctrine as well as in defense. For our humble part we will battle in all earnestness against those who somehow seek to smuggle the papistic principle of tradition into our beloved American Lutheran church and thereby, so far as they are concerned, wittingly or unwittingly, undermine our church's foundation.

Notes

Foreword to the 1856 Volume

1. Drawn up by S. S. Schmucker of the Gettysburg Lutheran seminary. The document also offered the Augsburg Confession in an "American Recension," revising it in conformity with "American Lutheranism." This was an attempt to adapt Lutheran teaching to the prevailing theological currents in America, which were principally Reformed. In this way the "Definite Platform" in effect destroyed the distinctive teachings of confessional Lutheranism. The "Platform" can be found in R. C. Wolf, *Documents of Lutheran Unity in America* (Philadelphia: Fortress Press, 1966), Document 44, pp. 100—104.
2. The June issue of this volume (pages 186—87) contains the following formal invitation (repeated with different signatures in the July, August, and September issues):

Call

for a general conference of all Lutherans who acknowledge the Augsburg Confession as the confession of their faith.

- - - -

The undersigned, preachers of the Evangelical Lutheran Church in the United States, convinced that the unity and welfare of our Lutheran Zion will be strongly furthered by a free exchange of views among brethren united in the faith concerning the various interests of our church in this country, herewith issue an invitation to all members of the Evangelical Lutheran Church in the United States who acknowledge the Unaltered Augsburg Confession as a faithful presentation of the teachings of the divine Word to come together in a free and fraternal conference on the current situation and needs of the church in America in the city of _____ , Wednesday, Oct. 1 of this year.

F. Wyneken, pastor, St. Louis, votes for Columbus, Ohio
G. Schaller, pastor, St. Louis, votes for Columbus, Ohio
F. Buenger, pastor, St. Louis, votes for Columbus, Ohio
C. F. W. Walther, prof., St. Louis, votes for Columbus, Ohio
A. Biewend, pastor, St. Louis, votes for Columbus, Ohio

Consubstantiation and Impanation

1W. Henry Suso (died 1365) certainly taught impanation. Cf. *Unschuldige Nachrichten* [Innocent Reports], 1748, pp. 812—13.
2W. It is as curious as it is important that Dr. Kurtz together with his cohorts openly acknowledges that in their midst there are people just like the so-called "Sacramentarians." In his tract, "Why Are You a Lutheran?" (1843), after stating that in America only a few, namely those coming from Europe, still believed in consubstantiation, Dr. Kurtz goes on to say: "The generally received opinion is, that the bread and wine remain unchanged in the Lord's Supper; that they are *merely symbolic representations* of the Saviour's body, but there is nevertheless a special spiritual blessing bestowed on all worthy communicants by which their faith and Christian graces are strengthened. This is the view which Melanchthon (?) and those Lutheran divines seem to have maintained who were termed Sacramentarians. With

the few isolated exceptions mentioned above, this is the common view of the great mass of Lutherans in the United States" (p. 223). [Walther gives this quotation in English. The emphasis and the question mark are his.]

3W. Hence it is not correct to say, as was said above, that Lutherans compare the union of Christ's body with the bread to "red-hot iron." This is the result of a confusion of the *sacramental* and the *personal* union. With regard to the latter, Lutherans, together with the ancient church, do indeed make this comparison. In the above-cited "imperfect" illustration of heat the only point of comparison is intended to be the illocality of the existence of something somewhere.

4W. Not through the keyhole, as some say; nor even through the window, as Peter Martyr unworthily alleges; nor through the entrance opening up by itself for Christ or through the walls opening up, as Beza and others claim!

5W. Cf. *M. Luthers geistliche Lieder mit den Singweisen* [M. Luther's Spiritual Songs with the Music], ed. Phil. Wackernagel (Stuttgart: Liesching, deluxe edition), 1848, p. 130.

1. Walther continues the quotation after the dots, but we are omitting that final part, which deals with Zwingli's and Oecolampadius' understanding of Luther.

2. Between "Unräumlichkeit" (illocality) and "Weise" (way) we have inserted the words "die Abstraction von Grösze, Schwere, Ausdehnung, Kurz von jeder...." We have also changed "himmlischen Welt" (heavenly world) to "sinnlichen Welt" (world of the senses). We did this on the basis of some old marginal notes found in a copy of this volume, and it yields better sense than the printed text does.

3. Walther's addition.

4. Since Walther's argument is based on the German text of the hymn, we have made a literal translation, which differs from the version in *The Lutheran Hymnal*, 311:2.

Is It Heretical to Question the Canonicity . . .?

1. This is an abbreviation of Walther's title, which may be translated: "Is He to Be Declared a Heretic or Dangerous False Teacher Who Does Not Hold and Declare as Canonical All the Books Found in the Scroll of the New Testament?"

2. These prefaces are given in English in *Luther's Works*, American Edition, Vol. 35, pp. 357 ff..

3. Martin Chemnitz, *Examination of the Council of Trent*, trans. Fred Kramer (St. Louis: Concordia Publishing House, 1971), First Topic, Section VI, paragraphs 15-25, pp. 180—90.

The Distinction of Estates in the Church

1W. Here we are obligated to defend Luther against the charge that he was responsible for the mingling of church and state in Germany, which has caused our church so much trouble and which gives offense to many in this country. On the other hand, there is now an attempt to show that such mingling is the right and normal condition of the church and even that it should be transplanted to America as much as possible. But we ought to thank God that we have been delivered from that sad condition of the church. The marriage between state and church in Germany is a marriage within forbidden degrees, of which we must say: What God has *not* joined together, let man put asunder.

2W. In the Smalcald Articles [Treatise] kings and princes are indeed called the "chief members of the church," but there is no mention of housefathers. It is therefore wrong to apply this expression to the *three* so-called *estates*.

3W. Here Pastor Grabau himself mingles the estates in order to defend *his* church government against the charge of mingling. . . . A sample of his constant logic.

4W. It seems that Pastor Grabau diligently studied the Council of Trent. For when the Council wants to anathematize a truth it always includes something false in the true statement and then condemns the whole. That is what Pastor Grabau is doing here. He wants to condemn the truth that every proper church government is representative of the whole Christian congregation. To be able to do this with some show of right he says that the judges must not be representatives of "the will of the crowd." This maxim recurs again and again in Pastor Grabau's polemics, whether he is trying to get rid of the pure doctrine of the church, or of the ministry, or some other teaching.

5W. The first one within the Lutheran Church to make the civil government, because of its estate, a partner in church government was Melanchthon, and he did it in—the *altered* Augsburg Confession!

6W. This explains the term "emergency bishops," which Luther applied elsewhere to orthodox princes of his day.

7W. Please observe that the last words are not intended to modify but to motivate the rejection of church government by Christians in general.

8W. Here Pastor Grabau may reply that in his theory the limits within which each estate has its function and authority are precisely defined. However, thereby he only reveals the impurity of his entire church politics; for either the limits are·pure pretense, or the concession that also the people in secular estates have part in the church's government is pure pretense. For if the secular estates as such are part of church government, the boundary has already been shifted and the mingling has taken place. We regard as most probable that Pastor Grabau does not really consider the people from the secular estates as belonging in the government of the church at all. The whole theory aims at getting the laity to believe that they participate in the church's government and that the reverend pastors are not sovereigns in the church. At the same time they, the laymen, are put off with the mere pretense of sharing in the church's government. It is clear that people in secular estates either share in the church's government as *Christians* or they have no share at all. Now, Pastor Grabau indeed accords them authority *in their estate and calling,* and he *calls* this participation in church government. But what is he doing? He is falsifying the doctrine of church government in order to appease the laity with mere phrases.

9W. . . . Let no one think it unnecessary to seek and to furnish detailed proof for the assertion that the civil government as an estate does not have a share in the government of the church, since the extent of participation granted to it by Pastor Grabau is reduced to virtually nothing. Bear in mind that we are concerned about following the principle: "Resist the beginnings!" (*Principiis obsta*). Pastor Grabau includes the civil government in his theory of church government only to demonstrate that the Christian takes part not as a Christian, but that Christians do so as members of estates. When we prove that the civil government as an estate does not share in the government of the church, we have preserved to the Christians the precious rights they have as Christians.

1. Pastor Johannes A. A. Grabau (1804—79) came to America in 1839 with a number of other Prussian Lutherans and settled at Buffalo, N. Y. While desiring to be a conservative, confessional Lutheran, he differed sharply from Walther on the doctrine of the ministry, as may be gathered from this article. Briefly put, Grabau favored the authority of *pastors,* while Walther upheld the rights of the *laity.* Grabau founded the Buffalo Synod, which became part of the American Lutheran Church in 1930. There are many references to Grabau in the *Selected Letters* volume of this series.
2. The omissions in the following quotations are ours.
3. We are omitting the last part of the quotation.

Foreword to the 1857 Volume

1. An excellent and detailed account of these Free Conferences is given by Erwin L. Lueker in *Concordia Theological Monthly,* XV (Aug. 1944), 529—63.
2. Walther is referring to the Religious Peace of Augsburg, 1555, between the Lutheran princes and Emperor Charles V. The treaty gave official recognition to the churches of the Augsburg Confession as legitimate and guaranteed them protection under the law. Since this provision applied only to those who were committed to the Augsburg

Confession some Zwinglians and Calvinists outwardly conformed by subscribing the Augsburg Confession. Those who continued to promote Calvinistic teaching under cover of the Augsburg Confession were labeled "Crypto-Calvinists."

Foreword to the 1858 Volume

1W. In 1854 it was this same v. Hofmann who united with several theologians of the Lutheran persuasion "to preserve the Confession of the Evangelical Lutheran Church against the confession of the Berlin *Kirchentag*," as may be gathered from a printed protest signed by v. Hofmann.

2W. Thus Pastor Loehe is even unwilling to subscribe everything in the symbols that is "said confessionally."

3W. Here Loehe is obviously angry with our church for declaring as symbolical what he calls Luther's originality and individuality; that is to say, our church *has* accepted that as its own teaching and is minded to cling to it against the devil and all the world, so help it God.

4W. Here Pastor Loehe does not cite the words of the Smalcald Articles [Treatise on the Power and Primacy of the Pope] as they read, and this is the cause of the misunderstanding. The actual words of the symbol are not open to misunderstanding, for in the cited passage it is stated explicitly: "In addition, it is necessary to acknowledge that the keys do not belong to one person or one particular individual but to the whole church" (Treatise 24, Tappert, p. 324). [Walther quotes the German, which reads ". . . . the keys do not belong and were not given to one person *alone* (emphasis Walther's) but to the whole church (*Concordia Triglotta*, p. 510)].

5W. Here Pastor Loehe is obviously, though without doubt unconsciously, misinterpreting the Smalcald Articles [Treatise] in order to argue with them in a courteous way and in order to be forced to criticize and reject as little as possible. The cited passage speaks not only of what the church may do in an emergency but, above all, what the church has the right and power to do "originally and immediately" (*principaliter et immediate*), aside from the *order according to which* both are to be handled in conformity with God's prescription.

1. To mark the 300th anniversary of the Reformation, King Frederick William III of Prussia in 1817 urged, and later ordered, the Lutheran and Reformed churches in his realm to unite into a single "Evangelical" church. It is this "Prussian Union" to which Walther refers.

2. In older editions of the *Book of Concord*, the Smalcald Articles, written by Luther, and the Treatise on the Power and Primacy of the Pope, written by Melanchthon, are often lumped together simply as the "Smalcald Articles," and are so cited, as Walther does here. For further details see Tappert, *Book of Concord*, pp. 287 f. and 319 f.

3. The bracketed words here and in the following sentence are Walther's.

Foreword to the 1859 Volume

[On Doctrinal Development]

1W. To say nothing of such theologizers as Dr. Benj. Kurtz, who wrote a few years ago that we are not the children of our old *teachers*, the fathers, but vice versa because of our naturally increased knowledge *we* are the fathers and the old teachers mere children compared with us.

2W. See *Kirchliche Mitteilungen aus und ueber Nord-Amerika* [Church News from and about North America], 1858, No. 8.

3W. See Walch, *Einleitung in die Religionsstreitigkeiten innerhalb der ev.-luth. Kirche* [Introduction to the Religious Controversies Within the Ev.-Luth. Church], IV, 518. Cf. Buddaeus, *Isagoge*, p. 259, regarding Wenceslaus Schilling, who resumed Hofmann's battle against every use of metaphysics in particular.

4W. Gerhard offers seven proofs that the church *can* err: 1. Because the Old Testament

182

church often erred; 2. because there are divine prophecies of a certain great seduction; 3. because the particular churches are warned not to err and not to lend their ear to the seducers; 4. because experience teaches that the New Testament church has erred; 5. because the knowledge of those who constitute the church is not yet perfect; 6. because the church can sin; 7. because all pastors can err (*Locus de ecclesia*, par. 111—115). In this way Gerhard annihilates the handy all-embracing argument of the Romans that as surely as they were once the church, so surely they cannot err, and that therefore everything that their church teaches may, indeed must, be accepted sight unseen.

5W. The point is important because if a thoroughly orthodox visible church does not *always* exist, it cannot be the church in the proper sense of the word, the church outside of which there is no salvation, but this must rather be the invisible church.

6W. So named explicitly in the Formula of Concord, Summary Formulation, 5 [Tappert, p. 504].

7W. It is extremely offensive for a Lutheran professor, as does Thomasius here and frequently elsewhere where he thinks he must depart from the teaching of our most enlightened fathers, to make short shrift of them by alleging that in this matter the fathers were again following the scholastics without realizing the consequences of such scholastic definitions. Would to God that there were in our day just one theologian who penetrated the organism of Christian doctrines as clearly and profoundly and was as quick to spot alterations as entire crowds of theologians were earlier in our church's better days.

8W. We have reproduced in special type [italics] only what Ebrard himself so gives.

9W. Here Rudelbach inserts some scattered remarks of Luther, Matthesius, Rhegius, Luke Osiander, and Schluesselburg which contain the familiar hypothesis for the interpretation of 1 Peter 3:19-20, that either all souls, or at least those surprised by the Flood, were in an intermediate state until Christ's accomplished sacrificial death; and now Rudelbach, without the slightest justification, exploits this hypothesis to support his teaching of a Hades as an intermediate place even after Christ's sacrificial death.

10W. This shows that we are here not dealing with a theological problem that could be debated pro and con, but with an article of faith in the proper sense of the word that only now, in this "great age," is to be brought into the light of day and cleansed of its dross.

11W. "Thus also *Abraham's bosom* in the parable of the rich man and poor Lazarus (Luke 16:22) receives its most satisfactory interpretation" (Rudelbach). According to Rudelbach, therefore, Christ's descent into hell is the journey into paradise and Abraham's bosom! This is doctrinal development!

12W. Already at the beginning of his essay Rudelbach had written: "It cannot be denied that an effeminate-sentimental, Pelagian concern was frequently, and especially in the 18th century, hidden behind the question concerning the *salvation of the heathen . . .*; it is, therefore, all the more necessary that it be given its due in a *Christian* way and be understood in its *true* significance."

13W. Scripture does not say one word about an "evangelizing of the dead" in connection with Christ's descent into hell. 1 Peter 4:6 does not speak of a proclamation of the Gospel to the dead after death, but when they were still alive; the kind of preaching referred to in 1 Peter 3:19 can easily be gathered from Colossians 2:15. Also in the interpretation of these passages the analogy of faith (Romans 12[:6]) dare not be violated, and "one's own interpretation" (2 Peter 1:20) must be avoided like hell itself. After giving his interpretation of 1 Peter 3:19-22, Luther remarks: "But I surely cannot believe that Christ descended to the souls and preached to them there. Scripture, too, is against this and states that every one, when he comes to that place, will receive as he believed and lived" (*Luther's Works,* American Edition, Vol. 30, pp. 114 f.) Likewise on 1 Peter 4:6 Luther writes: "I cannot accept the interpretation that the Gospel should be preached to the dead" (ibid., p. 121).

14W. For this assumption Kurtz appeals to Stier, G. H. von Schubert, Kniewel, M.

Baumgarten, *Rudelbach, Guericke!* Not to mention others like Jacob Boehme, M. Hahn, Fr. v. Meyer, Hamberger.

15W. So Kurtz interprets the Mosaic account of creation.

1. On this section from Gerhard see Donald P. Meyer, "John Gerhard on Philosophy in Theology," *Concordia Theological Monthly,* XXVII (Sept. 1956), 721—24.

On Church Language

1W. We are here using the expression "Bible language" in the sense of Biblical terminology.

2W. After the familiar distich:

Sint unum, doceant unum, fateantur et unum,
Qui unum de Christi nomine nomen habent.

3W. After the adage: *Dolosus versatur in generalibus,* that is, the deceitful man will speak in general terms. Incidentally, with regard to the church's language the symbols stand head and shoulders above all private writings, for, as Horace writes, "Even good old Homer will nap occasionally."

4W. This way of speaking is by no means supported by the words of the litany: "To accompany Thy Word with Thy Spirit and grace" [*The Lutheran Hymnal,* p. 111]. Here God is not asked to give the *Word* the power that is lacking, but to give power to *preachers* and *hearers,* so that the Word may be correctly preached and heard and thus its inherent power be manifested.

5W. An excellent model of proper church language about the mystery of the Holy Trinity is the Athanasian Creed, of which Luther says in his comments on Joel 3:1-2: "Which is so formulated that I do not know whether in the New Testament church after the time of the apostles anything more important and more glorious has been written."

6W. Dr. *Heinrich Mueller* writes on the Gospel of the good Samaritan: "What Christ says here has in our day almost entirely become a picture, interpreted parabolically as referring to Adam's fall and justification. Origen started it, Augustine followed in his footsteps, and subsequently the whole papacy adopted this gloss. From there springs the error about the powers of the free will which Pelagius also defended. This opinion is, for one thing, in opposition to the Savior's intent; neither in what precedes nor in what follows is He here speaking about Adam's fall and justification, but about *love,* and He wants to show the scribe who his *neighbor* is. This interpretation also runs counter to the rule of faith; for sin has left us in Adam not *half dead,* but has killed us altogether. Our powers have not only been weakened but completely destroyed" *(Herzensspiegel* [Mirror of the Heart]).

7W. The Formula of Concord says: "For although, prior to this controversy, not a few orthodox teachers used these and similar formulas in expounding Holy Scripture without in any way intending to confirm the aforementioned error of the papists, yet, since a controversy subsequently arose on this point which led to many offensive exaggerations, it is safest to follow the advice of St. Paul to maintain the pattern of sound *words* as well as the true *doctrine* itself (II Tim. 1:13). This would eliminate much useless wrangling and preserve the church from many offenses" (Formula of Concord, Solid Declaration, IV, 36, Good Works; Tappert, p. 557).

8W. We do not believe that we need to cite such expressions as are characteristic of the rationalists: The teaching of Jesus, the religion of Jesus, the sage of Nazareth, walk the path of virtue, we must be virtuous people, virtue is the life of the soul, an upright man, noble pride, a man of principle, etc. Just as little do we need to mention the expressions of the heavenly prophets like Carlstadt, Muenzer, *et al.,* who used the following words to describe the steps by which one ascends to the true knowledge of God: 1. refinement; 2. study, 3. astonishment, 4. boredom, 5. sprinkling (cf. John Gerhard, *Loci theologici, De ministerio,* par. 251). Finally, it would also be a waste of time and effort to list the unchurchly turns of speech with which current works in theology teem; they bear witness almost without exception to a revolution in the domain of ecclesiastical

184

language which reminds one of the confusion of tongues at Babel. Apart from the errors underlying the modern monstrous language, the familiar saying applies to most of them: *"Si non vis intelligi, non debes legi,"* that is, "If you don't want to be understood, you shouldn't be read."

1. We have not included all of Walther's footnotes, many of which give the Latin for certain sayings.
2. The phrase in parentheses is excerpted from a long footnote which gives extensive biographical information on Regius.

Foreword to the 1860 Volume

[Do We Draw the Lines of Fellowship Too Narrowly?]

1W. Here we make no mention of the Grabau group, which opposes our position as *hereticizing.* That group is its own judge inasmuch as it has even dared to make a heretical book out of our catechism, which was put together out of *Dietrich, the* Dresden Cross Catechism, and the Symbolical Books. By this act alone that group has branded itself as heretical.
2W. Pastor Loehe would have great difficulty documenting this assertion. Congruent modes of speech do not always support the same view. The decision can be found chiefly where doctrine is treated in thesis and antithesis. *Duo cum dicunt idem, non est idem* [When two people say the same thing, it is not the same]!
3W. When Pastor Loehe notes the practice of doctrinal discipline, he is already overwhelmed by holy horrors of an inquisition! He may be forgiven for that since this kind of church discipline has not been practiced in our church for more than a century. Whoever has respect for pure doctrine and knows the history of the inquisition will regard such "holy horrors" as both ridiculous and saddening. But perhaps these words are only a piece of tendentious rhetoric.
4W. It is true: Where there is no doctrinal discipline, there false brethren, who would otherwise insolently and openly pour contempt on the church's teaching, often become hypocrites and preach the truth which they themselves do not believe. So, when the Formula of Concord was introduced, many pastors who were inclined toward Calvinism listened to their wives who counseled:

> Schreibt, lieber Herre, schreibt,
> Dass Ihr bei der Pfarre bleibt.
> Sign, dear husband, sign,
> That you may keep your parish.

But if for that reason doctrinal discipline means rearing hypocrites, then Romans 7:9-13 is not true.
5W. In what follows Pastor Loehe speaks of his relations also to the Buffalo Synod and expresses this opinion: "According to their respective standpoints, Missouri and Buffalo could get together more easily than agree to his own views." Of the Iowa Synod he says: *"Its existence has no other purpose than to represent our own position in America,* that of a Lutheranism which continues to build ever *more fully* on the old (how old?) basis and producing ever more blessed results."
6W. Doubtless this year, in which plans are being made to conduct a year-long church celebration of Melanchthon's death, will still give us frequent occasion to show thoroughly that the later Melanchthon must be carefully distinguished from the earlier.
7W. How dishonestly Melanchthon had acted in Cassel is clear from a letter to Camerarius, where he says that there he had to present "our party's" teaching on the Lord's Supper, while *Bucer* had to bring his [Melanchthon's] views. Then Melanchthon adds: "Do not now ask me about *my* opinion, for I was the messenger of a foreign one" [cf. *Concordia Triglotta,* Historical Introductions, p. 177].

8W. We do not even have to appeal to such examples as this one, that in accordance with Luther's decision the preacher Moor in Naumburg was therefore deposed from office because in his sermons he had omitted doctrinal refutation against the papists, although he himself preached evangelically (cf. *Corpus Reformatorum*, V, 814—16).

9W. We hardly need to mention the short reprieve which the crypto-Calvinists in Electoral Saxony received under Christian I from 1586 to 1591, after the death of the cherished Elector August.

10W. He was the son of the good theologian Nicolaus Stenger, senior member of the Erfurt ministerium and later professor of theology, who died in 1680.

11W. At the latter two J. Musäus and Spener wrote the opinion.

12W. It is well known that, for example, Jacob Andreae was reminded and better instructed by Chemnitz in several points, and that the former gladly accepted this. See V. E. Loescher's detailed *Historia motuum*, II, 240, 245.

13W. In demanding agreement also in *non*fundamental articles, Loehe is evidently thinking of *secondary* fundamental articles.

14W. The Latin of the Solid Declaration reads: "in omnibus illius *partibus*," i.e., "in all its *parts*."

15W. It need hardly be said that this involves only such members of the church as are capable of discerning the doctrinal connection, and in the first instance only the servants of the church, the preachers, not simple laymen who have become confused.

16W. It is remarkable how highly even "decided" Lutherans esteem certain men within our church merely because they have distinguished themselves through eye-catching "works," even though those works are mostly child's play compared with the works of, for instance, earlier Jesuits like Xavier! To so great a degree has an appreciation of the true treasure entrusted to our church disappeared.

1. We give this quotation exactly (including capitalization, etc.) as it appeared in the article titled "The Future Position of the Lutheran Church."

2. Walther's addition.

3. This essay by Walther about confessional commitment is offered in a somewhat condensed English translation by Alex. Wm. C. Guebert, *Concordia Theological Monthly*, XVIII (April 1947), 241—53.

4. We have omitted a note giving references to the controversies about Huber.

5. We have omitted a lengthy note which gives further details about the theological opinion of the Jena faculty.

6. We have omitted a lengthy note which gives more examples of men removed from office because of chiliasm.

7. Here Walther observes that the synod has not explicitly condemned the so-called "subtle" chiliasm, if it conforms to the definition offered by Dr. August Pfeiffer, namely, that this kind of chiliasm does not look for an earthly kingdom of Christ, no double resurrection, but only a time of peace for the church, and leaves time and manner up to God. This kind of chiliasm may be erroneous but it does not affect the fundamental articles of faith.

8. Here Walther has a note which gives this quotation in the Latin.

Foreword to the 1862 Volume
[Do We Lack Creative Activity?]

1W. Yet even Winer must confess: "The controversy among exegetes has as a rule led back to an understanding which the Protestant church held earlier (in its initial period) as being the correct one" (*Grammatik* [Grammar], 3rd. ed., Preface).

2W. In his periodical Ehlers permits Fengler to write: "Christianity is always confession of faith, and confession comes from the innermost being, where faith dwells. *But* for the Missourians Christianity is more a recitation of all manner of correct, excellent statements of faith." Even our worst enemies have not written more presumptuously and judgmentally. Such a malicious remark is not nullified but becomes even more venomous when Pastor Fengler also writes the following: "In fact the Missourians are well versed and experienced in the wisdom of the Lutheran fathers. . . . Yet much good may be found also in the American periodicals. Everything possesses great clarity. And the zeal for Lutheran doctrine which the Missourians have in some things better than it is elsewhere is only worth imitating. Thus an article in *Lehre und Wehre*, December 1859, on a comparison of Luther with Johann Arndt and A. H. Franke was instructive for me. I think the presentation is excellent." According to this it seems that also in Germany there are people who praise the Missouri Synod, this thorn in the eye of false Lutherans, so that they can then defame it all the more as "impartial persons."

Opening Address at the 1866 Convention

1 W. On the advice and wish of several brothers in the ministry, the undersigned takes the liberty of here giving this address instead of a Foreword. Among other reasons which move him to do this, the thought is especially determinative that thereby the price of the synodical report will be reduced.   Walther

Foreword to the 1875 Volume

[Are We Guilty of Despising Scholarship?]

1 W. Already 25 years ago, Nov. 8, 1849, the writer delivered an address at the cornerstone laying of our college and seminary building in St. Louis in which he demonstrated in detail that "the church has always been and, according to its essence and calling must continue to be, a faithful and sincere friend and fosterer of art and science" (*Der Lutheraner*, VI, 161 ff.).

2 W. Hence Luther comments on Isaiah 61:6: "The wealth of the nations" here means the same as above in 60:6; that is to say, everything the heathen have, their riches, their power, their eloquence, etc., will be used, not in opposition to the church, as formerly, but in the service of the church" (St. Louis Edition, VI, 796).

3 W. Eusebius writes: "At that time (during the reign of Commodus) the school of the faithful in Alexandria was presided over by a man famous for his learning, named Pantaenus. For since ancient times a theological school was established in this city and still exists, where (as has been reported to us) there is a confluence of men expert in eloquence and theology" (*Church History*, V, 10 [13]).

4 W. Although the following rather long citation is undoubtedly, with very few exceptions, long known to our readers, we nevertheless for the sake of these few exceptions regard it as our duty to make room for the golden words of Luther contained therein.

5 W. Whom above all does the German nation have to thank (next to God) that it has not only lost this reputation for barbarism, in which it stood among other nations before the time of the Reformation, but on the contrary has become the most learned nation on earth? None other than Luther. For after Luther in the above-cited writing and in others had raised his voice like a trumpet for the establishing of institutions cultivating the liberal arts, the most glorious schools quickly appeared everywhere, almost overnight.

6 W. Reuchlin closes his book *De rudimentis hebraicis* [On the Rudiments of Hebrew], 1506, with the boastful words: "I have left behind a monument more permanent than the air."

7 W. See Heinsius' *Kirchengeschichte* [Church History], II, 372f., and *Consilia Witebergensia*, I, 867f., where the detailed retraction, which is worth reading, can be found.

8 W. In renouncing a material use of reason, philosophy, or science in theology, we self-evidently do not object to the use of these disciplines to *explain* things that Scripture mentions as belonging in the area of human knowledge. Here we find ourselves in

187

complete accord with our older orthodox teachers. For example, *Danhauer*, having stated that our theologians reject a material and magisterial use of reason in theology, adds immediately: "On the contrary, they acknowledge the use of reason which consists (1) in apprehension and retention; (2) in *explaining* matters in the areas of material philosophy, mathematics, physics, politics, and economics; (3) in drawing conclusions and passing judgment on the connection of the truths" (*Prodromus antichristosophiae*, p. 57).

9 W. Cf. *Die trunkene Wissenschaft und ihr Erbe an die Evangelische Kirche: Ein Beitrag zur Beurtheilung der neueren Theologi. In Briefen von Dr. C. Scheele.* [The Inebriated Scholarship and Its Legacy to the Evangelical Church: A Contribution Toward Judging the Newer Theology. In Letters by Dr. C. Scheele.] Berlin: G. Schlawitz, 1867.

1. This exposition of "the glorious mandate" was authored by Ambrose Moiban as an exposition of Mark 16:14-20, for which Luther wrote the preface.
2. Walther has "he said it" in Greek.

Foreword to the 1877 Volume
[On the 300th Anniversary of the Formula of Concord]

1 W. These concluding words, an integrating part of the Formula of Concord, indicate the sense in which the Formula desires to be, and should be, subscribed. According to the advice given Elector August of Saxony in a letter of March 14, 1577, by Chemnitz, Andreae, and Selnecker, every subscriber was asked simply to give "his name and surname and place of service," so that, as they put it, "no false teacher can hide under it" (Hutter, *Concordia Concors,* Frankfurt and Leipzig, 1690, p. 439).

2 W. God willing, we intend to report in the *Lutheraner* about other anniversary celebrations of the Formula of Concord, as far as the adequacy of our sources will allow.

3 W. Naturally also Luther's writings are not put on a level with God's Word. On the contrary, it says of them: "We also wish to be regarded as appealing to further extensive statements in his doctrinal and polemical writings, but in the necessary and Christian terms and manner in which he himself refers to them in the Preface to the Latin edition of his collected works. Here he expressly asserts by way of distinction that the Word of God is and should remain the sole rule and norm of all doctrine, and that no human being's writings dare be put on a par with it, but that everything must be subjected to it" (Solid Declaration, Rule and Norm, 9; Tappert, p. 505; cf. *Luther's Works,* American Edition, Vol. 34, pp. 327—38).

4 W. Leaders in Anhalt were the Crypto-Calvinists Wolfgang Amling, superintendent at Zerbst, and Peter Haring, superintendent at Koethen. In negotiations with them at Herzberg, Aug. 18, 1578, not only did Chemnitz, Andreae, Musculus, and Koerner tell them in private that their doctrine of the Lord's Supper was altogether Calvinistic and their doctrine of free will Jesuitical, but also one of the loyal Lutheran political counselors attending the meeting said to the colloquents: "Gentlemen, please do not become impatient, for our theologian (the 36-year-old Amling) is still jousting with his first sword; this is his first excursion; he has never attended such negotiations before." In fact, the other political counselor remarked: "It is with our theologian as with our young budding jurists, who know everything in the first year, have their doubts in the second year, and know nothing in the third year; our theologian is still in the first year" (J. N. Anton, *Geschichte der Concordienformel* [History of the Formula of Concord], Leipzig, 1779, I, 236).

5 W. He belonged more to the Crypto-Calvinist Philippists. Cf. Loescher's *Hist. mot.,* III, 266. *Unschuldige Nachrichten* (1715), pp. 1130 f.

6 W. This explanation regarding the Altered Augsburg Confession was included because in the time of confusion several orthodox princes had in good faith used the Variata

foisted upon them by Crypto-Calvinists (e.g., at the Day of Princes in Naumburg, 1561), so that the *Book of Concord* would not create the impression that by its rejection of the Variata it was labeling also these princes as earlier apostates from the pure Confession.

7W. This is that notorious letter of Nov. 1, 1559, in which Melanchthon, who had been asked by Elector Frederick III of the Palatinate for an opinion about a quarrel at Heidelberg between Heshusius and the deacon Klebitz on the Lord's Supper, in plain language accepted Zwingli's symbolic teaching *(Corpus Reformatorum,* IX, 960). As a result, the elector then strove to make his land Reformed, abolished Luther's Catechism, authorized and introduced a new one, the so-called Heidelberg Catechism, and deposed and exiled pastors who refused to accept it.

8W. Anton reports that according to the critiques of the Torgau Book that arrived in Bergen for the last redaction, "the theologians of *many* principalities and cities had wished that not only the errors but also their originators together with their writings would be mentioned" (I, 199).

9W. The suddenly surfacing opposition of Heshusius in fact struck the beloved Chemnitz like a bolt out of the blue. After Heshusius had subscribed the Formula with such great rejoicing, it is very difficult to explain how this highly gifted man, who had hitherto fought so heroically and with such glowing eloquence for the truth, all at once turned from an advocate to an opponent of the Formula. We cannot believe that the grave lapse of Duke Julius, who had his sons given the papal tonsure and had been reprimanded by Chemnitz in a letter of Dec. 19, 1578, had anything to do with it (cf. *Abgewiesener Demas* [Rebuffed Demas, 2 Timothy 4:10] by Loescher, p. 221.) Heshusius stands as a tragic figure of church history *after* the appearance of the Formula of Concord, as Flacius does *before* that event. H. E. Treiber, in his *Jubeljahrs-Posaune* [Jubilee-Year Trumpet], a history of the *Book of Concord* in verse, 1681, writes about Heshusius as follows (p. 178):

> ... What ever moved that man
> To turn away from what he had subscribed
> And even taught before—this no one knows
> But He who tries the hearts and will Himself reveal
> When He will gravely sit upon His judgment seat
> And bring to light what now is still concealed.

10W. According to Anton (I, 198) also Hamburg, Lueneburg, and Luebeck had remarked in their suggestions sent to Bergen that the words of the Torgau Book "were still much too mild" in their refutation of the false teachings.

11W. Even Anton, by no means rigidly orthodox, declares: "All who wish to judge impartially must admit that in its way and for the purpose for which it was prepared, it is very beautiful and excellent and that just that for which it has recently been criticized, namely that it goes into too much detail, to a certain extent makes it all the more valuable" (I, 260f.).

12W. At the Herzberg conventions in 1578 Andreae declared: "I can truly say that no one was coerced into subscribing nor banished in this matter. This is as true as the fact that the Son of God has redeemed me by His blood; or else I want no part in the blood of Jesus Christ" (Anton, I, 219). Nor was any coercion required, since the genuinely Lutheran confession was everywhere joyfully and gratefully subscribed, and only those few refused who revealed themselves as stiff-necked Calvinists and as enemies of the doctrine of the Augsburg Confession when they were invited to subscribe the Formula.

13W. There could be no question of accepting the Formula of Concord in Sweden between 1577 and 1580, because during that time the wretched John III sought to make his country papistic. Of a later time *Rudelbach* reports: "At the national council in Uppsala, 1593, in the fourth session (March 3), after firm theses on the general evangelical basis, Holy Scripture and the ecumenical Symbols of the church, they reviewed the Augsburg Confession article by article. At the end the bishop of

189

Strangnas asked the assembly whether all estates would remain faithful to this teaching and, if necessary, suffer for it. All arose and answered: 'For it we are ready to risk all that we have in this world, property and life.' Thereupon the presiding person shouted at the top of his voice: 'Now Sweden has become one man, and we all have one God' " (*Historisch-kritische Einleitung in die Augsburgische Confession* [Historical-Critical Introduction to the Augsburg Confession], Dresden, 1841, p. 202 f.). The Formula of Concord was not accepted until 1638, in a public parliamentary session (*Unschuldige Nachrichten* [Innocent Reports], 1730, p. 756).

14 W. Enemies have asserted that the king of Denmark had the Formula of Concord burned, but they cannot prove it. It is certain, however, that the king had been taken in by the Danish Philippists, much like Elector August had been by the Crypto-Calvinists, and consequently was filled with extreme aversion against the Formula of Concord. On Sept. 22, 1581, Paul Matthiae, bishop in Roeskilde, wrote to Jacob Runge: "We did not read the book [Formula] of Concord about which you want our opinion. For our illustrious and very pious king has issued an extremely rigorous decree in which he forbids anyone on pain of death (*sub poena capitali*) to import this book into our lands, or to read it if it has been imported" (Balthasar, *Hist. des Torgischen Buchs* [History of the Torgau Book], I, 18). Since already in 1570 *Norway* had been ceded to Denmark by the Peace of Stettin, it too did not accept the Formula of Concord. For that matter, of all non-German princes only the Danish king Frederick II had been invited to do so.

1. In view of the quadricentennials of the Formula of Concord and the *Book of Concord* (1977 and 1980) just past, Walther's reflections on the tercentenary jubilee appear highly interesting and instructive, and therefore deserve to be included in this volume. At the request of the Ev. Lutheran Synodical Conference Walther published a little book on the Epitome of the Formula of Concord entitled *Der Concordienformel Kern und Stern* [The Core and Guiding Star of the Formula of Concord] (St. Louis, 1877); see also *Denkmal der dritten Jubelfeier der Concordienformel im Jahre des Heils 1877* [Monument to the Tercentennial Celebration of the Formula of Concord in the Year of Grace 1877], ed. E. W. Kaehler (St. Louis, 1877).

2. This appeared in 1560. It was meant to be a collection of symbolical books, but besides the three Ecumenical Creeds it contained only writings by Melanchthon, including the Altered Augsburg Confession and the Altered Apology.

3. Here Walther has a long footnote to the effect that Paul von Eitzen's antipathy against the Formula of Concord was most likely motivated by his dislike of Jacob Andreae, one of the Formula's leading authors.

4. In the months that followed, the Formula was carefully reviewed throughout the Lutheran Church and subscribed by scores of princes and more than 8,000 pastors and teachers. Meanwhile a general Preface was planned to allow for last-minute additions, deletions, or further clarification. For further details see Tappert, pp. 463 f.; *Triglot Concordia*, "Historical Introductions," 235—56; Robert Kolb, *Andreae and the Formula of Concord* (St. Louis: Concordia Publishing House, 1977); Theo. R. Jungkuntz, *Formulators of the Formula of Concord* (St. Louis: Concordia Publishing House, 1977).

Foreword to the 1882 Volume

[The Only Source of Doctrine]

1 W. Mathesius in his first sermon on Luther's life, in which he pictures Luther's circumstance at the time he was studying at the University of Erfurt, writes: "When there were no public lectures he spent his time in the university library. On one occasion when he was carefully examining the volumes, one after the other, so that he might learn to know the best among them, he happened on a copy of the Latin Bible, which he had never in his life seen up to this time. Then he noticed with great amazement that it contained many more texts than those that were in the ordinary postils or were

customarily explained from the pulpits of the churches. As he was looking through the Old Testament, he chanced to see the story of Samuel and his mother Hannah, which he rapidly read through with great enjoyment and delight, and, because it was all new to him, he began to wish from the bottom of his heart that our good Lord would at some time bestow on him such a book as his own"[cited in E. G. Schwiebert, *Luther and His Times* (St. Louis: Concordia Publishing House, 1950), p. 120]. Luther is quoted as saying: "When I was twenty years old, I had not yet seen a Bible"[ibid.]. In his Table Talk Luther is reported to have remarked about Carlstadt: "Not until eight years after he received his doctorate did Dr. Carlstadt begin to read the Bible, because he and Dr. Peter Lupinus had been urged to read Augustine"(St. Louis Edition, XXII, 25). Again: "Dr. Carlstadt received his doctorate when he had never seen the Bible" (St. Louis Edition, XXII, 395).

2W. Evidently this happened by God's providence, as Luther himself observed later on, so that Luther in the simplicity of his heart did not need to think he had to keep his promise to remain silent. This would have done great injury to the work of Reformation which God wanted to accomplish through him. [Ed. note: For a detailed account of Luther's meeting with Cajetan, see "The Proceedings at Augsburg," *Luther's Works,* American Edition, Vol. 31, pp. 255—92].

3W. What Luther meant to indicate with the phrase "clear reason" is explained by what follows. He does not mean rationalistic arguments but the kind of arguments that would convince him that he had not correctly understood the Bible passages cited by him.

4W. This party was well aware that only in this way would it be able to cast suspicion on its opponent as a heretical church, and that it would have made itself ridiculous if it had appealed merely to the results of its own exegetical studies.

5W. The emphases are the author's [Walther's].

6W. By the way, the addition of the words "by and large" turns the confession even for those members who are conversant with the whole dogmatic literature into a wretched waxen nose that everyone can twist at will, as indeed the whole addition makes of commitment to the Formula óf Concord a meaningless game.

1. Here Walther has a footnote regarding the date of this writing of Luther's. It should be 1538.

2. In a footnote Walther gives this entire quotation in Latin.

3. In a lengthy footnote at this point Walther cites a listing by Martin Chemnitz of Melanchthon's doctrinal aberrations, followed by a very detailed catalog of his errors compiled by Leonard Hutter. Among them are errors of free will, Christ, the Lord's Supper, conversion, and predestination. In conclusion Walther comments: "This is the verdict of men like Chemnitz and Hutter on the great and revered teacher within our church, Melanchthon, who for so many years stood loyally at Luther's side and whom Luther had rated so highly. Indeed, he had been the blessed instrument in formulating our primary confession and in preparing the Apology. After Luther's death not only deceitful enemies of the truth appealed to Melanchthon but also many excellent men. What would have happened to our church if such appeals had not been permanently stopped by a solemn declaration on the part of our church? In its visible form our church would have perished 300 years ago. But, praise God, our precious Formula of Concord has for all time put an end to all appeals not only to Melanchthon but also to the private writings of all teachers of our church, even the most excellent, over against the Word of God and the Confessions, as well as all allegedly authentic interpretations of the latter on the basis of those writings."

www.ingramcontent.com/pod-product-compliance
Lightning Source LLC
Chambersburg PA
CBHW030639150426
42813CB00050B/185